ETHNIC IDENTITY

FROM THE MARGINS

ETHNIC
IDENTITY
FROM THE MARGINS

A Christian Perspective

DEWI HUGHES

WILLIAM CAREY
LIBRARY

Ethnic Identity from the Margins: A Christian Perspective
Copyright © 2012 Dewi Hughes

All Rights Reserved. No part of this work may be reproduced or transmitted in any form or by any means—for example, electronic or mechanical, including photocopying and recording—without prior written permission of the publisher. The publisher does not maintain, update, or moderate links and/or content provided by third-party websites mentioned in the book.

Scripture taken from the HOLY BIBLE, NEW INTERNATIONAL VERSION®. Copyright © 1973, 1978, 1984 Biblica. Used by permission of Zondervan. All rights reserved.

The "NIV" and "New International Version" trademarks are registered in the United States Patent and Trademark Office by Biblica. Use of either trademark requires the permission of Biblica.

Published by William Carey Library, an imprint of William Carey Publishing
10 W. Dry Creek Circle
Littleton, CO 80120 | www.missionbooks.org

Kelley K. Wolfe, editor
Brad Koenig, copyeditor
Alyssa E. Force, cover and interior design
Rose Lee-Norman, indexer

William Carey Library is a ministry of Frontier Ventures
Pasadena, CA 91104 | www.frontierventures.org

23 22 21 20 19 Printed for Worldwide Distribution

Library of Congress Cataloging-in-Publication Data

Hughes, Dewi Arwel.
  Ethnic identity from the margins : a christian perspective / Dewi Hughes.
     p. cm.
  Includes bibliographical references (p.   ).
  ISBN 978-0-87808-459-3
  1. Christianity and culture. 2. Ethnicity--Religious aspects--Christianity. 3. Church and minorities. I. Title.

I'r teulu

CONTENTS

Introduction ix

1. Context and Definitions 1
2. The Modern Understanding of Ethnic Identity
   from an Autobiographical Perspective 9
3. A Church, the Bible, and the Complexities of Ethnic Identity 31
4. The Bible, Christianity, Ethnic Identity, and Nationhood 59
5. Ethnic Identity and Human Rights 87
6. The Ethnic Cauldron of the Contemporary World 109
7. Not Just a Minority: The Case of Indigenous Peoples 133
8. Beyond Ethnic Conflict 157

Appendix: UN Documents 183
Bibliography 195
Index 205
Scripture Index 219

INTRODUCTION

THE title given to this book when it was first published was *Castrating Culture*. I pondered long and hard before deciding to go ahead with the title, and I'm now happy to admit that I took the wrong decision! But having confessed my mistake, I'm also happy to confess that the idea was not original to me. I took it from a statement by a Peruvian Quechua Indian, Artidoro Tuanama, that I found in a report he had written for Tearfund—an evangelical relief and development agency in the UK for whom I worked as theological advisor. Artidoro's statement takes us to the heart of the concern of this whole book:

> We simply want to take our place as indigenous and native Quechua people, understanding and living out the gospel. We assume our identity without shame, retaliation or indignation against those who have caused harm to our past and castrated our culture.[1]

Artidoro is a pastor and in 1996 was director of the Association of Quechua Evangelical Churches of the Jungle of North East Peru. His people continue to live most of their lives outside the boundaries of industrialism and globalisation. They are not numerous. In global terms and relative to the numerous and powerful nations of the earth, they count for nothing. In light of the majesty of God, a very sophisticated electronic scale would be required to even register their existence because all the nations of the earth with their splendour, glory, and power are but dust on his scales (Isa 40:15–17).

---

1 Tearfund Partners in Development Update File Number 24, June 1996, 1.

This may be so, but Artidoro has also understood something of the genius of the gospel with its revelation of a God who "has brought down rulers from their thrones but has lifted up the humble,...has filled the hungry with good things but has sent the rich away empty" (Luke 1:52,53). He has understood that, having welcomed the gospel, his little people by the world's standards have a responsibility to live out the gospel in the context of their history and culture. Sadly that history and culture has been harmed and castrated.

From the perspective of this book, which is Artidoro's perspective, history is the story of the terrible harm and violence that has been done to less powerful ethnic identities by the more powerful ones. I hesitated for a long time before deciding to use "castrating" in the original title because it is certainly not a nice word and I was afraid of offending Christian sensibilities—and as it transpired my worst fears were realised. However, it expresses so well the sort of violence that has been done to less powerful ethnic identities. Added to this I also feel strongly that if Artidoro, who has suffered much and has witnessed the suffering of his people, could use the term to express what has been done to his people, then who am I to question his wisdom?

It is impossible for a castrated creature to be fruitful and multiply and pass on its genes or genius to another generation. This is precisely what powerful ethnic identities do to less powerful ones. It is not surprising that many ethnic identities that have suffered such humiliation have answered violence with violence.

Not so Artidoro. He does not deny the harm and violence that has been done to his people and their identity. He is even able to identify those that have been guilty of the violence. He also accepts that what has been done has disabled his people from producing fruit for God's glory. One of the most devastating effects of ethnic oppression is to make people ashamed of who they are to the point that they try not to be who they are and adopt the identity of their oppressors. Artidoro believes that the gospel, as a glorious manifestation of God's love to him and his people, frees them inwardly from oppression. Any object of God's costly love cannot be worthless. Therefore, they can be who they are without shame and, in Christ's strength, they can do so without being angry, or wanting to hit back, at their oppressors.

My hope and prayer is that this book will help Christians understand Artidoro's concept of ethnic identity so that more of us will not only be concerned that individuals enter God's eternal kingdom, but that "the glory and honour of the nations will be brought into it" (Rev 21:26).

As I wrote this introduction almost ten years ago, "ethnic" Albanians, as the media described them, were creating mayhem in Macedonia and confirming the conviction that anything to do with ethnicity is bad news. Since then much blood has been spilt in ethnic conflict. Today—June 20, 2010—marks the first anniversary of the end of the long and very bloody ethnic conflict in Sri Lanka, but real peace between Sinhalese and Tamils remains as elusive as ever.

"Ethnic" and "conflict" have become closely linked in the minds of most people as a result of what happened in Yugoslavia and Rwanda. If one did a word association exercise with the word "ethnic," one would inevitably get a list including "cleansing," "genocide," "hatred," "cruelty," "rape," and so on. The common conviction is that it is an unmitigated evil. This book disputes this common conviction. It argues that the tree of ethnic identity is not essentially bad and that it can bear good fruit.

PERSPECTIVE

It seems to me that most of what I have read about ethnic identity, nationhood, and nationalism has been written by those who belong to the numerous and powerful nations of the world or who have been so thoroughly assimilated into their culture that they no longer have a minority perspective. In this work I consciously set out to write about the topic from the perspective of the minority. This is an attempt at a view from underneath. I believe strongly that those who belong to large and powerful ethnic identities, especially Christians, need to appreciate what it means to live at the ethnic margins.

I am a citizen of the United Kingdom who carries a British passport, but ethnically I am a Welsh person who had the privilege of growing up in an area where the Welsh language was still dominant. The whole of my sixty-five years has been lived in Wales, but for most of that time the powerful shadow of England and English has been a daily reality threatening my Welsh identity with extinction. As Jack Straw, a former home secretary of the British government said, the English have historically had a propensity for violence towards the less powerful nations of the British Isles—the Scots, Irish, and Welsh. To a Welsh person, this was such an encouraging statement. One often feels the reality of this "violence" when travelling outside Britain. A question I have been asked more than once when being introduced is, "Which part of England is Wales?" The question may just be the result of ignorance, but a Welsh person finds it difficult to avoid the conclusion that it is the result of an English campaign to deny our existence. After all, it is a historical fact that from the sixteenth to the late twentieth century there was a deliberate attempt on the part of the English state to assimilate Wales into England. This is epitomised by the following entry in an early edition of *The Encyclopaedia Britannica:* "Wales [see England]."

I suspect that what has been said above will sound to some readers like the beginning of a tract on Welsh nationalism. That is understandable, but what follows tries to dissociate the experience of belonging to a minority ethnic identity from the political ideology of nationalism. I attempt to do this by weaving together my own experience of growing up Welsh and a more objective examination of contemporary theories of ethnic identity, nationhood, and nationalism. The main purpose is to see what contemporary theory looks like for a Christian committed to the authority of the Bible who is looking on from the perspective of the margins. There are a great many people who, like myself, have access to English but who belong to national minorities and ethnic groups. My hope is that I have been able to express something of what it feels to belong to a national minority or an ethnic group in such a way as to encourage respect for their heritage. I also have in view those who belong to the powerful ethnic identities who have access to English. In their case I hope to elicit greater understanding and Christian love that will make a constructive rather than destructive contribution to the future life of ethnic and national minorities.

OUTLINE

The book begins by considering the context in which we now think about ethnic identity. Globalisation is one of the dominant realities of our time. It is clearly a force for cultural uniformity. However, it is also a force for a deeper appreciation of diversity. This paradoxical impact of globalisation has been called "globfrag." Some of the implications of both tendencies for ethnic identity are considered. The first chapter then ends with a brief discussion of definitions.

In the second chapter I try to understand how ethnic identity has been viewed in modern times from the perspective of my upbringing and family background in Welsh-speaking Wales. As I thought about my family, it was fascinating to realise that even we, as insignificant as we are in worldly terms, have been influenced by different currents of modernist European thought. On one hand, my father's side of the family was touched by industrialism and represented a socialist view of ethnic identity, nation, and state. To them, preserving identity was not a priority. On the other hand, my mother's background was more agrarian but also more deeply embedded in Welsh-language culture. For many of them, preserving identity was a priority, with some identifying themselves strongly with Welsh nationalism. Both the socialist and nationalist streams flowed from the river of European thinking since the Enlightenment, so an attempt is made to describe and compare the two streams. I argue that the "socialist" stream represents the belief that identity, including ethnic identity, is something human beings create for themselves.

This is the "constructivist" or "instrumentalist" view of collective identity. The "nationalist" stream represents the belief that identity is a given, an inheritance, and not a human creation, which is the "primordialist" view of collective identity.

I also believe that these two streams represent a fundamental tension that is found at the very foundation of modern thought as a whole, which is the tension between "freedom" and "nature." Because the foundational freedom claimed by modern thought is freedom from God's authority, as revealed in his word, it cannot transcend nature and is, therefore, continually threatened by absorption into it. What this means in the context of the constructivist/primordialist axis is that however much some say that identity is created, it becomes an irresistible "natural" force that determines human action. From a spiritual perspective this should not be surprising, because if God is rejected, then the construction of idols is inevitable. Freedom from God leads to the exaltation of something within nature to the status of "god," and gods by definition control human life. The industrialism that developed in Britain in the eighteenth century and gave birth to the idea that free markets in the context of democracy define the meaning of the state gave birth to nineteenth-century imperialism, which led to the terrible oppression of a very large proportion of the earth's peoples. The god that came to be worshipped was "civilisation," and even Christian missionaries were seduced into his service. Ideological nationalism, which has flourished since the beginning of the nineteenth century, clearly arises from the "nature" side of the modernist equation. Here the primordial reality of my collective identity must be served. It makes demands that cannot be gainsaid and as a true "god" demands ultimate loyalty.

What I try to do in the rest of the book is to deliberately explore the meaning of ethnic identity, not from the perspective of modernist thinking[2] but from the perspective of faith in a God who created human beings who, despite their rebellion against him, are the objects of his redeeming love. I believe that the real story of our collective identities, including our ethnic identity, is bound up in the great story of God's dealings with humanity.

The third chapter ("A Church, the Bible, and Complexities of Ethnic Identity") also begins autobiographically by telling something of my spiritual pilgrimage from conversion to sharing the leadership of a bilingual evangelical church. My conversion made my sense of ethnic identity more complicated because much of the spiritual vibrancy I now encountered was in English while, at the same time, I was also becoming more conscious of my rich Welsh-language spiritual heritage. I was faced with having to work out how expressing unity in Christ, which often meant living my corporate Christian life through the medium of English, fitted in with my growing appreciation of my Welsh-language Christian heritage. In my experience this very real tension for many Welsh-speaking Christians was resolved in the bilingual church that I had the privilege of contributing to the establishment and leadership of from 1969–75. It is reflection on this experience that forms the backdrop to a discussion of Paul's view of ethnic identity. Paul's teaching can be summarised as valuing ethnic identity in the context of risky inclusiveness. "Unity in diversity" is the standard phrase.

The implications of the new covenant in Christ, which is in the forefront of Paul's mind, are played out on the stage of God's providential care over humanity through history. In this context the Bible teaches that the formation of ethnic identities or nations was a part of God's purpose. The table of nations in Genesis 10 and other passages witness to this. However, this divinely guided process, like everything else in human experience, is severely impacted by sin. This is the main message of the story of the Tower of Babel in Genesis 11 that follows straight after the table of nations. Sin is the cause of

---

2 I would include postmodernist thinking under the heading of modernism because, as I see it, postmodernism represents a reemphasising of the "freedom" theme in modernist thought. Postmodernity may be in denial about "nature," but I expect that it will show its face again in due course. I can't accept that postmodernism represents a paradigm shift from the foundations of modernist thinking.

nations being judged and being used by God as the agents of judgement, although when God uses one nation to judge another it is not because one nation is more righteous than another. All nations that execute God's judgement are bent rods. The hubris that led to the building of Babel and the consequent confusion of language is also responsible for the confusion of identity in the world. So the chapter ends with a discussion of the complexities of Welsh identity at the beginning of the twenty-first century. Many *ethnes* in the world face the same confusion. The status of the *mestizo* in many Latin American countries is a good example. I argue that, faced with such confusion, as long as there is a strong trunk of ethnic identity with deep indigenous historical roots, there is no reason why a mixed people cannot be grafted onto it. In this context the flourishing of an ethnic identity is a human construct to a great extent.

While chapter 3 focuses on what the Bible says about ethnic identity, chapter 4 ("The Bible, Christianity, Ethnic Identity, and Nationhood") focuses on the impact of welcoming the Bible and its message. Having established that translating the Bible into heart languages was a characteristic of Christianity as soon as there was a Bible to be translated, the impact of this characteristic on England and Wales is considered. Christianity and the Bible undoubtedly contributed significantly to the transformation of the different Anglo-Saxon tribes, which invaded Britain after the collapse of the Roman Empire, into the English nation. The Bible and Christianity would have undoubtedly had the same impact on Wales if the development of the Welsh nation had not been hindered by England.

This historical evidence is then applied to the outworking of the Protestant missionary principle of translating the Bible into the heart languages of people. It is shown that Protestant missionaries were sometimes conscious, even over a hundred years ago, that what they were doing had implications for ethnic identity. But on the whole it seems that, as Protestants committed to ennobling ethnic groups through Bible translation, we have given very little thought to the consequences of our action.

If the Bible has saved Welsh identity in the past, as many claim in Wales, in my lifetime the survival of its legacy into the future has meant determined political action. In a small way I have been involved in this action, especially in the struggle for an adequate provision of Welsh-medium education in the area where I have lived for the last thirty-six years. In 1980 I was plunged into an unexpected conflict with the local authorities, which though never violent, was very heated and which taught me a great deal about what it means to be Christian when demanding something from the authorities that I believed was their obligation to provide. Looking back, it is now clear that we were in dispute on a matter of rights. Therefore chapter 5 ("Ethnic Identity and Human Rights") tells the story of the conflict over Welsh-medium education from the perspective of human rights and argues that there is nothing inconsistent with biblical truth in our demands.

I recognise that many Christians in the United Kingdom find it very difficult to accept that there is anything Christian in taking action to defend ethnic identity, and I suspect that this would be true among those who belong to, or who have been assimilated into, majority *ethnes* all over the world. They see a demand to respect difference as destroying Christian unity, and appeal to passages such as Galatians 3:28 and Colossians 3:11 to justify their attitude. However, a detailed analysis of these passages shows that Paul had precisely the opposite in view. He speaks of a unity that does not destroy but that respects difference.

As Christians we should take a critical stance towards the human rights movement focused on the United Nations (UN), not because the idea of human rights as such is questionable, but because some rights that are demanded are inconsistent with the gospel. We should rejoice when the UN advocates social justice that is consistent with the Bible.

From one perspective, the Declaration on the Rights of Persons Belonging to National or Ethnic, Religious or Linguistic Minorities, adopted by the General Assembly of the UN in September 2007, is a response to the unprecedented mixing of ethnic identities in our time. Peoples have always been on the move but never on such a massive scale as at present. Chapter 6 ("The Ethnic Cauldron of the Contemporary World") focuses on those people who move to live among another people but who seek to retain their ethnic identity. These are the "ethnic minorities" of the UN declaration. On the basis of biblical law concerning the stranger, which is founded on the theological principle of God's love and impartiality, I argue that the right of ethnic minorities to retain their identity should be respected, while recognising that inclusive Christian love tends towards assimilation.

The final section of chapter 6 considers two other results of ethnic mixing. Firstly, the growing number of people whose ethnic origins and location is so mixed that they have decided that they have no ethnic identity, that they belong simply to humanity. History suggests that such people will be given an identity by others, or in due course they or their progeny will find an identity. Globalisation may bring about a different scenario, but I have refrained from speculating about the possible meaning of the "mark of the beast" in this context. Secondly, the strong attachment of many migrants, even after a number of generations, to their land of origin. The popular search for roots witnesses to this, as does the support of violent and peaceful causes.

Chapter 7 ("Not Just a Minority: The Case of Indigenous Peoples") looks at those ethnic groups that have been where they are for a very long time but have been conquered and oppressed by stronger ethnic groups. Some say that only preindustrial societies qualify as indigenous peoples, but I prefer to include every group that has been conquered and survived, including my own people, who were among the first in the world to be industrialised. Sadly, the story of Christian attitudes towards such people, in both Catholic and Protestant traditions, is one of support for destructive policies. Happily, since the demise of the great European empires in the second half of the twentieth century there have been more encouraging signs, with contextualisation in mission theology as one example. From my experience on a visit to Bolivia, I am convinced that education in indigenous languages is crucial to the survival of indigenous peoples and that, as Christians, we should be in the forefront of the drive to encourage such education. We are well placed to do this because of our emphasis on providing the Bible in people's heart languages and the church structures through which education in indigenous languages could be encouraged. This is not to say that education in the majority language should be ignored. The idea is a thorough bilingualism that enables indigenous people to participate fully in a majority culture from the position of equality and not inferiority. This may mean that indigenous people will demand more self-determination, but we should not be fazed by such demands. Our only concern should be that such demands are not driven by ideological nationalism and its violent exclusiveness.

In the final chapter, entitled "Beyond Ethnic Conflict," I discuss the topic that many would consider the only relevant topic when thinking about ethnicity. To underline the constant theme of the whole book—that ethnic identity is not the cause of violent conflict—what happened in postcolonial Africa is examined briefly. Imperial rule in Africa encouraged "tribal" rivalries on the principle of "divide and rule." When independence came, the Western model of nation-state was adopted with its profound antipathy to ethnic diversity. "Tribalism," which had been encouraged by imperial administrations, now became a dirty word. The story of postcolonial Africa has not been a happy one, but with such a colonial legacy it is surprising that it has been as good as it has been. Rwanda is a particularly graphic example of the disastrous effects of colonialism. It was the colonial administration that converted what was becoming a class issue into an ethnic issue in Rwanda. That is not to deny that class conflict can be violent, but it is much more amenable to resolution by constitutional means than ethnic conflict.

Having deflected the blame for conflict away from ethnic identity, there is no doubt that there are millions of people all over the world who feel deeply that another ethnic group has violated their ethnic identity. Many would admit to hatred of another ethnic group because of what they have done to their own ethnic group. Feelings like these do fuel ethnic conflict. But then what should we say and do as Christians? The Croat theologian Miroslav Volf, having been challenged whether he could love a Serbian *Chetnik,* eventually published his response in a substantial volume entitled *Exclusion and Embrace.* Without doing justice to it in any sense, this final chapter summarises some of the key themes of this magnificent volume. Then in September 2000 I had the privilege of being present at one of the seminars of my friend Dr. Rhiannon Lloyd on "Healing the Wounds of Ethnic Conflict" in KwaZulu Natal. A description of that seminar in which I saw Volf's theological principles come alive, as Zulus, Welsh, Afrikaners, and English were reconciled in Christ, is a fitting way to end this volume on ethnic identity.

1

CONTEXT AND DEFINITIONS

CONTEXT

I want to take a step back in this book from the heat of ethnic conflict and ask whether it may be possible that denial and suppression of ethnic identity could be just as responsible for conflict as asserting its validity. A couple of questions about the Albanians points in this direction. Why are there Albanians living in Albania, Kosovo, Macedonia, and Montenegro? Why are Macedonian Albanians denied education in their own language? The answer to the first question would bring into focus the process of empire building that is the imposition of the will of one ethnic identity on others by force. To answer the second question we would need to understand a political philosophy that has been dominant in Europe since the end of the eighteenth century, which justifies the repression of minorities in the interest of state unity and individual freedoms. I believe that going behind ethnic conflict by asking and trying to answer such questions opens up the possibility that there are evils that have produced the evils associated with ethnicity. It is these evils that should be our target as Christians.

GLOBFRAG

The need for a critical assessment of the perception of ethnic identity is becoming acute because it is a reality that is showing no signs of going away, despite predictions to the contrary. In fact, as globalisation surges ahead, so does the rediscovery of ethnic identity. On one hand there is globalisation that is a technological and commercial movement that is uniting people all over the world. Many even talk of the creation of a global village, which implies that globalisation is creating a global community. If so, it may be worthwhile asking, what sort of community is being created? Is it not a consumerist community whose icons are Coke, McDonald's, and Nike and whose values are shaped by MTV and Hollywood?[3] If this is so, then globalisation is really the latest and most powerful expression of the spirit of empire that has blighted human existence since Babel. The frightening thing about this empire is that it can impact people everywhere through its immense commercial, technological, and cultural power. Unlike the great empires of the past, it imposes its will without the force of arms, although backed by the military might of the USA. Globalisation is driven by powerful commercial interests. At its heart is the need of massive Western transnational companies to expand their markets. In order to do this, they need to persuade more and more people that the goods they produce are desirable. The way this is now done is not by marketing the goods themselves but the lifestyle that is implied by possessing them. In this context globalisation is an attempt to lure more and more people into the pursuit of an Anglo-American cultural ideal that is profoundly materialistic. A good example of the success of this strategy is the fact that well-off young people all over the world are increasingly wearing the same clothes, listening to the same Anglo-American music, watching the same Anglo-American TV programmes, and reading the same Anglo-American magazines. As an expression of an aggressively materialistic Anglo-American identity this commercially driven "empire" destroys diversity more effectively than any previous empire.

---

[3] The reality of globalisation struck me very powerfully on a visit to South Africa in September 2000. Having spent the morning in an Assembly of God church where I experienced an exalted culture and Christian values, I spent much of the afternoon with the young adults of a black family in front of MTV with its gutter ethics and Anglo-American culture!

On the other hand there are aspects of the culture that is being globalised that encourage diversity. This tendency has been called "globfrag."[4] There seems to be a force pushing in the direction of fragmentation inherent within the culture that is being globalised. One source of this is the extreme individualism and relativism of postmodernist culture, which says that there is no religious, political, or any other creed that can make universal claims. The individual's freedom to choose any "creed" they like is the creed of postmodernity. I wonder what freedom of choice can mean in the light of genetic and historical endowment or if an individual chooses to identify with a strong collective identity that limits the freedom of others, but this approach undoubtedly opens the door to affirming ethnic diversity. If someone chooses their Yoruba or Karen identity, then their choice must be respected. People can be what they want to be.

In its spiritual, ecological manifestation postmodernist culture, which has strong links with New Age religion in this context, also becomes very affirming of difference. Having rejected the materialistic metanarrative of scientism, it has gone on a quest for spiritual reality to the exotic East and the "primitive" jungle. As a result, the defence of Tibetan identity from the assimilationist policy of China, or of indigenous tribal peoples in the Amazon basin from logging companies, have become popular causes in the part of the world that is driving globalisation. This manifestation of postmodernity sees the preservation of the identity of at least some ethnic groups as essential to the future spiritual and physical well-being of humanity.

Globalisation is also about a revolution in communications, which is not just about Coke, McDonald's, MTV, and Hollywood. When coupled with the growth in education worldwide, it makes possible the empowerment of ethnic groups through dissemination of information about their struggles to survive. Knowing that oth-

---

4 E.g., Gerard Kelly, *Get a Grip on the Future without Losing Your Hold on the Past* (London: Monarch Books, 1999), 160–171.

ers are facing the same problems is a great encouragement, but the communications revolution also makes possible the formation of networks of ethnic groups to defend the threats against them. An example of this is the way a network of indigenous peoples successfully lobbied the United Nations to begin a process of formulating international law to defend their rights. The drive behind this effort came from Latin American indigenous peoples and Native Americans, but the movement could impact the future prospects of the so-called tribal peoples of countries like India, Myanmar, and Thailand.

So while globalisation is unquestionably a powerful force for uniformity, the postmodernist view of freedom, the New Age and ecological movement, and the communications revolution create a current that is flowing in the opposite direction and makes the climate much more amenable than it was, even ten years ago, to a reassertion of ethnic identity.

There is one other factor, which is only loosely connected with globalisation, that has pushed ethnic identity to the fore in the last decade, and that is the collapse of the Communist "empire," especially in the former USSR and Eastern Europe. Once the restraint of the Communist party had been removed, the ethnic consciousness that must have been simmering under the surface burst into life again. This led to the peaceful formation of the independent Central Asian Republics, Belarus, and the Ukraine. Moldova on the other hand, which was seized by Stalin from Romania in 1940 and divided between the Ukraine and a new Moldovan republic, has descended into chaos, which is largely driven by old tensions between its majority Romanian and minority Slavic peoples. The united Russian Federation that remains faces an uncertain future as a number of its republics demand independence with Chechnya in the forefront. In Eastern Europe Czechoslovakia divided peacefully along ethnic lines into the Czech and Slovak republics, there is continuing tension between Romanians and Hungarians in Romania, Yugoslavia exploded in terrible ethnic conflict, and the Gypsies suffer persecution and discrimination throughout the area. The heightened sense of ethnic identity seems set to be a significant factor in this part of the world for the foreseeable future.

DEFINITIONS

Having already used the terms "ethnic," "ethnicity," "ethnic identity," and "ethnic groups," it will be helpful before going any further to discuss definitions.

I am eager, in the first place, to reject the negative definitions that sometimes appear. The following paragraph is a good example of what I would consider unhelpful:

> Ethnicity can be defined as a social phenomenon concerned with negative interactions between cultural-linguistic groups (ethnic groups). "It arises when relations between ethnic groups are competitive rather than co-operative"[5]...Ethnicity often manifests itself in phenomena such as cultural stereotyping and socio-economic and political discrimination...These labels result in prejudice, which encompasses negative assumptions and pre-judgements about other groups that are believed to be inferior...Ultimately, the feeling of exclusiveness as a group, and the negative images held about other groups, lead to discrimination, which Clements and Spinks[6]...see as "prejudice in action."[7]

This definition is a good example of "prejudice in action," the sort of prejudice that this book seeks to dispel. "Ethnicity" is not, by definition, about negative relationships but the characteristic of a certain type of human community. John Hutchinson and Anthony D. Smith, in their introduction to a volume of readings on ethnic-

---

[5] Okwundiba Nnoli, *Ethnicity and Development in Nigeria* (Aldershot, England: Avebury, 1995), 1.
[6] P. Clements and T. Spinks, *The Equal Opportunities Guide: How to Deal with Everyday Issues of Unfairness* (London: Kogan Page, 1994), 14.
[7] Tlamelo Mompati and Gerard Prinsen, "Ethnicity and Participatory Development Methods in Botswana: Some Participants Are to Be Seen and Not Heard," *Development in Practice* 10, no. 5 (November 2000): 626.

ity, list six main features of this type of community. They say that an ethnic identity is the name given to a specific type of human community that shares: (1) a common proper name; (2) a myth of common ancestry; (3) memories of a common past; (4) elements of a common culture, which normally includes religion, custom, or language; (5) a link with a homeland; and (6) a sense of solidarity.[8] I believe that this is a helpful working definition, and it is what I have in my mind when I refer to "ethnicity," "ethnic identity," and so on in this volume. It is also a pity that English has not adopted a noun like the French *ethne* as the name for the type of community that has "ethnic identity" or "ethnicity." I occasionally use it in the hope that it will be adopted as an English term.

There is obviously a close relationship between the meaning of "ethnic identity," as defined by Hutchinson and Smith, and "nation." Hechter claims that nations "are territorially concentrated ethnic groups (like the Quebecois and the Kurds), rather than ethnic groups—like American Jews, Algerians in France, and others often termed *minorities*—who are spatially dispersed in a given state."[9] I believe that Hechter is correct not to identify "nation" with the "state" in this definition, although Will Kymlicka's description of groups such as the Quebecois and Canadian Aboriginals as *national minorities* may be more helpful.[10] When these definitions are applied to the state in which I live, the United Kingdom or Great Britain, it is made up of four nations—the English, Irish, Scottish, and Welsh. In this state the English nation is dominant and the other three can be classified as national minorities. Added to this are substantial numbers of Asians and African-Caribbeans that are recent immigrants, mainly into England. I would describe these as ethnic groups or ethnic minorities.

---

[8] John Hutchinson and Anthony D. Smith, eds., *Ethnicity* (Oxford Univ. Press, 1996), 6–7.
[9] Michael Hechter, *Containing Nationalism* (Oxford Univ. Press, 2000), 14.
[10] Will Kymlicka, *Politics in the Vernacular, Nationalism, Multiculturalism, and Citizenship* (Oxford Univ. Press, 2001), 28

Something also needs to be said about "nationalism" at this stage in the light of the definitions that I have adopted. When the prime minister of the United Kingdom, as he often does, refers to "this nation" or the Evangelical Alliance announced a "National" Assembly of Evangelicals in 1997, meaning the United Kingdom, they could be guilty, maybe unwittingly, of betraying a state-building, nationalist attitude. The United Kingdom is not one nation but four. Ever since the sixteenth century, England has sought to impose its will on the other three historic nations in the United Kingdom and at times has aggressively attempted to destroy their identity and assimilate them. For many Irish, Scottish, and Welsh people, who belong to these threatened nations, to talk of "our nation" or "national," meaning the whole of the United Kingdom, smacks of this English nationalist state-building project that has done such terrible damage to our identity. This type of nationalism, which flows from a sense of superiority over other nations, is, from my perspective, a good example of a destructive ideology that is idolatrous. This type of nationalism is the direct cause of much so-called ethnic conflict. What has happened in the Basque country in Spain, Kosovo, and Macedonia are good examples of this.

Much more could have been written in this section on definitions but, hopefully, enough has been included to provide a framework that will be fleshed out in the body of the book.

2

THE MODERN UNDERSTANDING OF ETHNIC IDENTITY FROM AN AUTOBIOGRAPHICAL PERSPECTIVE

A WELSH CHILDHOOD

Small children don't learn, they absorb. Learning is a conscious activity. Perceiving a body of knowledge that I don't yet possess is required, followed by a conscious and often tedious process of learning. I didn't learn Welsh; I absorbed it. It was the language that my parents and sisters spoke to me while I was a baby. It was the language my mother sang to me as she lulled me to sleep. It was the language in which stories were told when neighbours and friends sat around the fire on winter evenings. One could go on to talk about the Congregational chapel we as a family attended three times every Sunday as well as our homemade entertainment, our concerts, and *eisteddfodau*,[11] big and small. All in Welsh. Even the infants school I attended was all in Welsh.

English was also a reality as long as I can remember in the gardener's cottage of Ciltalgarth farm overlooking the Tryweryn river, which is in the southeastern corner of the Snowdonia National Park. Books and the radio meant that English was always a part of my life. What came to be deeply etched on the memory is interesting: the radio Children's Favourites on Saturday morning and the Goon Show, neither of which needed much linguistic understanding to

---

[11] An *eisteddfod* is a gathering in which children and adults compete with each other mainly in singing, recitation, and poetry. The climax of many such gatherings is the awarding of a chair to the best poet. These gatherings are normally held annually and range from small local gatherings to the National Eisteddfod of Wales that is the biggest folk festival in Europe. These gatherings are tightly woven into the very fabric of Welsh-speaking cultural life.

enjoy. From the English books in the house the undoubted favourite was Arthur Mee's *Children's Encyclopedia*, and a distant second a comic-strip version of *Pilgrim's Progress*. Many hours were spent looking at the pictures in the Encyclopedia, and I had some inkling as to what *Pilgrim's Progress* was all about long before I could read the captions.

English became a greater reality when Ciltalgarth farm acquired a television in the early 1950s. This was the first television in the area and it was soon adopted by the whole district. Family viewing was impossible for the family of Ciltalgarth because they were invariably joined by others. At times their large living room was packed! It should be explained, maybe, that in rural Wales at that time our houses were definitely not our castles. Doors were never locked and visitors known to the family never waited outside to be invited in. One just knocked and walked in. So convention made it very difficult for a family to resist neighbours joining them to watch the television. In fact, at times some neighbours could be found watching the TV without anyone from the family being present! Interestingly, nothing I saw on the TV is etched on my memory in the same way as the radio programmes and the books.

What I absorbed through the radio, books, and the TV was certainly not enough to enable me to communicate in English. This became very apparent when the English cousins of the Ciltalgarth family came to visit. A close relative of Mrs. Evans Ciltalgarth had gone to live in England and married an Englishwoman. In those days Welsh speakers who went to England were generally committed to the principle of "when in Rome do as the Romans do," so the children of Mrs. Evans' relative were being brought up as monoglot English. When the family came to visit, the meeting of monoglot English and monoglot Welsh was almost inevitable for me because the gardener's cottage was almost in Ciltalgarth's farmyard, just beyond the pigsties and the wilderness that had once been an orchard.

I can still remember my feelings when the monoglot English children met us monoglot Welsh. I'm certain that fear was the predominant emotion in my heart. Having discovered that we could not speak to each other, I avoided them like the plague. But why should a child be afraid of another child just because there was no communication between them? Why should their strangeness have been felt as a threat? It may have been a fear of the unknown but it was more likely a reflection of the feelings of Mr. Evans Ciltalgarth.

Mr. Evans was a very successful sheep farmer who was almost illiterate and monoglot Welsh. He was also employed by the council to deliver me and one or two others to school in his van, which was used to carry sheep most of the time. When his wife's relatives were coming to visit, he left us in no doubt about his displeasure. He hated the thought. Then when they arrived, he was conspicuous by his absence. Every excuse to be away from Ciltalgarth was eagerly grasped. But then why should a mature adult and very successful farmer be so afraid of a couple of children who couldn't speak Welsh? Looking back, the only conclusion I can come to is that they made him feel inferior. Mr. Evans had received very little education as a child, but the little that he had experienced had been enough to teach him that English was superior to Welsh. English was the route to greatness, the way of "getting on in the world." It didn't matter that he had done very well without English, that he owned a number of farms and was living in a small mansion. When a couple of "kids" came to visit whose parents had neglected to make it possible to even speak a couple of words in Welsh with their wealthy uncle, he ran away in fear and embarrassment. It is not surprising that I did the same.

So one of my earlier experiences of ethnic diversity was a fearful experience. There was no sense of excitement at the prospect of meeting someone who belonged to another ethnic group. I had no idea that a lot of fun may be had in trying to overcome a linguistic barrier. It could be that I had already imbibed the country person's reticence when faced with the more sophisticated people of the towns and cities, but I'm convinced that a sense of ethnic inferiority was also present. This was to be heightened as I progressed with my education.

ENGLISH SCHOOLING

The first school I attended had two rooms shaped like a T with a maximum of thirty pupils on the school roll during my time there. One room was for infants (four to seven years) and the other for primary (eight to eleven years). We began sitting in a group of desks at the bottom of the T and progressed up the room from year to year until we got to the T junction. We then moved to the top of the T and progressed up the primary room from right to left. As far as I can remember, our formal English education did not really begin until we got to the primary room, by which time it was expected that we could read and write Welsh. But even at primary level, Welsh was the class language. The only non-Welsh speaking person in the school was the school cook, Mrs. Clayton. She and her two children had moved to live in a very remote cottage at the foot of the Garn hill about half a mile from our house and was treated as an "alien" by us children. She remained an alien because she never bothered even to attempt to learn Welsh and become integrated into our community. Her daughter, on the other hand, was young enough to come to the primary school. Since we were unable to speak English to her, she soon learnt to speak Welsh to us and was accepted, although her experience of another culture continued to mark her out as different.

In the 1950s in the UK, primary school ended with sitting an examination called the Eleven Plus which determined whether one went on to a grammar school or not. Since one had to be in the category of having special educational needs not to go on to the grammar school in our area. just about everyone passed the Eleven Plus. Ability was judged not so much by passing the exam but when one passed it. As it happens, I was put in for the exam a year earlier than most and found myself aged ten going daily on the train down the Tryweryn valley to the Bala Boys Grammar School.

From its foundation at the beginning of the eighteenth century, this had been an English and anglicising institution. Welsh was taught as an individual subject, and we had one enlightened teacher who insisted on teaching geography through the medium of Welsh in the first three years. Apart from that, everything was in English, including the whole ethos of the school. My exercise books from the first year at the grammar school, which I kept for many years, witnessed to the intense culture shock that I experienced when I made the transition from the primary school. It was very clear from the books that my grasp of English was tenuous to say the least. I had been plunged from the Welsh world of my everyday life into an alien English world. Added to this, the message that the school conveyed almost continually was that my Welsh world was inferior and that the English world represented by the school was the world that really mattered.

A significant proportion of the pupils, especially in the towns, had already succumbed to this intense cultural pressure and came from homes where Welsh was understood but where they chose to speak English. Some of the wealthier people in the area sent their children to private schools so that they would be trained to become English gentlemen and women. There was no doubt about the message given by the educational system—I belonged to a backward and inferior people that needed to forsake its language and traditions and become English.

MY FAMILY'S VIEW OF ETHNICITY

My Father's Family

The educational system that was designed to make me a good citizen of Great Britain was ultimately the result of a major upheaval in Europe and America. Unconsciously, my life was being shaped by the powerful forces that had revolutionised political theory and practice since the time of the Enlightenment in the eighteenth century. Interestingly, two of the major and opposing positions on the political significance of ethnicity, nation, and state were represented in my immediate family.

My father came from the slate-quarrying district of Ffestiniog. This was the only industrialised district in the whole county of Merionethshire, which was the main unit of local administration during my childhood. My grandfather had worked as a clerk in one of the slate quarries and had been active in the labour union there, which had been forced to fight hard for justice for the workers in the last years of the nineteenth and early years of the twentieth century. My grandfather died at the early age of thirty-five, leaving a widow and four young children to struggle to survive with very little welfare benefits to support them. It is not surprising that the family considered themselves socialist and that they were strong supporters of the British Labour Party.

Socialism, which is a child of the Industrial Revolution, does not believe that ethnic identity has any permanent significance. With liberalism it shares the conviction that industrialism will inevitably lead to the demise of ethnic and national identity. The socialist theory of ethnic/national identity, which is shared by the liberal tradition of free market economics as well, has been arranged by Gellner in the shape of a syllogism:

1. Ethnic hostility and separatism require cultural differences, for without them, how could ethnic groups ("nations") identify themselves and distinguish themselves from their enemies?

2. Industrial social organisation erodes cultural nuances.

3. Therefore the advancement of industrialism erodes the very basis of nationalism.[12]

There can be no doubt that something like what is described in this syllogism has often happened. People from different ethnic groups have migrated into the cities looking for work in the modern industrial sector. As they have been forced to mix with others from different ethnic groups and to fit their lives to the pat-

---

[12] Ernest Gellner, *Nationalism* (London: Phoenix, 1997).

tern demanded by an industrialised economy, their strong sense of ethnic identity has weakened. A good example of this is seen in the story of what happened to the hundreds of thousands of Welsh and Irish workers that migrated to Liverpool and other English cities in the nineteenth century. By the end of the century, Welsh-speaking Calvinistic Methodists had forty-two churches, many of them with a membership of five hundred or more, in their Liverpool Association, and there were many Welsh-speaking Congregational, Wesleyan Methodist, and Baptist churches as well. By the end of the twentieth century there were less than ten of these churches left, many of which were struggling to survive.

My wife's family is a good example of the way the industrial city can erode ethnic identity. Her grandparents were born in Wales and moved to Liverpool to find work. Her mother was born in Liverpool and was brought up in Welsh, and the family attended the local Welsh Calvinistic Methodist church. My mother-in-law married a man who was monoglot English, though of partial Welsh extraction. They were active members of an English-language evangelical mission church where my wife's mother found a spiritual vitality that was missing in the Welsh church in which she was brought up. My wife was brought up in English, educated in private schools, and feels strongly that she is an Englishwoman. There were undoubtedly powerful forces already undermining my wife's family's Welsh identity before they moved to Liverpool from rural Wales. When the pressure of the English commercial life of the industrial city was added, the result was the demise of the family's ethnic identity in just two generations.

This process of assimilation, which can be documented again and again, is claimed by liberals as proof that "getting on in the world" is the really important thing for human beings. What really drives us, they say, is the desire to satisfy economic needs. What humans need is democracy and a free market where individuals can pursue these needs. As long as they are satisfied, other things such as ethnic identity will be forsaken.

The socialist picture, especially in its Marxist form, is somewhat bleaker and less optimistic, at least in the earlier stages of their version of the human story. Whereas the liberals believed that a free market would lead to universal benefits, the Marxists could see that it was leading to hell on earth for a very large proportion of the working population. As far as they were concerned, industrialism was set up in such a way that the owners of capital would get richer and richer at the expense of their workers. This would inevitably lead to a class war in which the oppressed proletariat in the industrialised countries would unite to wrest control of industry from the hands of the capitalists. Marx believed that the victory of the proletariat was inevitable and ethnic identity was irrelevant in this development. The aim was the international unity of workers in the pursuit of industry with dignity. "Workers of the world unite."

In my father's case the liberal ideal was probably expressed primarily through the educational system, which was geared to making everyone in Wales thoroughly acquainted with English so that they could participate fully in the market. He learnt to read Welsh through Sunday school, but he never really mastered the art of writing the language, which was an embarrassment to him when his children left home and there was some pressure to write to them occasionally. In fact I can only remember receiving one short letter from my father.

Something of the socialist ideal must have filtered through to my father as a result of my grandfather's involvement with the labour union at the quarry. My father was only four when his father died but his older sister, who was only seven, always spoke with tremendous pride of my grandfather's involvement with the union, and she was an unyielding supporter of the British Labour Party. The purpose of telling this story is not to prove beyond question that my father's family had adopted a socialist view of the insignificance of ethnic identity. I have no real evidence for such a claim. But they had been touched significantly by a movement of thought and action which enabled them to relegate their ethnic identity to a low level in their list of priorities. When the Welsh nationalist movement was gathering a head of steam in the 1960s, they were terribly opposed to what it represented. I was then old enough to realise that my father was being pulled in two directions because some of my mother's family leaned strongly in the direction of nationalism.

My Mother's Family

While my father was brought up in an industrial setting, my mother's was agrarian. Her father rented a very small farm from the local council. He was employed by the council to keep the sides of roads tidy, and he did some home butchering for local farmers. Having been spiritually renewed in the 1904 revival, he was a respected elder of the local Calvinistic Methodist church. As the youngest child of his youngest child, I was denied the pleasure of getting to know my grandfather on earth because he died aged seventy-five before I was born. Sadly, I was also denied the pleasure of having my mother influence my development into adulthood, because she died when I was ten. From what I know of her, she shared her father's spirituality and was immersed in Welsh cultural life, which was mainly centred in the chapels. After my mother's death, the main influence on me from her side of the family came through her only brother, my Uncle Bob. I spent at least some of my summer holidays each year with him and my Auntie Annie from about eight to sixteen.

My Uncle Bob was a skilled carpenter who, by the time I used to stay with him, held the tenancy of the small farm which his father had held before him. Like so many, as a young man he had gone to Liverpool in England to seek employment. He really enjoyed life in the city but was forced to return to Wales in 1928 because work had become very scarce as a result of the Depression. He eventually found employment as a fitter in a local milk factory in 1938 and remained there until he was forced to give up work because of ill health in 1951. His daughter, who was one year old when the family returned to Wales from Liverpool, cannot remember my uncle being anything politically other than a very enthusiastic nationalist.

Although a carpenter by trade, he had a deep love of Welsh history, literature, and current affairs and read widely. He was familiar with the discussions that led to the formation of the Welsh nationalist party, Plaid Cymru, in 1925 and was among its earliest members. Since nationalism in Wales in the 1920s was also a protest against British militarism and imperialism, my uncle was a convinced pacifist. He joined in a number of protests to try and stop the establishment of an artillery practice range near Trawsfynydd in North Wales and was even taken into custody on one occasion.

On the basis of what I as a young boy heard said in conversations at my uncle's home, the humiliation of his ethnic identity by Englishmen, as well as intellectual conviction, had made him into someone who was committed to seeing Wales become an independent nation with its own government. He believed very strongly that political self-determination was the only way ethnic identity could be preserved and developed. My uncle had no doubts at all about the distinctiveness of the Welsh people. It was so obvious to him that the English and the Welsh were different. What was not so obvious to many of his Welsh-speaking compatriots was the nationalist conviction that a distinct ethnic identity needs to go hand in hand with a distinct political identity if distinctiveness is to survive and flourish. This is the idea that the *ethne* as nation needs a state in order to authenticate and preserve its existence. Added to this, he believed that there was a very strong hegemonic tendency in the English which was very corrosive of other ethnic identities. I heard him speak on a number of occasions about the Englishman who was the manager of the milk factory in terms which implied that he was typical of what Uncle Bob perceived as the Englishman's need to be the boss.

However, by the 1950s the Wales which Plaid Cymru was campaigning to free from English rule was losing its linguistic identity at an alarming rate—by that time less than a quarter of the population spoke Welsh. But Plaid Cymru was and is a party committed to constitutional change by democratic means. It accepts that the only valid basis for government is the voice of the people. In order to succeed, therefore, Plaid Cymru had to persuade the majority of the population of Wales, who had either lost or never possessed one of the key elements of a Welsh ethnic identity, that they needed political independence in order to regain or acquire it. Added to this is the fact that the industrialised areas of South and North East Wales had been anglicised partly as a result of immigration of English-speaking people from England and Ireland. They and their descendants in those areas were being asked to value an important characteristic of a historic Welsh ethnic identity that they had never shared.

My uncle had no doubts whatsoever about his ethnic identity and the way to preserve it, but the political reality was complex. The support of the majority who did not share his experience of identity was required in order to secure it. This type of complex political reality is in fact the context in which ethnic identities subsist all over the world, especially where industrialism has arrived. It is also the context in which ethnicity has to be defined.

ETHNIC IDENTITY, NATION, AND STATE IN EUROPE SINCE THE EIGHTEENTH CENTURY

Modernists and Primordialists

Just a very sketchy outline of my uncle's position is enough to indicate that he was swimming in the mainstream of European thinking about ethnic identity, the nation, and the state. The clear tension in his political philosophy between the real (that is, Wales is ethnically diverse) and the ideal (that is, Wales belongs to the Welsh) is also something that historians and political philosophers and theorists have struggled with and disagreed about, especially during the last quarter of the twentieth century.

The debate has been going on for a long time, is spread across a number of disciplines, and has become extremely complicated. In anthropology the two poles of the argument are represented by the primordialists on the one hand and the instrumentalists on the other. The primordialists believe that ethnic identity is of the essence of what human beings are. It is not something which humans create; it is a given, the assumption on which they build their lives. The instrumentalists argue that ethnic identity is a human creation. It is something which societies construct in order to pursue political or economic ends.

In the context of political theory, philosophy, and history, what is called "instrumentalism" in anthropology is called "modernism," or "constructivism." Modernists believe that what we understand by ethnic identity, nations, and nationalism are modern ideas originating in the Enlightenment of the eighteenth century. Constructivists believe that nations and ethnic identities are constructed out of the social circumstances in which they emerge. This brings us back to the modernism which we touched on briefly in thinking about my father's political background in industrialised Blaenau Ffestiniog. The story needs to be told a little more fully at this point.

THE ROOTS AND FRUITS OF MODERNISM

Modernism as expressed in the liberal and socialist approaches, which had an impact on my father's background, had its origin in the Enlightenment of the eighteenth century. The Enlightenment elevated reason to the seat of authority in human affairs. It declared the freedom of the human mind and spirit from traditional authority, especially the authority of the church as a force for conservatism that was often linked very closely to the power of the state. By the end of the seventeenth century the persecution of Galileo by the Roman Catholic Church and the Vatican state had become a *cause celebre* of the type of religious oppression allied to the power of the state that needed to be overthrown.

Because church and state had been so closely linked in the mediaeval model of Christendom, to challenge the authority of the church, which happened during the period of the Reformation in the sixteenth century, inevitably led to challenging the authority of the state. The most significant European challenge before the eighteenth century came in the English Civil War.

The intellectual root of the Civil War was the political theology of Protestants like George Buchanan and Samuel Rutherford who argued against the doctrine of the divine right of kings. James I and Charles I, like other European kings, believed that they were above the law. As the ultimate lawmakers, they could not be subject to the law that they made. The theologians argued that there was only one lawmaker who is not subject to his law and that is God, and kings as well as their subjects are under his law. In fact kings rule by God's permission and are expected by God to see that justice is done towards their subjects. If justice is not done, then their subjects have the right to remove them from office in favour of someone who will rule justly under God. By the eighteenth century this type of thinking, which had been put to the test in the English Civil War, had developed into the social contract theory of government. According to this view, there is nothing primordial in a form of government. Kings and an aristocracy don't rule because that is how things are. They rule because there is an implied agreement between the rulers and the ruled that this is the best way to preserve civil society. If the root of government is a social contract, then there is no reason why the shape of government cannot be a social construct. With the American Declaration of Independence and Constitution and the Constitution of the Republic after the French Revolution, this theory became a historic reality.

There is one other key belief of the Enlightenment that needs to be grasped in order to understand political developments since, and that is the belief in the universal of "humanity." This is the belief that human beings have limitless ability to master the natural world and to order their own lives; the belief that human reason operates along the same lines everywhere and that if we were left in freedom to follow reason we would come to the same beneficial conclusions about how we should order our lives in this world. "Man, the measure of all things," given freedom, is able to shape his destiny in this world for the good of all.

According to the modernists, the political dimension of the Enlightenment as encapsulated in the American Constitution and the French Revolution's cry of "Liberty, Equality and Fraternity" gave birth to the modern nation-state when combined with the great social changes brought about by migration and the Industrial Revolution. When the founders of the United States of America came to define their new state, everyone within the boundaries of the state, except for slaves and Native Americans, became citizens irrespective of social status or ethnic origin. The same was true in France. At the Revolution everyone within the boundaries of France became French citizens possessing equal rights before the law. However, the equal rights enjoyed by citizens of the United States or France did not include the legal right to ethnic diversity. In the United States the law spoke English only, and the large community of people of German or any other origin would have to be anglicised in order to enjoy equality. Likewise in France the Bretons and other ethnic minorities had to become French.

The fact that English was the dominant language of the United States or French of France is not seen as that significant by the modernists. A common language is an administrative convenience that facilitates the pursuit of material prosperity, which is the fundamental "freedom" of modernism. Language as a marker of ethnic identity is not that relevant. So ethnic identity is not significant in the construction of the modern nation-state. An *ethne* is merely a creation of those who are looking for a power base within a state; it will inevitably melt away in the warmth of practical efficiency. What is important is the freedom of the individual to associate, produce, and influence the nation-state's development through a democratic process. As already stated, modernists expect ethnic diversity to diminish as nation-states get bigger and bigger, with the ultimate ideal being one universal nation-state where everyone can enjoy the freedom to create and consume. It is at this point that the idea of humanity will be finally realised. This echo of Babel is a frightening thought in a world where human beings are not very good at handling power.

This "freedom" stream of modernist political theory has been, and continues to be, very influential. It has brought many blessings to many people but at a heavy cost to a host of small and marginalised peoples. It was the theory which motivated most of the movements that struggled for freedom from colonial oppression in the twentieth century. It led to the formation of many new "secular" states, such as India and Nigeria, that are now threatening to fall apart because of the failure to recognise the reality and value of ethnic identity. But it was not the only idea of the relationship between ethnic identity, nation, and the state to emerge from the Enlightenment.

THE ROOTS AND FRUITS OF PRIMORDIALISM

The Enlightenment made a great deal of noise about freedom. Liberty was the cry of the revolution. But there is a profound paradox at the very heart of modernism. "Freedom" is continually threatened by "nature." "Freedom" represents the modernist confidence in human capacity to construct history, while "nature" represents the idea that human beings are constructed by history. Paradoxes are inevitable. Biologists try their best to claim that what we are as human beings is not really included within the inevitable process of evolution. Karl Marx looked forward to the predetermined victory of the proletariat. Social scientists blame the most heinous crimes on everything other than the will of a free and responsible individual. We cry "freedom" but seem to be ruled by "nature." In political theory the free individual of the revolution can become lost in the corporate identity of *ethne*, nation, or state.

In its German idealist form, Enlightenment political theory from the perspective of "nature" saw the progressive history of the world in terms of the organic evolution of the idea of humanity. Each nation or *ethne* has something to contribute to this gradually unfolding history of humanity, but some nations or *ethnes* have more to contribute than others. This was particularly true of the powerful European nation-states that came into being in the nineteenth century. Many came to believe that these nation-states had developed a genius or spirit which represented most perfectly the progressive evolution of humanity and therefore had a duty to share their genius with less-developed nations/*ethnes*. It is this type of thinking that has fuelled the fires of "nationalism" and imperialism since the nineteenth century.

"Nationalism" is an emotive and confusing subject over which a lot of ink, and blood, has been spilt. Modernists hate it and lift up their self-righteous hands in horror whenever it is mentioned. But in fact it is their shadow, the other side of their coin. Human beings are incurable worshippers. Having made "man" the measure of all things, it is not at all surprising that modern man should make some aspect of human life an object of worship. Often in "nationalism" it is the nation, the *ethne,* that is worshipped.

There have also been plenty of modernists who have been happy to combine the creed of freedom with that of nature. They came to believe that their democratic, industrialist, and bureaucratic institutions gave them a right to oppress others. The doctrine of Manifest Destiny, which was developed by policy makers in the USA in the first half of the nineteenth century, is a good example of modernist imperialism. The following quotation from the *Cheyenne Daily Leader* of March 3, 1870, is a good example of the doctrine:

> The rich and beautiful valleys of Wyoming are destined for the occupancy and sustenance of the Anglo-Saxon race. The wealth that for untold ages has lain hidden beneath the snow-capped summits of our mountains has been placed there by Providence to reward the brave spirits whose lot it is to compose the advance-guard of civilisation. The Indians must stand aside or be overwhelmed by the ever advancing and ever increasing tide of emigration. The destiny of the aborigines is written in characters not to be mistaken. The same inscrutable Arbiter that decreed the downfall of Rome has pronounced the doom of extinction upon the red men of America.[13]

---

[13] Dee Brown, *Bury My Heart at Wounded Knee: An Indian History of the American West* (London: Vintage, 1991), 189. First published 1970.

Similar ideas drove the expansion of the British Empire. It was a common belief well into this century that Britain had been blessed by God or fate with the most advanced civilisation in the world. Therefore it had a duty to share those blessings with as many as possible. That gave Britain the right to annex vast tracts of land to the crown of England and rule over the people of those lands. Empire builders believed that it was the destiny of Britain to spread the blessings of modern civilisation all over the world. But those whose destiny it was to enjoy British rule paid very handsomely for the privilege! Modernists can protest and deplore empire as much as they like, but many of the great empire builders were modernists in their thinking about government and the state. They differed only in the way they thought the message should be disseminated.

To return to the idealist view of nationalism which originated in Germany, it differed from the North American or French model of nationhood in that its starting point was not territory or the state but the people. In France everyone within the boundaries of the country constituted the nation, be they Breton, French, or whatever. In Germany the nation was constituted by ethnic Germans alone. There are various reasons for this difference in emphasis. One reason is that in France, the USA, and Britain the modern nation-states were formed with a diversity of ethnic groups, while in Germany and Italy it was a case of amalgamating a number of separate German or Italian states into one. The process of German and Italian unification was not completed until the 1870s, and even then Austria remained independent from Germany. The idea of uniting all Germans or Italians under the one government and flag was a strong motivation for unification.

Another reason was the idealist philosophy alluded to above. According to this philosophy every ethnic group had its own unique contribution to make to the development of the idea of humanity. They called this the genius or spirit of a people. In order for this spirit to be fully manifested, it needed to be embodied in a state. It was through the institution of the state that an ethnic group made its unique contribution to the historical realisation of humanity. This is the origin of the idea that an *ethne* must have its own government or state in order to make its own unique contribution to history. The potential for evil in this view has been more than fully realised by those who have developed it in ways that may have horrified its original formulators.

The most famous is Nazism. While the original idea that the spirit of an *ethne* or nation, as manifested in language, history, and political institutions, does subject the individual to the will of the whole, it did not preclude those who were from different ethnic origins from belonging. So Jews like the eighteenth-century Enlightenment philosopher Moses Mendelsshon could be accepted as fully German, as could his composer grandson, Felix. The Nazis denied this possibility with their doctrine of ethnic/racial purity. While the idealists believed that individuals found their identity in the corporate institutions of the state, the Nazis insisted that the individual will should be totally subject to the will of the party, which they believed embodied the essence of the state. This idea is not a million miles away from the jingoistic views, which were common in Britain and the USA in the twentieth century, that it is the duty of all citizens to be prepared to die for their country. The terrible treatment of pacifists who refused to conform witnesses to this.

The other obvious relative of this view is the contemporary view of ethnic purity that has led to the horrors of ethnic cleansing. This is a development of the idea that an *ethne* needs a territory and a state in order to realise its potential. It says that members of other ethnic groups have no right to be in a particular territory and that they must be removed either by death or banishment. So the Croats murdered and drove the Serbs from the Krajina, the Serbs murdered and drove Bosnians from parts of Bosnia and Kosovars from Kosovo, Kosovars are now murdering and driving Serbs out of Kosovo, and in Rwanda ethnocentric Hutus set out to solve the Tutsi "problem" through genocide. The terrible atrocities perpetrated in the name of ethnic cleansing shock us, but there is nothing essentially new in what is happening. After all, the Celtic peoples of what became known as England were ethnically cleansed by Anglo-Saxons, as were the overwhelming majority of the native peoples of the United States, Tasmania, and Australia, and then there is the continuing saga of the destruction of South American peoples at the hands of Europeans of mainly Portuguese and Spanish origin.

UNCLE BOB'S "NATIONALISM" IN THE LIGHT OF THE MODERNIST-PRIMORDIALIST DEBATE

I want to apply what has been said about ethnic identity, nation, and state in European political theory to the memories of the times I spent with my "nationalist" favourite uncle. The only conclusion I can come to is that modernists would think that he, at best, was making a fuss about something of little consequence and, at worst, that he was a dangerous subversive.

It is true, as the modernists could point out, that my uncle was living in a country where he could enjoy many freedoms such as the freedom of movement and association, the freedom to trade, the freedom to vote for the candidate of one's choice in elections at local and national levels, the freedom that comes from living in a welfare state with a National Health Service and so on. Modernists would say that these economic and political freedoms are the key freedoms. As long as people can eat, work, and vote, celebration can take care of itself. The language of the newspaper, the radio programme, the poem, the song, or the play is not important. One universal language and idiom will do fine for the modernist utopia. Death to ethnic diversity.

This is all very well for the dominant *ethne* in a multiethnic state like Britain. But what modernism means for minority ethnic identities in the British context is that we ought to forsake whatever ethnic roots we have and become English. They argue that this is not what they are saying but that, in adopting the English language and ways, those who are not from an English ethnic origin will contribute to the creation of a new identity which they call "British." This again is the dominant voice speaking. It does not feel like this at all to many of us who belong to minority ethnic identities. For a Welsh person to become "British" means cutting off life-giving links to the past. Sadly, many have done it as a result of the sustained campaign through the educational system to breed a sense of inferiority in us. The belittling of his heritage and the severe discrimination against those who valued it was the cause of my uncle's resolute determination to cling to it. He may have been wrong to tar all English people with the same brush, and he was certainly wrong to show hatred towards the English as he sometimes did, but his strong desire to cling to his ethnic identity in the face of tremendous pressure to forsake it is commendable. "Nationalists" are more often than not those who stand against a wrong that has been perpetrated against them.

However, the modernists are not yet finished with my uncle. Those of the constructivist sort would say that his idea of ethnic identity and nationhood was only a social construct anyway. Some would have said to him that he was just being exploited by a group of power-hungry, middle-class Welsh leaders who felt excluded from the British establishment. His Welsh identity had been created by this group so that they could establish a power base for themselves. There is some evidence at least from other situations to corroborate this thesis. Many now believe that the genocide perpetrated in Rwanda was the result of the cynical manipulation of ethnic hatred by a group of power-hungry Hutus. But it is difficult to believe that this Hutu caucus created Hutu ethnic identity. It is much more likely that they exploited something that was there already. It is the same in Wales. Plaid Cymru was indeed formed by a group of middle-class people, which included a large proportion of Christian ministers, but it is difficult to accept that they were simply driven by a desire for power and that principle played no part in their motivation. In the early days especially, to join Plaid Cymru was a sure way of not gaining any power, and there are a number of well-known cases of politicians forsaking Plaid Cymru for British parties in order to have a better chance of grasping power. There is more validity in the opinion that the leaders of the Welsh nationalist movement were set on creating a Welsh identity. Yet it would be nonsense to say that there was nothing there for them to work with. They were unquestionably standing for something which had a long history and which they had inherited, but they were shaping that inheritance for life in the twentieth century. That shaping continues, and the identity which seemed very close to death in 1950 is showing more signs of life by 2010, thanks to people like my uncle Bob.

Finally, the idea that my uncle could have been a dangerous subversive is very amusing because he was a kind and gentle man and a very convinced pacifist. It is true that pacifists have been treated as subversives by modern nation-states because they refuse to accept that the state cannot make ultimate claims on people's loyalty. In Britain, for example, pacifists were put in prison until the Second World War because their refusal to kill Britain's enemies was considered treasonable! Interestingly, the whole Welsh nationalist movement was pacifist from its foundation and explicitly rejected any violence against people in pursuit of its ends. It may have been a movement that has inherited something of the rhetoric of the idealist tradition in its belief that an *ethne* needs a political expression in order to preserve and enhance its existence, but it has been totally committed to gaining that expression by means of the ballot and not the gun.

CONCLUSION

There is a deep division in contemporary thinking about the meaning and significance of ethnic identity. On the one hand, there is the modernist-constructivist-instrumentalist camp which tends to relegate ethnic identity to a low status in the scale of significant human values. In this stream of thinking flowing from the Enlightenment in both its liberal and socialist forms, political and economic freedoms are supreme. They seem very reluctant to admit that it has been the pursuit of such freedoms, often at the expense of ethnic freedom, that has been the direct cause of many conflicts in the last two hundred years. Nationalism, which modernists see as a supreme evil, would not exist without the oppression and injustice that has been perpetrated in the name of modernism.

On the other hand, the primordialists represent the "nature" end of the fundamental tension between "freedom" and "nature" that is endemic in modern thought. Here the tendency is for ethnic identity to take the place of God in the scale of human values. Individuals lose themselves in the corporate ethnic identity that then makes ultimate demands on their lives. The exaltation or survival of the *ethne* becomes the ultimate value, and any means become justifiable to serve that end. Some aspects of imperialism, the American idea of Manifest Destiny, Nazism, the activities of the Irish Republican Army (IRA) and other paramilitary groups in Ireland, and ethnic cleansing in the Balkans and Rwanda witness to the horrors that have been and are being perpetrated when this tendency becomes dominant.

As the pendulum has swung between "freedom" and "nature" in the world that has fallen under the spell of the West since the eighteenth century, it is fair to ask for another path. Maybe there is an alternative route. Since it is now acceptable to look for a third way, the rest of this volume is really an attempt to do so. The alternative path that I propose between nationalism and indifference to ethnicity is based on the revelation that God created human beings and that, despite our rebellion against him, he has a redemptive purpose in Jesus Christ even for the nations.

A CHURCH, THE BIBLE, AND THE COMPLEXITIES OF ETHNIC IDENTITY

CONVERSION

In August 1962, aged fifteen, an event occurred which has decisively shaped my life ever since—I experienced an evangelical conversion. In my consciousness this was the culmination of a two-year-long struggle with my conscience. Even though I had been brought up to attend a Congregational church three times every Sunday, it was at a youth camp run by the Evangelical Movement of Wales in the summer of 1960 that I first realised that Christianity was not something one inherits automatically as a result of one's upbringing. I saw that I was not a Christian and that to become one I needed to consciously turn my back on what could only be described for me, even at thirteen, as the way of the world and follow Christ. The decisive event took place appropriately during another camp which by 1962 was held at Bryn y Groes, the Evangelical Movement of Wales' centre at what was by then also my hometown of Bala. In the meeting the night before I submitted, the speaker had been contrasting Adam and Zacchaeus—Adam hiding in the trees from God because of his shame and Zacchaeus climbing into the tree so that he might see Jesus. Even after this meeting, I admitted to the camp leader that I was inclined to identify with Zacchaeus. The following night I had no doubt and I gladly bowed the knee to Jesus.

My spiritual awakening preceded my ethnic awakening and in many ways made the latter more complicated. Since first realising the implications of evangelical religion at the camp in 1960, I had regularly attended a Scripture Union group at Bryn y Groes. The meetings were mainly in Welsh but all the audiovisual material used, such as the excellent "Fact and Faith" films, were in English. After my conversion, my involvement with the Scripture Union group intensified. We went to National Young Life Campaign (NYLC) English-language meetings in Wrexham, which was the nearest big town; we became familiar with the Billy Graham campaigns and the then-popular songs which were sung by George Beverly Shea; we used English Scripture Union notes for our daily Bible reading; and most other books and booklets we read to help us on our way were also in English. Much of what seemed to be real and lively and relevant to youth in my newfound faith was in English.

Yet this was not the whole story. At that time in Evangelical Movement of Wales circles, an evangelical conversion did not mean a weakening of our denominational commitment.[14] To the contrary, it was expected that we would be more committed than ever. So I faithfully attended all the meetings of the Congregational church, while others attended the Baptist and Presbyterian churches. On top of this, we also met together as evangelicals every week for a *seiat*. This was a small group meeting which was consciously linked to the model of the "experience meetings" or "society meetings" that had been such a powerful force for growing the church during the eighteenth-century revival in Wales.[15] In these meetings we shared our experience of God, studied the Bible, prayed, and often sang spontaneously. These meetings were held in the Welsh language and thoroughly infused with the spirit of Welsh revivalism. It was here that I began to learn to appreciate my rich Welsh Christian heritage.

On March 15, 1963, Emyr Llywelyn Jones, a student at University College, Aberystwyth, appeared before the magistrates' court in

---

[14] The situation changed after Dr. Martyn Lloyd Jones called on evangelicals to "put their fellowship with other evangelicals above other church loyalties" in a meeting of the National Evangelical Alliance Assembly in October 1966. See O. Barclay, *Evangelicalism in Britain 1935–1995* (Leicester, England: InterVarsity Press, 1997), 83.

[15] They were similar to the "class meetings" of Wesleyan Methodism in England.

Bala, accused of causing an explosion that destroyed a transformer at the Llyn Celyn works on February 10 of the same year. As school prefects, we were allowed to go into town during the lunch hour, so I accompanied a number of friends into the crowded public gallery of the court to witness history in the making. But we must go back a few years in order to understand why Emyr Llywelyn was standing before the court.

Capel Celyn was a little hamlet about seven miles north of Bala in the Tryweryn valley. It consisted of a chapel, a school, a post office, and a few houses, and was the focus of the farming community around. My family lived in Tynybont, the next little hamlet down the Tryweryn valley, so there were close links between us and the community focused on Capel Celyn. In the mid-1950s Liverpool Corporation came to the conclusion that Lake Fyrnwy, the reservoir that they had built in Wales earlier in the century, was not going to be able to satisfy their needs for water in the future. They decided that they needed another reservoir, so they began looking in Wales for suitable sites. The site that was eventually decided upon was the Celyn valley. This was done without any reference to the people that lived there. I can remember test drilling being done in the field where I learnt to ride a bicycle while no one really knew what was going on. Permission would have been granted by Colonel Price of Rhiwlas who owned most of the Tryweryn valley and who was destined to be a major beneficiary from the scheme. He was from impeccable Welsh origins, but like almost all the landowning gentry in Wales, his family had become totally anglicised and alienated from his tenants and their culture.

When the people of Cwm Celyn found out what was going on, a vigorous campaign was mounted to oppose the scheme and preserve their community. Since Liverpool Corporation needed an act of Parliament to be able to drown the Celyn Valley, the climax of the campaign focused on the passage of the bill in 1957. In the crucial debate, every Welsh member of Parliament except one voted against the bill, but despite this the bill was passed because of the massive majority of English members in the Westminster Parliament. The door was now open for the final tragedy of the indigenous Welsh community of Celyn, but the campaign had been a defining moment in the history of Wales. Wales had spoken with one voice and had been ignored by an English-dominated Westminster Parliament. Of course, being only ten at the time, I was largely oblivious of what was going on but by 1963, with the work on the dam well advanced, I understood a little better. Yet I certainly did not approve of Emyr Llywelyn's violent protest. In fact I felt that in the campaign against drowning the valley an idealised picture of the community and its environment had been created which was far from the truth. The land was poor, the chapel was in decline, and the young were leaving. I should have appreciated more than I did that the destruction of any Welsh community against its will was a cause worth striving against, but because of my intimate knowledge of the place I struggled with the idealised constructions that seem to be needed in the political battle. I was also struggling with how culture and politics fitted in with my newfound faith.

UNIVERSITY

This struggle intensified when I found myself a student at the University College of North Wales, Bangor, in October 1964. I happened to arrive as a member of the lowest intake of Welsh speakers to the college in its history up to that point. With the expansion of the universities in the '60s, we had become a drop in a sea of Englishness. It is not surprising that the Welsh-speaking college community laid a very heavy emphasis on its distinctiveness. Because of my evangelical faith, I found myself included but not embraced.

It is one of the mysteries of Welsh history that by the 1960s evangelical Christians, who represented the dominant religious tradition in Wales from about 1750–1930, were generally considered as distinctly odd by most Welsh people. Theological liberalism had done its work very thoroughly, and evangelicals had become a marginalised minority in the church. Then the narrow-minded fundamentalism of some of us further helped to push us to the margins. In the college context where young people were tasting freedom from the constraints of home and formal religion for the first time, there was no hope whatsoever that a somewhat narrow evangelical like myself would be embraced by the Welsh-speaking community.

My Christian community in college was the Christian Union which was affiliated to the InterVarsity Fellowship.[16] There was a very small group of us who were Welsh speakers, and who struggled to maintain a Welsh evangelical witness in the college, but the overwhelming majority of CU members were English. On Sunday at first I went to more evangelical English-language churches in the morning and to a Welsh church in the evening. Attendance at the Welsh church soon fell away, and I went with my CU friends to an English church in the evening as well. My corporate spiritual life came to be conducted almost entirely in English except in the vacations. This reflected my conviction that spiritual life is paramount and that fostering my relationship with God must take precedence over anything else. Even so, I was very aware that I was something of a spiritual schizophrenic, torn between my Welsh upbringing, my Welsh devotional life, and rich evangelical history on the one hand and my English corporate spiritual life on the other. In fact I have lived with this tension for all my spiritual life except for an all-too-brief episode from 1969–75.

BUILDING A BILINGUAL CHURCH

In the autumn of 1969 I was starting my sixth year as a student at the university in Bangor. I had graduated in Welsh Literature in June 1967 and married an English fellow student from Liverpool

---

[16] This organisation is now called the Universities and Colleges Christian Fellowship in the United Kingdom.

in September of the same year. By September 1969 we had moved with our five-month-old daughter to Bethesda which is four miles from Bangor. This was the time when many evangelicals in Wales were responding to the call made by Dr. Martyn Lloyd Jones in 1966 to leave their denominations and establish evangelical churches. Geraint Jones, a research student in the Welsh department of Cardiff University, who was fired by the doctor's vision, was sent by the Heath Presbyterian Church[17] in Cardiff to plant an evangelical church in Bangor. We joined the little group that was meeting in a student flat on their second Sunday together. The following week we discovered that a group of English-speaking students had started meeting together at the same time in another student dwelling. When we decided to come together and form one bilingual church, we began what I believe to be a very significant experiment in bi-cultural church life which was a marvellous example to the whole of Wales and even beyond. I still consider that it was a tragedy that the church decided to divide along linguistic lines shortly after I had moved from Bangor.

The worship of the church was arranged as follows: English and Welsh speakers met separately for the morning service. Initially this was in separate places, but when the church bought an old Congregational church building, we met consecutively in the same building. Eventually, because space was available, the two congregations met simultaneously in the same building, which was the ideal situation because they could meet for coffee after their services. In the evening the whole church came together for an English service. During the week there were separate Bible study groups and a united prayer meeting with freedom to pray in the language of one's choice. Church business meetings were in English. As leaders we had to contend with complaints from both sides. The Welsh speakers were unhappy about those aspects of the church's life that were

---

[17] Heath Presbyterian was in the process of leaving the Presbyterian Church and becoming Heath Evangelical Church at the time.

exclusively in English, while some of the English speakers could not understand the need for anything in Welsh at all, since all the Welsh speakers could understand English!

THE SHADOW OF HISTORY

Personally I believe that this bilingual church was a powerful witness to the gospel in a bilingual and multiethnic situation. A little bit of Welsh history is needed in order to understand this claim. Though generally united in terms of ethnic origin and language, Wales had hardly existed as a political or geographic unit when the Acts of Union with England were ratified by the English Parliament in the sixteenth century. These acts made Wales administratively a part of England and explicitly commanded a policy of destroying the Welsh language.[18] Happily the explicit English policy of ethnic assimilation was thwarted by the Reformation conviction that faith comes by understanding. The New Testament was published in Welsh in 1567 and the whole Bible in 1588. In the eighteenth century the flames of revival brought home the truths of the Bible to a large proportion of the population and led to a flourishing Welsh language Christian culture. But in the nineteenth century the shadow of ethnic assimilation returned with a vengeance.

South East Wales with its rich coalfields was one of the centres of the Industrial Revolution in the United Kingdom. In the second half of the nineteenth century in particular, there was massive English and Irish immigration into this area. There was also significant im-

---

18 To quote the Act: "Because that in the same Country, Principality and Dominion [of Wales] divers Rights Usages Laws and Customs be far discrepant from the Laws and Customs of this Realm [of England], and also because that the People of the same Dominion have and do daily use a Speech nothing like, nor consonant to the natural Mother Tongue used within this realm…The king's purpose in uniting Wales with England is to reduce them [the Welsh] to the perfect Order, Notice and Knowledge of this his Realm, and utterly to extirp [destroy] all and singular the sinister Usages and Customs differing from the same." This law advocating enforced ethnic assimilation was finally repealed by the Westminster Parliament in 1993.

migration into the industrial belt of North East Wales. The Welsh language was literally swamped by the sheer number of immigrants in many places.

More sinister was the increasing involvement of government in education in the second half of the nineteenth century. Towards the end of the century a strong anti-Welsh language campaign was mounted through the primary education system that had by then become state funded and compulsory. Children were commonly punished for speaking Welsh. The most pernicious form of punishment that has sunk deeply into the ethnic psyche of Welsh speakers was the use of the "Welsh Not." This was a piece of wood with "W. N." engraved on it, which a teacher would hang around the neck of the first child that he caught speaking Welsh on any school day. It was the task of the child to pass on the hated object to anyone else that he/she heard speaking Welsh. Children would be keen to pass on the "Welsh Not" because the child in possession at the end of the day would be beaten.[19] This was a very effective way to discourage the speaking of Welsh and to devalue the language, but it could breed resentment—and still does in ethnic folk memory. This devaluation of the language in education permeated right through the system. Some years ago someone gave me the notes taken by a relative in classes held by Sir John Morris-Jones, who was the first professor of Welsh at the University in Bangor. The subject was Welsh, the students were Welsh speaking, but the notes witness to the fact that the lectures were in English!

The fact that Welsh speaking was strongly discouraged through the educational system meant that English-speaking immigrants had no incentive or need to learn the language. The result of this was that by the middle of the twentieth century Welsh was in crisis

---

[19] Mexicans who became US citizens after the end of the Mexican War in 1848 and Native Americans were treated in a similar way in the American educational system. See James A. Banks, Race, Ethnicity and Schooling in the United States: Past, Present and Future, in *Multicultural Education in Western Societies*, eds. James A. Banks and James Lynch (London / New York: Holt, Rinehart and Winston, 1986), 32.

in the industrial areas. Interestingly, however, this mixture of indigenous people who lost their grasp of their Welsh language and the immigrant English and Irish have come to think of themselves as Welsh. They speak their own distinctive English dialects and the overwhelming majority of them have no doubt whatever that they belong to the Welsh nation. They now represent at least 70 percent of the people of Wales.

Let's return to Bangor and the bilingual church which was called Ebenezer Evangelical Church / Eglwys Efengylaidd Ebeneser. Though not an industrialised area, the tiny city of Bangor[20] is similar to the industrial areas of Wales in that the majority of its population would be non-Welsh-speaking Welsh. This would be made up of a similar mixture of indigenous people that had lost the language and the descendants of historic immigrations. The second largest group is the Welsh-speaking Welsh. Then in contrast to the industrialised areas of Wales, Bangor has a significant population of recent immigrants who are mainly English. Many have moved into the area because of its beauty and others to find employment, especially in the university. Finally, as a witness to the reality of globalisation, the university and the large general hospital attract international students and medical personnel. Even a small city like Bangor is quite a complex multiethnic and multicultural community. Ebenezer Evangelical Church reflected this diversity in one congregation of followers of Jesus. On one hand, the church declared that people from different ethnic and cultural backgrounds are one in Christ; on the other hand, it also declared that it is right and proper to respect cultural and ethnic difference. The unity that Christians enjoy is not assimilationist and oppressive but unity in diversity. This, I believe, is what we find taught in the Bible.

---

20 The population in the 1991 census was just over 12,000.

PAUL AND JEWISH IDENTITY

Paul was specifically called by Jesus to take his gospel to the Gentiles, and in doing so he fulfilled what Jesus had commanded should happen after his resurrection and ascension (Matt 28:18–20; cf. Matt 8:5–13; 24:14; Mark 11:17; 13:10; 14:9; Luke 11:29–32; John 16:10). A crucial part of this calling was his explanation of the meaning and significance of such a radical step in the history of redemption. It is possible to argue that this matter is one of the central themes of his letters, especially to the Galatians, Romans, and Ephesians. The whole point of the letter to Galatians is that Jews and Gentiles, even though they have a different history of relationship with God, are now spiritually on exactly the same plane. The way to God is exactly the same for both. Paul also draws the inevitable conclusion from this that those who have come to God through faith in Jesus are one—be they Jews or Gentiles, they are children of Abraham and heirs of the promise. "There is neither Jew nor Greek," he says, "for you are all one in Christ Jesus" (Gal 3:28). For Paul, one crucial consequence of this spiritual unity was the annulment of the Jewish laws of ritual purity. The table fellowship which was such a significant part of the church's life from the beginning could be extended to the Gentiles. Jews and Gentiles were free to eat the same food off the same table.

It is not at all surprising that many Jewish Christians were initially very reluctant to accept Paul's position, because behind the surface issue of adherence to law lay the deep issue of identity. The Jewish dietary laws which prevailed in New Testament times were a development of the laws about clean and unclean animals, birds and reptiles found in Leviticus 11 and Deuteronomy 14:3–21. There is no command in these passages which forbids a Jew from eating with a non-Jew. It was the way the laws were interpreted that led to the prohibition. The interpretation of the command that a young goat should not be cooked in its mother's milk is a good example (Deut 14:21; cf. Ex 23:19). This is the basis of what is still a prohibition in

Judaism against mixing meat and dairy products in cooking. Strict observance of this rule demands separate cooking utensils for the two types of food. The social implications of this interpretation are obvious. It makes it almost impossible for a Jew to eat with a Gentile without breaking what was considered to be God's law. This interpretation, when added to others, left Jews with only one alternative, and that was to withdraw from any table fellowship with Gentiles.

That the type of interpretation which led to the need for two sets of utensils in the Jewish kitchen was developed after the collapse of Jewish political independence in 586 BC is not without significance. After 586, to be Jewish meant increasingly to live as an exile from the land of Israel. By New Testament times there were large Jewish communities in the main centres of the Roman Empire such as Alexandria in Egypt, Syrian Antioch and, of course, Rome itself. Smaller communities were found all over the Eastern Empire. Paul himself hailed from Tarsus in Cilicia (modern Turkey), and he found a synagogue in many of the places he visited on his missionary journeys. The separate identity of these Jews of the dispersion was unquestionably preserved by their faithful adherence to rules such as those pertaining to diet.

Enter the message that Jesus is the Messiah. As in many other places in the early days of the Christian mission, the first Christians in Syrian Antioch were Jews.[21] But non-Jews were also attracted. In time these Gentiles were coming to believe in Jesus in such numbers that Barnabas, who was leading the mission, went all the way to Tarsus[22] to persuade Paul to come and help. Paul came and found what we would call a revival in full force. Just as in Jerusalem, when the Spirit was first poured out on the disciples at Pentecost, the proclamation of Jesus as Messiah gave birth to a people who loved to pray together, learn together, and also eat together. Antioch was

---

21 The section on what happened in Syrian Antioch is based on Acts 11:19–26; 15:1–35; Galatians 2:11–21.
22 A round trip of over two hundred miles by boat.

a huge, cosmopolitan city, but the separate identity of those who came to believe in Jesus could not hinder their mutual joy in Christ, expressed in their love feasts together. At some point Peter came to see what was going on and was swept along in the tide of revival, which is not surprising in the light of his very significant experience with Cornelius, the Roman centurion (Acts 10).

There was anxiety as well as joy when news of the revival reached Jerusalem. A group of those who were very anxious decided, without authorisation from James, to go to Antioch to find out what was going on. This "unofficial" delegation was made up of those who were very eager to preserve Jewish customs (Acts 15:24). As soon as they arrived, they got to work on Peter and managed to persuade him to withdraw from eating with Gentile Christians. In due course even Barnabas, the encourager, followed suit. Soon there was the making of two Christian communities, Gentile and Jewish, with increasingly restricted social contact between them.

Paul was resolute in his opposition to these developments. He opposed Peter publicly, charging him with hypocrisy and subverting the gospel. "You are a Jew," Paul said to Peter, "yet you live like a Gentile and not like a Jew. How is it, then, that you force Gentiles to follow Jewish customs?" (Gal 2:14). Before the strongly Jewish Christians had come up from Jerusalem, Peter had eaten with Gentiles, but then he had backtracked—not out of conviction, according to Paul, but out of fear, which may have been rationalised as respect for Jewish Christians. This hypocritical approach was in Paul's eyes very dangerous, because it threatened the very heart of the gospel which he and Peter proclaimed. Peter's action in withdrawing from table fellowship was saying to the Gentiles that there was something other than Christ as the basis of their unity. To become one with Jews, Gentiles had to become Jews first. Now if Gentiles had to keep all the Jewish regulations before they could be united with Jews in Christ, then law is put before grace, and the fundamental Christian belief that faith in Christ alone is the means of justification is subverted.

But what has all this to do with ethnic identity? After the very bitter experience of apostasy, defeat, and dispersion, the Jews came to focus on what set them apart from other nations. They built more and more fences around themselves in order to exclude the other. The dietary regulations are an excellent example of this principle of exclusion at work, because adherence to them would make Jewish assimilation into a host identity impossible. It is impossible for one ethnic group to become assimilated into another ethnic group if they can't eat together. Paul was adamant that the gospel has swept away this fence against assimilation. Christ makes table fellowship between Jews and Gentiles a necessity, because if a person is in Christ that person is united in faith with every other person who is in Christ, irrespective of ethnic identity or anything else that may divide people from each other.

The key question in the context of this chapter is whether this unity in Christ, which was so precious to Paul, undermined all ethnic difference. Did he think that Jews had to stop being Jews now that they were Christians? In ethnic terms, did Christian unity mean that a minority ethnicity like Judaism should be assimilated into a bigger ethnic identity?

Paul certainly believed that what marked the Jews off as different had lost its religious significance with the coming of Jesus Christ. Circumcision, for example, had been a sign of belonging to God's people. In Christ it ceased to be so. The new sign was "circumcision of the heart," which is faith and trust in Jesus for salvation. Being able to prove that one was a blood member of one of the tribes of Israel, and hence descended ultimately from Abraham, was also considered proof of belonging to God's people. Paul argues that the true descendants of Abraham are not those who share his genes but his faith. Even those Jews who had been dispersed throughout the Roman Empire looked to Jerusalem and especially to the temple and its ritual as an important focus of their religious life. Though he does not say so explicitly, Paul's conviction that Jesus had through his death dealt with the problem of sin and opened a way directly into God's presence makes the temple and all its ritual redundant. When all this is added to the annulment of the dietary regulations, then much of what distinguished a Jew from a Gentile would seem to have been swept away.

What then was left? Circumcision could be left as a mark of ethnic if not religious identity. The case of Timothy is interesting. He hailed from the town of Lystra in Asia Minor, which Paul visited on his first missionary journey. It was there that Paul healed a crippled man and had a real problem persuading the locals not to sacrifice to him and Barnabas as divine manifestations because of a language barrier. The people spoke Lycaonian, and it took Paul and Barnabas a while to realise what they were intending to do. Since they could not speak Lycaonian, they had a real problem communicating the fact that they were mere humans bearing a precious message about the true God (Acts 14:8–18).

When Paul returned to Lystra on his second missionary journey, he was very impressed with the spiritual growth of the young man Timothy, who had been converted during his first visit. Timothy's mother was a Jew, but his father is described as a Greek. It is unlikely that his father hailed from Greece. He was probably a Lystran who had adopted the Greek language and culture of the empire. That he had married a Jewish woman witnesses to the difficulty for immigrants of preserving ethnic fences. However, according to rabbinic law, the child of a mixed marriage whose mother was a Jew could consider himself a legitimate descendant of Abraham. So Timothy had a legitimate blood claim to being a Jew. He had also been brought up in the Jewish faith by his mother and grandmother. Therefore, when it was decided by prophetic affirmation that Timothy should join the missionary team of Paul and Silas, Paul arranged for Timothy to be circumcised so that there would be no doubt about his Jewish identity. Of course, Paul's reason for doing this was not to solve a crisis of identity from which Timothy might have been suffering but to make it easier for him to be fully involved in the mission, especially in those places where the Jewish community was very prickly about identity. It was a case of working out his principle that one can take part in aspects of a people's culture without compromising the faith in order to make it easier for the faith to get a hearing. This approach does not yield a very positive view of ethnic identity, but to be able to say that there is nothing inherently wrong in certain ethnic practices at least suggests that there is nothing wrong with having a specific ethnic identity. So, for Paul, circumcision was acceptable as a badge of identity but not as a badge of salvation.

It remains to be seen whether Paul was positive about anything in his Jewish identity. He was. For Paul the glory of his own people was that they had been privileged to be the recipients of God's revelation. In the middle of his sustained argument in the early chapters of Romans, to prove that every human being, Jew and Gentile, was in need of being justified before God, he asks: "What advantage, then, is there in being a Jew, or what value is there in circumcision?" He answers his own question: "Much in every way! First of all, they have been entrusted with the very words of God" (Rom 3:1,2). He expands on this when he comes to deal with the present state and future hope of his own people in Romans 9–11. It is here that he expresses his intense love for his own people. "For I could wish," he says, "that I myself were cursed and cut off from Christ for the sake of my brothers, those of my own race, the people of Israel" (Rom 9:3,4). There is an obvious case of rabbinic hyperbole here, but Paul would have been prepared to give up his own life for his own people, whom he calls "brothers," and "kinsmen according to the flesh," which is incorrectly translated as "those of my own race" in the NIV. Paul is not thinking of "race" here but common ancestry, which is one of the key characteristics of ethnic identity.

He then goes on to give the reason why he loves his own people so much: "Theirs is the adoption as sons; theirs the divine glory, the covenants, the receiving of the law, the temple worship and the promises. Theirs are the patriarchs, and from them is traced the human ancestry of Christ, who is God over all, for ever praised! Amen"

(Rom 9:4,5). Here is a succinct outline of the most significant ethnic history in the history of the world, which began with Abraham and reached its climax with Jesus of Nazareth. However, Israel, as represented by their leaders, rejected the Messiah Jesus. So Paul is exercised by the problem of his people's future in the light of this rejection. The conclusion he reaches in Romans 11 continues to be a matter of debate. Some say that Paul is prophesying the salvation and exaltation of the whole Israelite nation before the second coming of Christ, while others say that all he claims is that the promise of salvation in Christ is as available to Israel as it is to anyone else. Those holding these two positions have engaged in fierce debate, but there is one thing that is common to them both. In both Paul is envisaging the persistence of Israel as a people. Whether the whole nation is going to be saved, or salvation is going to be available to them, he believes that there are going to be Jews around to be saved.

The link between the story of God's dealings with an ethnicity or nation, its history, and its future will be the subject of the next chapter. It is enough at this stage to say that for Paul his own people's future is strongly tied up with God's dealings with them in the past. But what of the future? Does Paul suggest that, having preserved their identity as a people by clinging to the traditions that kept them from believing the gospel, they will lose their identity as Jews when they turn to Christ?

Paul certainly insisted on pulling down some of the fences that the Jews had put up to preserve their identity. Initially the purpose of the fences had been the preservation of faith. They had been put up by the faithful after the destruction of Jerusalem in 586 BC who believed, rightly, that the cause of that disaster was the adoption by Judah of the religious beliefs and practices of its neighbouring nations. In time the fences that had been put in place to preserve the Jews from idolatry became idols themselves. When this happened, the emphasis moved from faithfulness to God to preserving a superior identity. What Paul was doing in his preaching of the new covenant in Christ was calling the Jews back to their faithfulness to

God. He was calling them to a glorious fulfilment of their history and not to its abandonment. That there seemed to be a risk attached is entirely consistent with the spirit of the gospel which involves losing life in order to gain it.

So far the emphasis has been very much on unity, on the gospel as a means of breaking down barriers between people. The only positive point that has been made about diversity is the reference to the legacy of history that is to be developed in the next chapter. The focus has been on the impact of redemption in Christ. However, the drama of redemption is played out on the stage of God's creation and providence. God redeems people whom he created to live and make history in his world.

GENESIS 10: THE TABLE OF NATIONS

In this context the existence of ethnic identities is a direct result of the outworking of God's command to the original human beings to multiply and fill the earth (Gen 1:28). The fulfilling of this command is twice interrupted, but God's purpose eventually prevails. The first interruption was the flood, which destroyed most of humanity. After the flood, God reasserts his command to "be fruitful and increase in number" and "to multiply on the earth and increase upon it" in his covenant with Noah (Gen 9:7). The evidence that this command was effective is found in the table of nations in Genesis 10. As the families of Noah's son's became more numerous, a process began which has persisted ever since. Greater numbers created economic pressure which drove some clans to go in search of a new place where they would be better off. Very early in the history of humanity, some even crossed the sea in this search.[23] Distance and geography lead to the development of an identity different from that of the place of origin, so that in time distinct peoples come into existence "spread out into their territories by their clans within their nations,

---

[23] From these the *maritime* peoples spread out (Gen 10:5, emphasis added).

each with its own language" (Gen 10:5; cf. vv. 20,31,32).

It is interesting that the description of what happened as human beings spread over the earth in Genesis 10 corresponds very closely with what are claimed as the main features of ethnic identity. As stated in the introduction, there are six main features of ethnic identity: (1) a common proper name; (2) a myth of common ancestry; (3) shared memories of a common past; (4) elements of a common culture, which normally includes religion, custom, or language; (5) a link with a homeland; and (6) a sense of solidarity.[24]

Many of the names in Genesis 10 are somewhere on the road between a proper name for an ethnic group and the name of an ancestor. For example, Japheth's son Gomer is the ancestor of what is known historically as the Cimmerians, an Indo-European people who lived in southern Russia and who were a severe challenge to the Assyrians in the eighth and seventh centuries BC. On the other hand, Madai (or Medes) is the proper name of an Indo-Iranian people who may have established themselves on the Iranian plateau as early as 1300 BC.[25] In vv. 8–12 there is a break in the genealogy to tell the story of Nimrod, one of the descendants of Cush the son of Ham, who was the founder of Babylon and Nineveh among other great cities in Mesopotamia. This is a good example of the type of historical memory that forms an ethnic identity. The diversity of languages that followed the scattering is mentioned after the genealogy of each son of Noah, while a number of the names in the lists are also names of territories. Mizraim/Egypt, Seba, Havilah, and Dedan are all examples of known territories. The only feature in the list that is not clearly witnessed in Genesis 10 is a sense of solidarity.

The impression that we get from Genesis 10 is that the development of ethnic identities as a result of the spread of human beings over the earth was simply the fulfilment of the divine mandate to Noah and his family after the flood. There is no hint of evil in this

---

[24] Hutchinson and Smith, *Ethnicity*, 6–7.
[25] Gordon J. Wenham, *Genesis 1–15 Word Biblical Commentary*, vol. 1 (Waco: Word Publishers, 1987), 216–7.

development. Then, as soon as the genealogies are finished, we have the story of the Tower of Babel, which seems to imply that the scattering of the people over the earth and the formation of ethnic identities was a judgement of God. Whatever view we hold of the authorship and compilation of Genesis, it is reasonable to believe that the redactor must have placed the table of nations (Gen 10) and the story of the Tower of Babel (Gen 11:1–9) side by side for a purpose.

It is possible to get the impression from Genesis 10 that the spread of human beings over the earth was a perfectly natural process, as was the development of ethnic identities. Genesis 11, the story of the Tower of Babel, reminds us that history is severely impacted by human sin and divine judgement. As is the case throughout the biblical book of origins, the pattern is one of divine goodness requited by human rebellion and followed by judgement. The story of the Tower of Babel is primarily not about the origin of languages, which is one of the features of ethnic identity, but about human wickedness and pride and God's judgement upon it. Like everything else, the formation of ethnic identities has been severely affected by sin.

GENESIS 11: THE TOWER OF BABEL

The building of the Tower of Babel is the second interruption to the story of the scattering of humanity. We find humanity, early in its history after the flood, with one common language, moving east from Ararat until they come to the broad and fertile plain of Mesopotamia. There they settle down and multiply in numbers and skills as they establish the world's first civilisation. Soon they feel that they can usurp the prerogative of God, so they set about building a tower reaching to heaven in order to make a name for themselves. This is probably the first proclamation of empire in human history with, in this case, one city seeking to dominate the rest of humanity and, in the process, trying to usurp a position that belongs only to God. The city and its tower was also meant to be a magnetic centre of power that would keep people from moving apart from each other and filling the earth as God had intended they should. Seeing that a united humanity with one language would have an endless capacity for rebellion, God confused their language so that they could not understand each other. Without understanding, collaboration is impossible, so the tower is abandoned as the people scatter in every direction "over the face of the whole earth" (Gen 11:4). The final outcome is precisely what God had intended for humanity in the first place, and the process that we saw at work in Genesis 10 occurs.

On the one hand, this understanding of the Tower of Babel story makes linguistic diversity a blessing to humanity, even though it is a consequence of God's judgement on sin. It also explains why empire building always involves a drive towards linguistic and cultural uniformity. Empire needs the ability of the best minds from a variety of backgrounds to increase its power and boost its image. What Nebuchadnezzar did in gathering to Babylon the cream of his conquered nations so that they could be taught "the language and literature of the Babylonians" before entering royal service is typical of the way imperial power works (Dan 1:1–5). English is now the language of the greatest empire ever seen that does not wield power territorially but economically and culturally. The increasing capability to collaborate in rebellion against God that the spread of this Anglo-American "empire" affords should fill us with fear and trepidation.

On the other hand, that there is a diversity of languages in the world is unquestionably a hindrance to the spread of the kingdom of God and its values. I have often felt the terrible frustration when travelling of being unable to share the kingdom with people. How much easier it would be for us to further the cause of Christ if there was no need to struggle for years to master a language, to translate the Bible, and so on. How many mistakes could be avoided if there was no need to translate ideas from one language into another? In this context, Christian missionaries have been right to take advantage of those languages that have come to be used internationally as a result of the spread of imperial power. This was true of the New Testament era itself with the spread of Greek in the Eastern Roman Empire and Latin in the West. This made it much easier to introduce Christianity into a large number of ethnic groups, although the work of evangelisation could only be completed through indigenous languages. Russian served the same purpose to facilitate the spread of Christianity through North Asia, and English has been widely used as an access into the lives of many ethnic groups in the last three hundred years. However, this opportunity afforded by imperial power is an accidental consequence of that power itself whose focus is on self-aggrandisement at the expense of the less powerful.

There are two more important points to be made in reflecting on our post-Babel world. The first is that God's cultural mandate still prevailed, even after the judgement that led to the confusion of tongues. That is, human beings, despite their sin, are still commanded by God to fill the earth, subdue it, rule over it, work it, and take care of it. This is what humans do. All too often the whole process is soured by sin, but there is much in human achievement as well which is noble and praiseworthy. After Babel this celebration of God's creation had to be embodied in a diversity of languages. This historic and contemporary source of wisdom and beauty cannot be thrown away as if of no significance. Sin might have been the ultimate cause of linguistic diversity, but the languages that developed after Babel testify to the active engagement and glory of God in his creation.

Secondly, language is only a subcategory of one of the main features of ethnic identity. The two most terrible examples of ethnic conflict at the end of the twentieth century happened between people who spoke the same language; the Hutus and Tutsis speak Kinyarwanda, and the Serbs, Croats, and Bosnians speak Serbo-Croat. What happened in Babel happened, and we cannot avoid the consequences, but there is every likelihood that ethnic identities would have developed even if diverse languages which made understanding impossible had not appeared. All six features of ethnic identity can be in place without a distinctive language. A group could have a common name, ancestor, historical memories, customs, homeland, and sense of solidarity and speak basically the same language as everyone else in the world. The development of ethnic identity, therefore, can be divorced from the sin of Babel and its judgement as something which was an inevitable consequence of God's providence. In fact Scripture testifies to God's overseeing of the process. Deuteronomy states that "when the Most High gave the nations their inheritance, when he divided all mankind, he set up boundaries for the peoples" (Deut 32:8). And Paul, in his sermon to the Areopagus, says that "from one man [God] made every nation of men, that they should inhabit the whole earth; and he determined the times set for them and the exact places where they should live" (Acts 17:26). Of course ethnicity has developed under God's providential care in a sinful world and is as affected by sin as everything else.

GOD'S RULE OVER THE NATIONS

The rest of the Bible witnesses to God's sovereignty over the destiny of the communities of peoples with common names, history, culture, homeland, and sense of solidarity which, in English translations, are called "nations." These biblical "nations" are usually what modern English would call "ethnic groups," rather than political communities, as is implied in the modern understanding of "nation."

Deuteronomy 2:9–12, 19–23 contain what, on first sight, seem like obscure notes, which the NIV puts in parentheses, about the movements of nations in the area east of the Jordan, which the Israelites passed through on their way to the Promised Land. Christopher Wright comments:

> These notes unambiguously assert Yahweh's multinational sovereignty. The same God who had declared to Pharaoh that the whole earth belonged to God (Exod. 9:14, 16, 29) had been moving other nations around on the chessboard of history long before Israel's historic exodus and settlement. This universal sovereignty over the

nations mattered a great deal to Israel in subsequent centuries as they themselves joined the ranks of the dispossessed. Later prophetic understanding of Yahweh's "use" of the Assyrians, Babylonians, and Persians as agents of Yahweh's purposes in history is in fact consistent with this deeper theme of God's ultimate, universal direction of the destiny of nations (cf. Deut. 32:8; Jer. 18:1–10; 27:1–7).[26]

Two further points need to be made on the basis of these passages in Deuteronomy. First, it is clear that in the long view nations are not permanent entities. They begin, grow, flourish, decline, and die like human beings. There is no room for the idolatrous absolutising of the nation as happens in ideological nationalism. Second, God has a moral purpose in his dealing with nations. For example, repentance can save a nation from oblivion (Jer 18:7–10; Jonah 3), and one nation can be used by God to punish another nation for its sin. As Deuteronomy 9:4,5 states, the wickedness of the Canaanite nations was a key reason for their expulsion and destruction by the Israelites. Later on, the Persians drove the Israelites themselves out of Israel as punishment for their sin. But as Wright states, "The 'rod of God's anger' (Isa 10:5) did not have to be straight."[27]

If we try to view conflicts, which lead to the destruction of nations, from the perspective of God's sovereign moral purpose, we soon pass beyond the point of human understanding. In the case of the destruction of the Tasmanians, for example, all we can say is that it could have been a divine judgement. That says nothing about the "bent rod" that caused their destruction or about the judgement that awaits them. All we can say now is that what happened must have been ultimately under God's control. It may be a cliché, but the clock cannot be turned back. The past is unchangeable. All we can do is leave it to God's just judgement, and garner examples that can help us to do things better in the future. The future is also held

---

[26] Christopher Wright, *New International Biblical Commentary: Deuteronomy* (Peabody MA: Hendrickson, 1996), 36. Some other passages that make the same point are Deut 26:19; Job 12:23; Ps 22:27,8; 47:8; 86:9; Dan 12:1; Acts 17:26–28.
[27] Ibid., 133.

within God's sovereign purpose, but our opportunity to have an impact on what has not yet happened is very real. Learning from the past, responding to God's goodness, and working in God's strength, we can shape the future. Having learnt from what happened to the Tasmanians, Native Americans, and many others, God's goodness should now motivate us to labour in his strength to protect indigenous peoples so that they may have the opportunity to respond as nations to God's love in Christ.

We also reject any attempt by any nation to adopt a position of judge over other nations on the grounds of inherent moral superiority. All nations are "bent rods." There is no biblical justification whatsoever for ideas such as Manifest Destiny, which justified the terrible treatment of Native Americans in the United States, or apartheid, which justified the horrible abuse of blacks in South Africa.

So far the focus has been primarily on Old Testament teaching on the destiny of nations. In the New Testament two major themes emerge. On the one hand, there is the theme of the nations being offered and welcoming the good news of the kingdom of God. In fact this New Testament theme is but a continuation of the Old Testament prophetic theme that in the last days the nations would flock to Zion to present their gifts to God (Isa 60:1–11). The climax of this process is seen in John's vision of heavenly glory in Revelation 21:24–26: "The nations will walk by its light, and the kings of the earth will bring their splendour into it. On no day will its gates ever be shut, for there will be no night there. The glory and honour of the nations will be brought into it." On the other hand is the counterpoint theme of the nations finally conspiring together to destroy the kingdom of God. Jesus promises that throughout the rest of history there will be "wars and rumours of wars" (Matt 24:6–7). Nations will clash until the time when they come together to attack God's people. In Revelation, again echoing Old Testament prophecy, this is pictured as the battle of Armageddon that ushers in the end of the world. Reconciling these two themes seems impossible. All we can say is that, while wars and rumours of wars abound, we are yet free to invite the nations to bring their treasures to Zion. The day of "national" redemption is not passed. Repentance is still a live option.

Something needs to be said at this point about the collectivist view of humanity in the Bible that is so alien to our individualistic Western culture. This is not to say that the Bible devalues the worth of an individual human being. That is impossible for a creature made in the image of God. What the Bible teaches is that the meaning and purpose of human life is worked out in the relational context of collectivities—of family, tribe, people, nation, and humanity. "All flesh" is a phrase used in the Old Testament to express the idea of "all humanity," although it sometimes includes animals as well (as in Gen 7:21; Ps 136:25). But "all nations" is probably the most common phrase for expressing the whole human race, beginning with the promise to Abraham that all the nations would be blessed through his seed in Genesis 18:18[28] and ending with the prophecy of the coming of the "desired of all nations" in Haggai 2:7. In the New Testament, humanity is divided between the people of God, meaning Israel first and then the church, and *ethnoi*, which is translated as "Gentiles" more often than not, but really means "nations other than the nation of God." It follows that Christians have dual citizenship. On one hand, they belong to the heavenly kingdom, which is already manifested in Jesus but is yet to be revealed in all its glory. On the other hand, they also belong to earthly nations and have a responsibility to ensure that, when the kingdom is revealed, those nations will be able to make a worthy contribution to the praise of the Lamb. In his vision of the glory of the eternal kingdom, John sees that "the glory and honour of the nations will be brought into it" (Rev 21:26).[29]

---

[28] Interestingly, when this promise was first made to Abraham in Genesis 12:3, it was all the "families" of the earth that would be blessed through him. The term used here could be translated "clan"—a collective unit that was bigger than a "father's household" but smaller than a "tribe."

[29] For a comment on the significance of this verse, see D. Hughes, *God of the Poor* (Carlisle, England: Paternoster, 1998), 226–7.

LANGUAGE AND ETHNIC IDENTITY

One question which I have had to face as a Welsh person who wants to be biblical in his thinking about ethnic identity is, who belongs to the Welsh nation? As a leader of a bilingual church from 1969–75, I believed that to be truly Welsh a person had to be Welsh speaking. It took a move to a thoroughly anglicised South Wales valley in 1975 for me to appreciate fully that there were people who were enthusiastically Welsh who did not speak the language. In Bangor I had no understanding of the ethnic implications of what we were doing. The ethnic was merged into the linguistic that simplified the situation but avoided facing up to important issues of reconciliation. In South Wales the issue is more difficult to ignore because it is much more acute. Here the small Welsh-speaking community and the large non-Welsh-speaking community see each other as a threat. The non-Welsh speakers feel that the Welsh speakers don't believe that they are really Welsh while the Welsh speakers feel marginalised. Sadly, the evangelical churches that are predominantly English speaking see no need to address the issue, so the unchristian feelings that exist in society at large are left to simmer in the churches as well.

To be Christian in this context, I believe that we need to sail between the two rocks of saying, on the one hand, that the Welsh language is not crucial to Welsh identity and, on the other, that it is only those who speak Welsh that belong to the Welsh ethnic group or nation. The Welsh language needs to be recognised as an important historic and contemporary component of what it means to be Welsh. Even those who cannot speak the language should want to point to it as a part of their distinctiveness. Those of us who speak Welsh should have a profound sense of responsibility because we are able to provide vital links for our whole ethnic group with important aspects of our history that are crucial to our survival in the future. We also have a responsibility to make sure that future generations will have access to that history and to enrich the tradition in the present.

At the same time we must recognise and value the *Welsh* history and customs that have developed among our non-Welsh-speaking compatriots. That history and those customs are as genuinely Welsh as anything we have to offer in the Welsh language.

CONCLUSION

The situation in the bilingual church in Bangor was far more complicated than I imagined at the time. Looking back I am amazed at the way those of us who were responsible for the work were led and preserved by God. I also believe that we created something that could be a model in many situations where the church needs to model true Christian reconciliation across ethnic and linguistic divides. Granted, from the perspective of hard ethnic divisions it was a compromise, but I prefer to view it as a Christian example of mutual self-sacrifice. Christian unity is not meant to destroy but to celebrate diversity.

There can be no closer unity than that between a man and wife, because they are one flesh, but, as Paul makes clear, that unity is only achieved with mutual self-sacrifice (Eph 5:22–33). The wife voluntarily renders herself up to her husband's control as she submits to the control of Jesus. The husband offers himself up even unto death for the sake of his wife as Christ offered himself for him. Such mutual self-giving is the secret of the joy of marriage and the path along which both husband and wife discover their true identity. So it is in the church when Christians discover their unity in Christ. In my experience, when Welsh speakers forsook their right to worship entirely in Welsh and the English speakers were content for the church's life not to be conducted entirely in English, true unity was being modelled. The key phrase is "unity in diversity." That is what Christian unity across the ethnic and linguistic divide is about. Sometimes, as with the Jews in the New Testament church, it would seem as if one side was being asked to give up more than the other. Paul was really asking his fellow Jews to take a big risk by abandoning those fences that had been so crucial in preserving their identity. He did so because he believed, like his Master, that salvation is from the Jews and that what they were doing was inviting the Gentiles into their house. But the Gentiles also had to give up a lot, especially their pride, in stepping over the Jewish threshold.

The redemptive drama of reconciliation between Jew and Gentile, and between Gentile and Gentile, which does not involve their assimilation, is played out against the background of God's purpose for the nations. That there are "nations," which in the Bible means something much nearer to "ethnic groups/identities," is a part of God's purpose for humanity. They come into being, relate to each other in different ways, and come to an end under his direction. As divine creations, to elevate them to a position of ultimate authority is idolatry. Like other primordial collective identities such as the family or clan, an ethnic identity can ask much of an individual, but it can never be the ultimate authority.

Finally, the divinely guided movement of history which sees the birth, growth, maturation, and demise of ethnic identities means that the definition of an ethnic identity is often problematic. History means that there is a strong element of human construction in the way an ethnic identity is defined. In my own case, through my experience of living in different parts of Wales, I have come to the conclusion that those people living in Wales who speak Welsh, those who do not speak Welsh but are of Welsh origin, those who are of English, Irish, Scottish, Italian, Chinese, or other origin but have lived in Wales for generations, those who are the progeny of mixed marriages between any of these peoples living in Wales, and those who have recently come to Wales from another country but choose to call themselves Welsh, are Welsh if they want to be. There is a trunk to the Welsh ethnic tree that is ancient and with very deep roots, but it has a number of large and small branches and can even accommodate any number of grafts.

4

THE BIBLE, CHRISTIANITY, ETHNIC IDENTITY, AND NATIONHOOD

THE BIBLE: A TRANSLATABLE BOOK

What the Bible says about ethnic identity is not the only significant contribution made by the Bible to this issue. The book itself as well as its content is significant. Christianity, with a book at its heart, has a long history of impacting nations all over the world with a message that was considered translatable from the beginning. Christianity inherited a book, the Old Testament, which had already been translated from its original Hebrew and Aramaic into Greek, the official language of the Eastern Roman Empire, by the second century BC. From the perspective of ethnic identity, the translation of the Old Testament into Greek is interesting since it became necessary because the Jewish community living in Egypt in the second century BC was losing their Hebrew/Aramaic and needed a Greek translation of the law to remain faithful to their traditions. The translation, having been made for the benefit of Jews, also made possible a better appreciation of the Jewish religious tradition by non-Jews. In this way a significant number of non-Jewish people were attracted to the Jewish faith and attached themselves with varying degrees of commitment to the Jewish communities that were scattered in the main centres of population all over the Eastern Empire in particular. These people were often the most receptive to the message of Christian missionaries.

Jesus and his disciples were Aramaic-speaking Jews, but when the disciples were filled with the Spirit on the day of Pentecost, the large crowd of Jews of the dispersion and non-Jewish God-fearers that had come to Jerusalem for the festival heard about the wonders of God in their own languages. It is significant that the wonders of God were not heard in Greek, the official language of the empire that would have been understood by all, but in their mother tongues or heart languages. What was experienced at Pentecost was supernatural symbolism that is yet to be fully realised. The everyday work of mission has always run on more pragmatic lines. Greek was just too convenient for the likes of Paul, Barnabas, Silas, Timothy, and others. By using it, they could guarantee that the gospel could be proclaimed to a significant section of any community in the Eastern Empire. A more profound impact could then be made by the local Christians, who would have been at least bilingual, once a church was established. Not surprisingly, all the components of the Christian book—that was coming to be recognised as authoritative by around a century after the death and resurrection of Jesus—were in Greek.

The official language of the Western Roman Empire was Latin. This meant that a significant portion of the populations of the whole of North Africa west of Egypt and much of what has become Europe west of Greece could be reached with the gospel by using Latin. So the New Testament was translated into Latin. There were Latin translations of the Gospels circulating in North Africa before the end of the second century AD.

Fulfilling the prophetic symbolism of Pentecost also began very early in the history of Christianity. Translating Scripture into more local languages is clear evidence of this. Not surprisingly, deeper penetration into local culture occurred first in the Eastern Empire. The oldest translations of parts of the Greek New Testament into Syriac, the main language of the Roman province of Syria, were probably made in the second century AD. The earliest translations into Sahidic Coptic, the dialect of the southern part of ancient Egypt, was made early in the third century. Interestingly, early translations were made into at least four Coptic dialects. By the middle of the fourth century Ulfilas, the apostle of the Goths, had translated the whole Bible into Gothic. To do this he had to create a Gothic alphabet and reduce the language to writing for the first time. This was the first literary product of any Germanic dialect. The Armenian Bible appeared in the fifth century. Producing this again required the invention of an alphabet and the reduction of a language to a written form for the first time. Well over a thousand manuscript copies of this translation have been catalogued and many more are known to exist. Armenia was the first state to become officially Christian in the late third century, and there can be no doubt that its literary tradition, which is heavily influenced by the Bible, has been one of the key factors in its almost miraculous survival as an ethnic identity against heavy odds. The story of ancient Bible translation continued with the appearance of the Georgian, Ethiopic, Old Slavonic, Arabic, Nubian, Sogdian, Anglo-Saxon, and Old Persian versions.[30]

THE BIBLE AND THE FORMATION OF ENGLISH IDENTITY

Telling something of the story of ancient Bible translation is not a deviation from the subject of this volume. It proves that from the beginning of its story Christianity, while happy to ride the linguistic tiger of empire in its use of Greek and Latin, also saw the need to contextualise the gospel into the heart language of the people. The thesis of this chapter is that this contextualising characteristic of Christianity has been a crucial factor historically in the solidifying of ethnic identity and the creation of nations. England provides one of the best examples of this process at work.

Adrian Hastings devotes a whole chapter in his book on nationhood to the history of England as a prototype of the development of nationhood.[31] Hastings approaches the whole issue of ethnic identity from a historical angle. He thinks of ethnicity as a phase in

---

[30] Information on the early versions has been drawn from Bruce M. Metzger, *The Text of the New Testament* (Oxford: Clarendon, 1964), 67–86.
[31] See *The Construction of Nationhood: Ethnicity, Religion and Nationalism* (Cambridge Uni. Press, 1997).

the story of a people that can either lead to nationhood or oblivion. This movement from ethnicity to nationhood is a movement from instability to stability. He shares this idea with modernists. But in opposition to the modernists he believes that some nations at least existed for a long time before the nineteenth century. In seeking to prove his point, he describes the factors that he thinks proves that there is a move away from ethnicity in the direction of nationhood. This is the context of his examination of the history of England as what he calls the prototype nation.

The question that he seeks to answer is, when was England? At what point in history can it be said that the mixed Teutonic tribes of Angles, Saxons, Jutes, and Danes that invaded and populated the major part of the Roman province of Britannia, that had previously been populated by Celtic peoples, become the English nation? He argues that a number of the key unifying and stabilising factors were the result of the influence of Christianity. Even as early as the eighth century, Bede could write a book entitled *The Ecclesiastical History of the English People*.[32] At that time England was divided into a number of kingdoms originating in different tribal invasions, but Bede could already view it as a unit because the church for the whole country was administered from Canterbury. Then in the ninth century Alfred, although threatened throughout his reign by pagan Danes, managed to secure a measure of legal unity with a law code based on the Old Testament. The century following Alfred's reign saw an explosion of mostly Christian literature that further consolidated the identity of the English people. But with the Norman Conquest in 1066, the flourishing of English literature was halted for around two hundred years as French became dominant among the ruling classes.

In due course English reasserted itself and was shaped to a great extent by Wycliffe's Bible. This was an English translation of the Latin Vulgate version of the whole Bible by Wycliffe and his associ-

---

[32] Written around AD 730. The last word of the title is sometimes translated as "nation," but the Latin original has *gens*, not *natio*.

ates and finished in 1388. The fact that two hundred copies of this manuscript version of the English Bible still survive today witnesses to its wide circulation. But the Bible came into its own as a crucial factor in nation formation in the Reformation period in defining England as a Protestant nation. There was a political reformation and the right to have a vernacular Bible was linked to that process. But there was also a spiritual reformation in the sixteenth and seventeenth centuries that saw the Bible taken deep into the hearts of English people.

Between 1560 and 1640, 240 editions of the English Bible were printed as Tyndale's prophecy in the 1520s that even ordinary people would be able to read God's word was realised. As the Bible became more accessible, the description in it of Israel, which is probably the most significant "nation" in history, began to impact political philosophy. The arguments, which raged between the establishment and the Puritans and their more radical stepchildren, are full of Old Testament precedents. It was in these debates that some of the key ideals of the modern nation-state, such as freedom of conscience, were shaped.

The point Hastings is making, correctly in my opinion, is that Christianity in general and the Bible in particular made a vital contribution to the shaping and stabilising of English identity. A simple reason for this is the fact that written traditions are more stable and fixed than oral ones. So if what defines and guides the life of an ethnic group is written down, then that group is likely to be more unified, have a clearer understanding of its own identity, and to last longer. In the case of England, from the eighth century on, its written traditions were dominated by the Christian church and the Bible. There can be little doubt that in the case of England the Christian church and the Bible played a significant role in defining English identity, probably until well into the twentieth century.

THE BIBLE AND THE WELSH

What about Wales? For around 1,500 years Christianity has had a profound impact on the life of the Welsh people, but during the whole of that time the Welsh have lived under the threatening shadow of their more powerful English neighbours. The Welsh are descended from the Britons, who were a Celtic people that once populated the whole of what is now England, Wales, and southern Scotland. By the beginning of the Christian era, the Britons had been incorporated into the Roman Empire. Christianity had gained a foothold in the Roman province of Britannia by the third century AD, because there were British bishops from York, Lincoln, and London present at the Council of Arles in 314. Most of this Christianity was swept away by pagan Anglo-Saxons, who invaded and occupied most of Britannia as the Western Roman Empire collapsed under pressure from Germanic tribes in the fourth century AD. Christianity survived among the Britons of Strathclyde and South Wales. The vale of Glamorgan in particular, through the efforts of monastic teachers such as Illtud, became the breeding ground for itinerant missionaries like Cadog and Dewi.[33] They belonged to that Christian revival movement of the "Celtic saints" that saw wave after wave of ascetic missionaries win the Celtic world of Scotland, Northern England, Ireland, Man, Wales, Cornwall, and Brittany to Christ. By the end of the sixth century, Wales had been thoroughly Christianised.

The growth of the Celtic churches was a spontaneous revival movement that was not driven in any sense from an ecclesiastical centre. It was not a movement that looked to Rome and its pope for inspiration. Matters were different among the English. It is true that the Scottish missionary centre in Iona did much to bring Christianity to the English of Northumbria, but the dominant centre of English Christianity came to be based in Canterbury in the kingdom of Kent. It was here in 497 that Augustine arrived with

---

[33] Saint Dewi is the patron saint of Wales although better known internationally in the English translation—Saint David.

his missionary band, having been sent directly by Pope Gregory to convert the English. When the task was eventually completed, not surprisingly the English church, as the fruit of its mission, had a very special relationship with Rome and came to be viewed as the central ecclesiastical authority in the islands of Britain and Ireland.

With the growth of the military power of the English tribes, Wales became the first of the Celtic ethnicities to be forced to succumb to the authority of Canterbury. This proved crucial in the development of Welsh identity. In many ways, up to the twelfth century Welsh identity was developing in parallel with England. As in England, there was no stable political unity, but there was one church for all the Welsh people, and after the reign of Hywel Dda (d. ca. 950), who managed to unite most of Wales under his rule, there was also one law code.[34] The critical role of Canterbury in hindering the development of Welsh identity becomes apparent in the twelfth century in the story of Gerald of Wales' (1146?–1223) attempt to get the see of St. David recognised as a metropolitan see responsible for the government of the church in Wales. When St. David's became vacant in 1198, the chapter wanted Gerald as their bishop. The archbishop of Canterbury and the king of England did not want him. The controversy lasted five years, during which Gerald made three visits to Rome to argue before Pope Innocent III that St. David's should be independent of Canterbury. Gerald lost the argument. Gerald was undoubtedly driven by his ambition, but he could also see that the Welsh were a unique and different people who needed to be given the responsibility for their own destiny before God. The closing passage of *Gerald's Description of Wales* recounts what an old man from Pencader told Henry II: "It is my belief that on the sharp and bitter day of Judgement in the presence of the Supreme Judge, whatever may happen to the rest of the earth, no other nation than this Welsh one, and no other language but Welsh, will answer for this little

---

[34] Hywel paid homage to Edward, king of Wessex (the son of Alfred the Great). It is possible that he followed Alfred's example in promulgating a legal code for all the Welsh people.

corner of it."³⁵ This opinion was unquestionably shared by Gerald.

With the church subject to an English archbishop, the government of Wales was also grasped by the king of England with the defeat of Llywelyn II in 1282. There was a rebellion under Owen Glyndwr in 1400 that came tantalisingly close to succeeding. If it had succeeded, Wales would have had its own parliament, independent church, and university. With the accession of Henry VII in 1485, many in Wales believed that the prophecy of Merlin, from the time of King Arthur, that the Welsh/British would ultimately have the victory over the English had been fulfilled as a Welsh nobleman became king of England. It was a hollow victory indeed, because his son Henry VIII in the Act of Union of 1536 legislated for the total destruction of Welsh identity. But miraculously we are still here.

It has been said that the Welsh Bible saved the Welsh "nation." As a student of Welsh literature and then of theology at the University College of North Wales, Bangor, I had ample opportunity to reflect on this claim. Even before arriving at the university, I had studied the history of the Reformation period at school, including some Welsh history. I had also learnt to appreciate something of my religious heritage as a living reality through my contact with the Evangelical Movement of Wales. Wales is often unjustly caricatured as a land of bards in funny costumes and male voice choirs, but there can be no doubt that poetry and song has played an important part in preserving Welsh identity. Unlike England, where the tide of secularisation banished the likes of Watts, Wesley, Cowper, Toplady, Montgomery, and many other fine hymn writers from poetry anthologies, in Wales we have continued to believe that it is a valid poetic exercise to write beautifully about God and his grace. I had been brought up in the Congregational chapel to appreciate good hymn singing.

---

35 R. Tudur Jones, *The Desire of Nations* (Llandybie, Wales: Christopher Davies, 1974), 82. For a discussion of the struggle against the domination of the Welsh church by Canterbury and to get metropolitan recognition for the see of St. David, see Glanmor Williams, *The Welsh Church from Conquest to Reformation* (Cardiff: Univ. of Wales Press, 1962), 232.

What happened when I was converted was that the beautiful poetry of the hymns of William Williams, Ann Griffiths, Morgan Rhys, and many others came alive in my own experience.

In the university I came to appreciate more fully the crucial role of the Bible in the formation and preservation of my Welsh cultural heritage. The Welsh literary tradition has its roots as far back as the sixth century, and much of our best poetry is mediaeval, but it was the printing press and the Reformation that gave Wales a stable literary tradition. That this happened at all is due to the application of the Reformation principle that salvation comes through hearing the word of God found in the Bible. Administrative convenience had led the government of Henry VIII in the Act of Union to attempt to wipe away Welsh identity. Mercifully, some Welsh clerics and laymen in the reformed Church of England, especially after the accession of Elizabeth I, were concerned enough about the eternal destiny of their fellow countrymen to push for the translation of the Bible into Welsh. The "missionaries" got their way with the result that the New Testament in Welsh was officially published in 1567 and the whole Bible in 1588. So by the end of the sixteenth century there was a Welsh Bible in most parish churches in Wales. Since the Prayer Book had also been published in Welsh in 1567, it was now possible to deliver the whole liturgy in the only language understood by the overwhelming majority of people in what is now known geographically as Wales, and also a large section of the English county of Hereford.[36]

Making the Bible available for the people and getting the people to value it are two different things. The Welsh Bible may have been placed in most parish churches in Wales by the end of the sixteenth century, but it took more than a century for significant progress to be made in getting it into the people's hearts. Significant steps were taken in the seventeenth century. In 1630 an edition of Bishop

---

[36] The act commissioning the translation of the Bible into Welsh passed in 1563 and gave the responsibility for the work to the four Welsh bishops and the bishop of Hereford.

Parry's revised version of 1620 was published in a size and at a price more suitable for home use. Sadly, few people could read, and there were very few clergy in the church that were really committed to improving the biblical knowledge of their parishioners. In 1650, during the period of Puritan ascendancy, what was by then the remains of a parliament that had sat since 1641 passed "An Act for the Better Propagation and Preaching of the Gospel in Wales." This set up commissioners all over Wales who were to be responsible for using church funds to make sure that good ministers with Puritan sympathies were appointed to the churches. Interestingly, this was the first act of an English parliament since the Act of Union that treated Wales as a distinct administrative unit. Sadly, Puritanism was not popular in Wales, and its imposition by military might did not increase its popularity. With the restoration of the monarchy in 1660, a persecuting Episcopal hierarchy was restored, but the short period of Puritan freedom left a legacy of independent churches dotted about the country.

The leaders of the Great Awakening[37] in Wales, which began with the conversion of Howell Harris in 1735, looked back on the fifty years before the revival as a time of great spiritual darkness. Compared to the brilliant light of the revival, it was really dark before, but it was a long way from being totally dark. Five editions of the whole Bible were published between 1678 and 1727, as compared to three between 1620 and 1677, and the number of Bibles printed in four of the five editions was larger than the editions before 1678. In 1718 the Society for the Propagation of Christian Knowledge (SPCK) was responsible for publishing ten thousand copies of the Welsh Bible, and in 1727 they published another five thousand. The growth in Bible production during the fifty years before the Great Awakening

---

[37] I have decided to call the revival in eighteenth-century Wales the "Great Awakening" rather than the "Methodist Revival" for two reasons: (1) The two main leaders of the revival in Wales, Howell Harris and Daniel Rowland, had been awakened and were active as revivalists some years before the Wesleys were converted. (2) Though they became good friends of the Wesleys in due course, they were theologically identified with Whitefield.

is significant, although it witnesses to the fact that, for a population of about half a million, the desire for God's word was not intense.

Griffith Jones of Llanddowror

Among those who were driving the SPCK's activity in Wales at this time was a man called Griffith Jones, who became a corresponding member of the Society in 1713. Griffith Jones (1683–1761), the shepherd who became an Anglican cleric, developed into a visionary educationalist that made an enormous contribution to taking the Welsh Bible to the heart of the people. Ordained in 1708, he became a very popular preacher. In 1714 his bishop was complaining that he was "going about preaching on week days in Churches, Churchyards, and sometimes on the mountains to hundreds of auditors."[38] The bishop would probably have been glad to lose him to mission work in India, which had been a real possibility in 1713. Around 1709, after his appointment to minister in Lacharn, he took charge of the SPCK school that had been established in the parish by Sir John Philipps of Picton, who became a close friend and patron. This link with SPCK led him to apply for the post of schoolmaster and missionary with the East India Mission in Tranquebar, India. Having appeared before the SPCK board in London, he was offered the post. For some unknown reason he turned down the offer, for which those who value the cause of the gospel in Wales will be eternally grateful.

Griffith Jones' experience as a schoolmaster in an SPCK school convinced him that teaching people to read in a language other than their mother tongue was not very effective. Education in SPCK schools was through the medium of English. This policy was consistent with official government policy to stamp out the use of Welsh. Mercifully, Griffith Jones' missionary heart got the better of him, and he realised that a lot more Welsh people could be taught to

---

[38] John Edward Lloyd, R. T. Jenkins gol., *Y Bywgraffiadur Cymreig* (Llundain: Cymdeithas y Cymmrodorion, 1953), 436.

read the Bible much more quickly if teaching was done through the medium of Welsh. So he decided to train teachers at Llanddowror, where he had become rector in 1719, and send them out during the winter to hold evening schools/classes for three months at a time. The schools were to be held in the evenings between September and May, because that was a quieter time in the farming year and so more people, both adults and children, would be able to attend. His aims for the schools were limited—to teach the pupils to read the Bible and to say the Creed. No one knows exactly when or where the first schools were held, although it is more than likely that he began at his feet in Llanddowror. He wrote to the SPCK suggesting that they sponsor a "Welch School" in Llanddowror in September 1721, but nothing is known of the response. By 1737 we know for certain that he had thirty-seven schools with 2,400 pupils. We also know from the last report of the work published before he died in 1761 that his circulating Welsh schools movement had for over thirty years or so been responsible for running 3,495 schools in which around 158,000 pupils had had the opportunity to learn to read the Welsh Bible.[39]

The amazing extent of Griffith Jones' achievement was made possible by the Great Awakening that created a desire to read the Bible. Almost from the beginning the Great Awakening in Wales was, in contemporary terminology, a church growth movement operating on "cell group" principles. Because it began as a renewal movement within the established Anglican Church, with hardly any clerical support, the little group of leaders that had gathered around Howell Harris and Daniel Rowland by the late 1730s were forced to make their own arrangements for the discipling of the increasing number of converts. They did this by forming "societies," which were little groups of converts that met on a regular basis for prayer, singing,

---

[39] The work was carried on very successfully by Griffith Jones' friend and patron, Bridget Bevan, until her death in 1779. Tragically, the endowment that she left to carry on the work was contested by relatives, and the money that was left gathering interest in the Court of Chantry for thirty years was rendered useless.

Bible teaching, and to share their experience of God. Harris had started early and, according to George Whitefield, had established nearly thirty societies by the time they met in March 1739. After Whitefield's breach with the Wesleys in 1741, the former and his supporters joined with the Welsh leaders of the revival to form one general association to regulate the life of the increasing number of societies. When the first General Association met under George Whitefield's chairmanship in Caerphilly in 1743, there were probably over a hundred societies to be supervised in Wales alone. This movement was destined to grow steadily for the next hundred years, creating generation after generation of mainly young people with a profound desire to read the Bible in their mother tongue.

The ideological overlap between the objectives of Griffith Jones and the revivalists is obvious, so it is not surprising that there should be some overlap in personnel. Harris himself acted as a supervisor of Jones' circulating schools from sometime in 1736 until 1738, which was the time when he was beginning to establish his societies. The relationship between the two movements was not always easy, because Jones was dependent for his support on the goodwill of clerics, who were often suspicious of the revivalists and their irregular ways. For the sake of the work, he was sometimes forced to distance himself from the revival, but there is no doubt that his heart was with them and that the two movements were of mutual benefit to each other. The impact of the combined effect of revival and growth in literacy on Bible production in the eighteenth century is striking. Correct figures are very difficult to ascertain, but thirty-five thousand is a very rough estimate of the total number of Bibles and New Testaments printed in the seventeenth century. In the eighteenth century, twenty thousand Bibles were printed before the circulating schools and the revival got underway. Between 1730 and 1800 it can be estimated that between 85–100,000 Bibles and New Testaments were printed.

Thomas Charles, Mary Jones, and the Bible Society

By the last quarter of the eighteenth century the centre of gravity of the Great Awakening had moved to my hometown of Bala in North Wales, where Thomas Charles was based. The mantle of Griffith Jones fell on Thomas Charles who, after establishing his own circulating schools, pioneered an even more effective tool for increasing literacy—the Sunday school. By the end of the eighteenth century the supply of Welsh Bibles was a long way from being adequate to meet the demand. This fact was brought home very powerfully to Thomas Charles when a young woman called Mary Jones arrived at his door, probably sometime in the autumn of 1800, wanting to purchase a Bible. Born of poor parents in 1784, Mary had learnt to read through one of Thomas Charles' schools. She became an ardent Christian, but her family did not possess a Bible, so her access was limited to a visit to a nearby farm once a week. Determined to own her own Bible, she saved whatever she could over a number of years. Then when she had enough money saved, she walked the twenty-five miles from the hamlet of Llanfihangel y Pennant to Bala, because she had been told that Thomas Charles had Bibles for sale. She bought at least two Bibles from him; one for herself, which has found its way to the library of the Bible Society, and another for an aunt, which used to be in the library of the Calvinistic Methodist College at Bala.[40]

The story of Mary Jones and her Bible, in a somewhat romanticised form, achieved international celebrity through the part played by Thomas Charles in the founding of the British and Foreign Bible Society.[41] In its romanticised form, Thomas Charles told Mary that he had no Bible to give her; Mary cried bitter tears when she heard the bad tidings; then Charles gave her a Bible that he had promised

---

[40] For a scholarly account of Charles' encounter with Mary Jones and his role in the founding of the Bible Society, see D. E. Jenkins, *The Life of the Rev. Thomas Charles of Bala*, vol. 2 (Denbigh, Wales: Llewelyn Jenkins, 1908), 492–529.

[41] Now called "The Bible Society" in the UK. This society was the mother of an international movement which saw the founding of Bible societies in many countries and continues to be one of the most significant producers of Bibles in many languages today.

to someone else. These events are embellishments without historical foundation. However, there is no reason to doubt that Thomas Charles used this story of a poor young girl being so desperate to possess a Bible to challenge evangelical leaders in London to make sure that such a desire could always be satisfied by establishing a Bible society. One thing is certain: Mary Jones has been Wales' most effective public relations officer, especially in the evangelical Christian world! The result of Thomas Charles' challenge was the formation of the British and Foreign Bible Society, which was established in 1804, and its first fruit was twenty thousand copies of the Welsh Bible published in 1806. By 1855 it had published 933,222 Bibles and New Testaments in Welsh. When it is considered that others, such as the SPCK, also published Bibles in that period, it is true to say that in 1850 there was no nation on earth that was so well supplied with the Holy Scriptures in its own language as the Welsh nation.

Industrialism and the Decline of Welsh Identity

The total population of Wales in 1811 was around 600,000. That figure was destined to grow dramatically, especially in the second half of the nineteenth century, but it is fair to say that the demand for Bibles in the first half of the century is indicative of an indigenous ethnic identity that was becoming thoroughly infused with and formed by biblical and Christian values. Its cultural expression was somewhat narrow because of the pietist element in "Methodist" spirituality, but it was extremely vigorous. An increasing flood of material poured from the presses. There was a lot of theology, church history, and hymnody, but there was also an increasing amount of general information and current affairs, and in 1843 a newspaper, *Yr Amserau* ("The Times"), was launched in Liverpool by William Rees, the author of the Welsh original of the famous hymn, "Here Is Love Vast as the Ocean." Welsh identity seemed very secure, having been provided with a stable linguistic foundation in the Welsh Bible. In 1850, at least it is true that the Bible had created a Welsh identity that seemed rock solid. Yet just over a hundred years later Welsh identity was in crisis, and assimilation with the English seemed inevitable.

The impact of the Bible on Welsh identity was reaching its zenith as Britain was going through the process of modernisation. South East Wales in particular became one of the major centres of the Industrial Revolution in Britain, beginning with the development of the iron industry in Merthyr Tydfil in the eighteenth century. Rural Wales emptied its population into the industrial areas. The prospects of work and a better standard of living also attracted many from England, Ireland, and many other countries. The population of Wales grew from nearly 600,000 in 1811 to almost 2.5 million in 1911. By 1891 one in seven of the population was English. According to the 1891 census 139,031 English people had moved into Glamorgan, as compared to the 121,653 that had moved from other parts of Wales. In Gwent there were 61,061 English and only 30,504 Welsh migrants. The total number of Welsh speakers continued to grow to reach its highest total ever in 1911 at 977,366, but by then their proportion of the whole population of Wales had dropped to 43.5 percent.[42] There was still plenty of life left in revivalist religion in Wales in 1911, but its distinctive Welsh life was being swamped in the industrial areas by the sheer weight of numbers of non-Welsh migrants.

The political theory that had been developed to fit in with the rationalisation of industry was more concerned with production and democratisation than with ethnic identity. The key word became "progress," which meant better material circumstances and more say in the way a country is governed. More nonmaterial cultural values could be sacrificed on the altar of this new god. This philosophy had its most devastating effect on Welsh identity in the area of education.

---

[42] Statistics taken from R. Tudur Jones, *Ffydd ac Argyfwng Cenedl: Cristionogaeth a Diwylliant yng Nghymru 1890–1914*, vol. 1 (Abertawe: Ty John Penry, 1981), 20–21. A translation of this two-volume work has been published under the editorship of Robert Pope, entitled *Faith and the Crisis of a Nation: Wales 1890–1914*, (Cardiff: Uni. of Wales Press, 2004).

The efforts made by Griffith Jones and Thomas Charles succeeded in giving a rudimentary education to a considerable proportion of the population of Wales. Even in 1850 the great majority of those who could read and write had learnt to do so through Sunday schools. Still around 50 percent of bridegrooms were not able to sign the marriage register by 1850. Tragically, education had also become embroiled in what became a very acrimonious, ecclesiastical debate. The 1851 census shows that Wales had become a Nonconformist[43] country, with at least 75 percent of the population having links with a Nonconformist denomination, which included Calvinistic Methodists as well as the older Congregational and Baptist groups. Nonconformists were very suspicious of the state getting involved in financing education, because of their fear that state education would mean education dominated by the Anglican Church.

The Treason of the Blue Books

The fear that the Anglican establishment was intent on using education to undermine Nonconformity was confirmed in what came to be called the Treason of the Blue Books. In 1846 the Education Committee of the British government, at the instigation of a London Welshman who was member of Parliament for Coventry, commissioned a report on the state of education in Wales. Three young English barristers were appointed to do the work and after three months or so in Wales staying with local gentry, who were thoroughly anglicised, and with Anglican clergy, many of whom were very antagonistic towards Nonconformists, they presented their massive report of over 1,200 pages in three folio volumes bound in blue boards. The commissioners were undoubtedly very able men, and their work does present a very thorough review of the state of

---

[43] The term originated in 1662. When the monarchy had been restored after the English Civil War, all clerics were asked in 1662 to conform to the reestablished Anglican Church structure. The two thousand or so who refused to conform were ejected from their churches and became Nonconformists. They and their flocks constituted the Presbyterian, Congregational, and Baptist denominations.

education in Wales in 1846, albeit from the perspective of English imperialists who delighted in expressing their contempt of Welsh. The following extract from the report by the commissioner J. C. Symons is a good example of its general approach:

> The Welsh language is a vast drawback to Wales, and a manifold barrier to the moral progress and commercial prosperity of the people. It is not easy to over-estimate its evil effects…It dissevers the people from intercourse which would greatly advance their civilization, and bars the access of improving knowledge to their minds. As a proof of this, there is no Welsh literature worthy of the name.[44]

Six of the report's 1,200-plus pages also expressed the conviction of some Anglican clerics that Nonconformity was keeping people ignorant and fostering immorality, especially among women. To add insult to injury, the London press, just as they would today, focused heavily on these insinuations and used the report to pour scorn on the Welsh. The storm of protest went on for years and confirmed the suspicion in many minds that the interference of the state in education was but part of an Anglican plot to regain ground lost to the Nonconformists in Wales.[45]

The report succeeded in denigrating Welsh-medium education, because one of its contradictory effects was a determination in many quarters to make sure that the Welsh could never again be called ignorant and immoral because they had no knowledge of English. When primary education became a statutory responsibility of local government in 1870, Wales acquiesced in a deliberate policy of anglicisation. Welsh was either banished altogether or became very peripheral in the curriculum. Welsh could be tolerated as the

---

[44] R. R. Lingen, J. C. Symons, and H. R. Vaughan Johnson, *Reports of the Commissioners of Inquiry into the State of Education in Wales* (London: HMSO, 1848), 309–10.
[45] The controversy gave tremendous impetus to the movement working for the disestablishment of the Church of England which was eventually successful in Wales when the Church in Wales was disestablished by Act of Parliament in 1928. However, the bitterness generated by the campaign on the Nonconformist and Anglican sides did tremendous damage to the cause of the gospel.

language of the home and chapel,[46] but English was the language of commerce and material success. English was the key to "getting on in the world." The cultural effect of this policy was devastating. By the 1971 census, the proportion of Welsh speakers in Wales was down to 20.9 percent. Although the language is not the only aspect of ethnic identity by any means, the loss of it is some indication of a loss of identity. When the domination of the industrial areas of Wales by a political ideology firmly wedded to modernist materialism is added to the loss of language, the situation became critical.

The Impact of Socialism

As a direct result of the greed and inhumanity of the masters of industry, socialism became the dominant political creed in Wales in the twentieth century. Some Welsh socialists favoured a measure of Welsh independence throughout the century, but they failed to gain any significant support in the Labour Party until the 1990s. For most of the century the Welsh Labour Party was firmly wedded to the idea that Welsh prosperity was dependent on the absorption of the Welsh economy in the English economy. In 1979 Welsh Labour supporters even came out strongly in a referendum campaign to oppose a proposal to devolve government to a Welsh assembly proposed by their own Labour government. Name, history, culture, language, place, solidarity—those aspects of corporate existence that make for identity and a sense of belonging—could be sacrificed to the gods of material prosperity. Then in the 1990s something remarkable happened when the majority of the Welsh Labour Party came out in favour of limited devolution for Wales. This time, in May 1999, a referendum was won by a whisker, and a Welsh Assembly was established to democratically control government spending in Wales. Some Christian reflection on this event

---

46 "Chapel" means different things in different contexts. In Ireland and Scotland a chapel is a Roman Catholic place of worship, while in Wales it is a Nonconformist and very Protestant place of worship.

would take me way beyond the scope of this volume, but it does generate hope that the Welsh, in God's providence, are being given some more time and opportunity to add to the treasures that they have already built up to present to the King of kings.

The purpose of this brief and inadequate sketch of the fate of Welsh ethnic identity since the high point of Christian influence upon it as a result of the Great Awakening is to prove that factors other than Christian influence play a part if an ethnic identity is to mature into nationhood. In the case of Wales, English rule again and again provided a very powerful block to the full development of Welsh identity. While the Protestant tradition with its emphasis on Bible translation has been very good at fostering ethnic identity up to a point, it seems to have given very little thought to the implications of doing so or has even resisted the idea that an ethnic identity ennobled by the Bible could possibly mature into nationhood.

CHRISTIAN MISSIONS AND BUILDING ETHNIC IDENTITIES

Evidence is available that missionaries engaged in Bible translations were sometimes conscious of the ethnic and political implications of what they were doing. We shall look briefly at three cases. The point of looking at these cases is to show that Protestant missionaries, especially through their work of creating written languages, have contributed to the creation of ethnic identities, and that at times they even understood clearly that they were doing this.

The Tsonga of the Transvaal, South Africa

There were many communities in Africa by the nineteenth century, such as the Ethiopian kingdom or the Baganda in Uganda, which shared many of the characteristics of European "nations" before the Industrial Revolution. There was also a lot of instability with large numbers of people migrating, particularly as a result of war that was the result of the "imperial" expansion of the more stable or powerful groups. It was such conflict in the main that brought various groups from southern Mozambique and the coastal regions around Delagoa Bay into the hill country of northern Transvaal in the first half of the nineteenth century. The Swiss Mission started work among these peoples in 1873. By the early 1890s the mission had published a grammar and parts of the Bible in the local language that they called Gwamba. The Swiss Mission then extended its sphere of operation and established a work near Lourenço Marques among a people that they believed spoke a very similar language to that they had called Gwamba. Henri Junod, who pioneered this second branch of the mission, came to the conclusion that Gwamba was not adequate and that the people spoke a different though related language. So from 1894 he produced a language primer, readers, and Bible translations in this new language that he called Ronga. His doing so set off a heated debate with the original mission in the Transvaal, and in particular with its leader Henri Berthoud. What was said on both sides in this debate gives a fascinating insight into the impact of missions on ethnic identity and also the way that missionaries have been influenced by secular theories.

Berthoud was conscious of the fact that the Gwamba language was not precisely the language that was spoken by many in the area that the original Swiss Mission station served but his approach was pragmatic. He believed that a written language that was not entirely understood, through devotional use, would come to predominate and become the language of a people who spoke a number of different but related dialects. He was influenced in this by economic considerations, because his approach would need much less outlay on printing and translation work. He was also motivated by European political history where languages such as Jacobin French or Castilian Spanish had been used to unify large numbers of people into one ethnic group, even though they were linguistically not very closely related.

Junod, on the other hand, was motivated by his desire for evangelistic success and was probably spurred on by the fact that the Wesleyans who operated in the local dialect were very successful.

He was also familiar with the work of contemporary anthropologists like Sir James Frazer who believed that classifying languages and the social customs related to them was the key to understanding the history of national development. At this point the missionary was plugged in to the idealist approach to ethnic identity and nationhood already mentioned. Junod was in the business of identifying and describing ethnicity.

Junod's position prevailed, especially following Berthoud's untimely death in 1904. Ronga has become the dominant language in southern Mozambique, while Tsonga (Thonga/Shangaan) became dominant in the northern Transvaal and central-southern Mozambique.[47]

The Baganda of Uganda

What happened in Uganda is similar in many ways to what happened in Southern Africa. The mission this time was the Church Missionary Society (CMS). When they first arrived in Buganda in 1877, the missionaries worked through Swahili, which some thought could be encouraged as a *lingua franca* for the whole of East Africa. Bishop Tucker[48] abandoned this idea, and by 1896 the whole Bible had been translated into Luganda, the central dialect of Buganda. However, as mission activity expanded beyond the area where Luganda was dominant, an argument arose as to whether work should be done in other languages/dialects as they were encountered.

The case of Toro is a good example. After his first visit Tucker came to the conclusion that Luganda would suffice to evangelise

---

[47] Patrick Harries, "Exclusion, Classification and Internal Colonialism: The Emergence of Ethnicity among the Tsonga-speakers of South Africa," in *The Creation of Tribalism in Southern Africa*, ed. Leroy Vail (London: James Currey, 1989), 82–117; and Patrick Harries, "The Roots of Ethnicity: Discourse and the Politics of Language Construction in South-east Africa," *African Affairs* 87 (1988): 25–52. There is a helpful discussion and critique of Harries in Adrian Hastings, *The Construction of Nationhood: Ethnicity, Religion and Nationalism* (Cambridge: Cambridge Univ. Press, 1997), 152–55.

[48] Alfred Robert Tucker (1849–1914), who went to Africa in 1890 as bishop of Eastern Equatorial Africa, a massive diocese including Kenya and Tanzania. He became bishop of Uganda alone in 1899. He retired in 1911.

Toro because it was well understood by the people, even though he himself could not even speak Luganda very well! The local missionaries Fisher and Maddox, and later Edith Pike and Ruth Hurditch (who became Mrs. Fisher), disagreed. Not only did they believe that there was a need to evangelise the Toro in their own language of Lunyoro, but they were also convinced that Buganda was scheming to annex Toro. Walker, a senior missionary, supported Tucker in his original decision using arguments similar to Berthoud in the Transvaal: it would be cheaper and more efficient if everyone used Luganda; it would be easier for missionaries to move from one station to another; with the development of communications, that is, with modernisation, differences between "tribes" would be minimised and they would come to speak the same language; and later he added the sad argument that since the colonial authority was being centred on Buganda, it was the duty of all missionaries to cooperate with the imperial authority.

Maddox was the chief advocate of Lunyoro. Like Junod he argued that effective evangelism demanded its use, and by 1905 he had plenty of evidence to support his position because of the dramatic success of Lunyoro-speaking evangelists. Maddox was also concerned for the preservation of the Toro as an ethnic group and saw Bible translation as a means to preserve their identity. It was Maddox who prevailed eventually, and the door was opened for Bible translation to other minority languages in Uganda. Really this was but the triumph of the Reformation and evangelical principle that the gospel is heard most effectively in the language of the heart. Since the battles of the turn of the twentieth century, evangelical mission has been totally committed to translating the Bible into as many heart languages as possible. Interestingly, in the case of Uganda and a number of other countries, this policy insured that a native language could not become the administrative language in the postcolonial era.[49]

---

[49] Tudor Griffiths, "Bishop A. R. Tucker of Uganda and the Implementation of an Evangelical Tradition of Mission" (PhD thesis, Univ. of Leeds, 1999), ch. 7.

The Yoruba of Nigeria

By today the Yoruba are a large ethnic community of over 18 million people that inhabit much of Western Nigeria. Before the Western colonisation of Africa, they were the only people south of the Sahara whose social organisation was based on cities that dominated a large tract of surrounding land. By the end of the eighteenth century many cities were incorporated into the empire of Oyo, but Yoruba city-states inside and outside the empire looked to Ife as their mother city. Although the various city-states shared a common origin, many customs, and even language, there was no real sense of unity between them, and they did not even have a common name by the beginning of the nineteenth century. It was the coming of Christianity in the nineteenth century that changed the situation and gave the Yoruba their name and the consciousness of being a single people. Interestingly, in their case, Africans worked the change. Samuel Ajayi Crowther, the first Anglican bishop on the Niger, translated the Bible into Yoruba, and Samuel Johnson, another Anglican priest, wrote *The History of the Yorubas from the Earliest Times*,[50] doing for the Yorubas what Bede had done for the English. Here again the creation of a literature was crucial in making a vague sense of identity into something far more concrete. That Christians were responsible for this is particularly noteworthy in this case because a substantial minority of the Yoruba are Muslim.

There has been a movement for independence among the Yoruba since the beginning of the nineteenth century, even though on the whole they have remained faithful to the federal state of Nigeria that was established at decolonisation. There was much Yoruba frustration when the Yoruba chief Abiola was hindered by the Muslim-dominated Hausa-Fulani military elite from taking up his position after he was elected president in 1994. This frustration was assuaged with the election of president Obasanjo who was also a Yoruba.[51]

---

[50] Composed in the 1890s but not published until 1921.

In the Transvaal and Uganda the case for translating into heart language prevailed over any economic or political considerations. However, the question needs to be faced as to what will be the future of the increasingly numerous ethnic groups, many of which have relatively small populations, that Protestant missionaries are continuing to ennoble through Bible translation. The testimonies of people receiving a Bible in their own language for the first time are striking. I have taken just two recent examples from the publications of mission agencies:

1. An elder of a Falam church: "We never imagined it possible to have a Bible in our own language. We'd accepted that reading it in other [languages] was good enough for us. But when the Falam Bible was made available we discovered the wonderful richness of reading God's word in our own language…We now realise that the Bible freed us from the 'slavery' and domination of other ethnic groups. We have come to realise that we are special, one of the races our God created."[52]

2. The second testimony concerns the publication of the New Testament into Chorote, which is one of the languages of the indigenous people of the Argentinean Chaco. "At last," a Chorote pastor exclaimed, "God speaks to us in Chorote." Other reactions were: "It is like waking up from a long sleep." "Now we no longer need to be like parrots, we can actually understand the words." However, there were misgivings among the Chorote about the whole project. Some felt that to emphasise their ethnic difference through bolstering their language would disadvantage them in a political and economic community dominated by Spanish. They had to be encouraged by Western outsiders to value their own distinct identity. To quote Bill Mitchell, a Bible Society consultant involved with the project: "When you're a little people, when you

---

[51] Hastings, *The Construction of Nationhood,* 158–59; James Minahan, *Nations without States: A Historical Dictionary of Contemporary National Movements* (Westport, CT / London: Greenwood, 1996), 626–28.
[52] Quote from a Bible Society publication.

live on the margins, and you're forgotten, receiving the Word of God in your language is tremendously affirmative: it says you matter. You might not matter in world politics, but you matter to God and your language matters. This gives a new sense of identity to people, it helps them to lift up their heads and stand tall."[53] The mission strategy that prevailed in the 1890s prevails still.

CONCLUSION

Christianity has a history of almost 2,000 years and has spread very extensively over the face of the earth. It is fair to expect that it has had a significant impact on the way human beings view their collective identity. This may sound like a truism, but it is amazing how secular historians and observers of current affairs are able to ignore religion in their observations. Christianity is also a literate religion. Everywhere it goes it has created a people with a literature. Now since a people with a literature have a much stronger and more stable sense of identity, giving them the beginnings of a literary tradition by translating the Bible is a key factor in moving a people from an amorphous ethnicity to clearly defined nationhood. England is a good example of the way Christianity gave an amorphous mixture of Teutonic migrants a strong sense of identity as English people. The Reformation principle of providing the Bible in the vernacular was particularly significant in the solidifying of English ethnic identity and nationhood. In the case of Wales the same Christian factors that had solidified English identity prevailed, but Wales was hindered by English oppression from developing its identity fully.

The Protestant principle of vernacular translation of the Bible was a fundamental policy of the missionary movement from the English-speaking world that really got under way with the founding of the Baptist Missionary Society in England in 1793. There was a

---

[53] "At Last, God Speaks to Us in Chorote," *Share: The Magazine of the South American Mission Society,* issue 3, 1997, 4–5.

significant debate among missionaries at the turn of the twentieth century as to whether translations should be made into "created" languages that corresponded with areas of colonial administration or into the "heart language" of every people, irrespective of size or convenience. The second alternative prevailed, especially among evangelicals. The work of translating into more and more languages is ongoing. This means that more and more groups are being given the ability to create their own literature and thus move from a more amorphous to a more defined stage of ethnic identity. Historically, in many cases, the end of this development has been nationhood that involves political autonomy. While evangelical missiology has given very little thought to the collective implications of its Bible translation policy, the human rights movement, rooted in the United Nations, has focused a great deal on ethnic identity in the last twenty years. The next chapter will begin to explore a possible evangelical approach to the flourishing of ethnic identity by examining the issue from the perspective of human rights.

ETHNIC IDENTITY AND HUMAN RIGHTS

RIGHTS AND OBLIGATIONS

I have noticed that evangelical Christians are a bit nervous about talk of human rights. The standard response is that the biblical emphasis is not so much on human rights as on human obligations and responsibilities. The language of rights, it is said, is the language of people demanding something for themselves while at the heart of the gospel is the principle of giving up our life for the sake of others. But the gap between rights and responsibilities may not be quite as large as is supposed. To say that someone has a particular responsibility implies an obligation to supply something that someone else is lacking. It is someone else's lack that creates the responsibility.

Christian responsibility towards the poor is a simple example. The apostle John makes it very clear that seeing a Christian brother in physical need creates an obligation in a brother/sister who has more than they need to supply the needs of the needy brother (1 John 3:17). The obligation is not a legal obligation but an obligation of love that heightens rather than diminishes the right of the needy brother. What John is saying is that when someone who has material possessions knows of a needy brother, that knowledge creates a demand of love which can only be satisfied when the want of the needy brother is satisfied. This is not that far from saying that the needy brother has a right to expect help from the one who has plenty. In the context of Christian love at least, obligations and rights seem to be two sides of the same coin.

So if the concepts of rights and obligations can be found within the perfect law of love as revealed in Christ, we should not be surprised to find shadows of them in the way human relationships are organised in a fallen world. Even here obligations and rights are the two sides of one coin more often than not. For example, just about any article in the United Nations Universal Declaration of Human Rights could just as easily have been formulated as a series of obligations. A couple of articles will suffice to illustrate the point. Article 3, "Everyone has the right to life, liberty and security of person," could just as easily have been "Every state has the obligation to protect the life, liberty, and security of its citizens." Article 19, "Everyone has the right to freedom of opinion and expression," could be "Every state has the obligation to allow its citizens freedom of opinion and expression."[54] The obligation is implied in the right and vice versa.

The crucial question in the Christian context is not whether or not rights language is legitimate but whether the right that is being demanded is legitimate. The demand of homosexual couples to have their civil partnership recognised as marriage illustrates the need to assess the rights that are being claimed in the light of God's revelation. What is at issue for us Christians in this case is not rights and obligations but the legitimacy or not of a perceived right that the state has an obligation to treat homosexual couples in exactly the same way as heterosexual. Most Christians would argue that the state has no such obligation. In the context of this chapter, the key question is whether a state has an obligation to foster ethnic diversity. If it has, then an ethnic group has a right to expect a state to provide conditions in which its unique identity can flourish. One key way of doing this would be to provide education in its language, even though that language is not the official language of the state.

---

54 See www.un.org/en/documents/udhr/.

CONFLICT OVER THE RIGHT TO A WELSH EDUCATION

In the autumn of 1980 I was unexpectedly plunged into an intense controversy over the right to a Welsh language education, in the area where I live, that gave me very little opportunity to think whether the specific right being demanded was legitimate or not. Maybe this is the norm when, as Christians, we seriously attempt to be in the world though not of it. I had in fact thought quite a lot about the legitimacy of Welsh-medium education before that time. What took me by surprise was the intensity of the specific conflict into which I was plunged as a result.

The Struggle for the Recognition of Welsh as an Official Language

Though not the type to become a political activist or to welcome suffering in the cause of the Welsh language or any other cause, I was a passive supporter of the movement to get official recognition for the language that was gathering momentum during my time as a student. When I became a student in 1964, a period of massive expansion in the provision of university places was beginning in the United Kingdom. The number of students at my college in Bangor, North Wales, was increasing, but the proportion of Welsh speakers was falling. My year saw the lowest number of Welsh speakers that had ever registered. We were a small stream in a flood of Englishness engulfing the college. This was a college of the federal University of Wales that had been built in the nineteenth century by collections from quarrymen and other workers in North Wales to provide a good education for their children. Sadly, from its foundation the whole ethos and administration of the college had been totally English. The year I arrived, it felt as if the Welsh student ethos of the college was also being swept to one side. The campaign to reform college administration began in earnest and eventually succeeded, though not without a long struggle, in making Bangor University more of an institution serving Welsh people than an instrument to destroy their identity. I played a tiny part in that struggle by supporting those who threatened to boycott lectures unless courses were offered in Welsh. Since there was a lot of support for us among the staff of the Faculty of Theology, the success of this little campaign was almost complete in a very short time.

The 1960s also saw the formation of the Welsh Language Society (*Cymdeithas yr Iaith Gymraeg*). The census figures of 1961 showed that the number of Welsh speakers was declining at an alarming rate. By that time Plaid Cymru, the Welsh "nationalist" party—now officially called the Party of Wales in English—had been in existence for over thirty years, but its attempts to influence the fate of Wales through the ballot box seemed to be getting nowhere. Plaid Cymru had not succeeded in getting even one member of Parliament elected. For some members of Plaid Cymru, there seemed to be nothing hindering Wales from being totally assimilated into England. The Welsh Language Society was established in 1962 as a campaigning organisation that was prepared to contemplate civil disobedience and even destruction of property to get Welsh recognised as an official language in Wales. One of their early campaigns was in favour of bilingual road signs. All instructions and names of places on road signs in Wales were in English, or had anglicised versions of Welsh names where there was no English name. *Caergybi* was Holyhead, *yr Wyddgrug* was Mold, *Porthmadog* was Portmadoc, and so on.

The Society campaigned constitutionally for four years to persuade the authorities to put up bilingual signs. It was only after all constitutional means had proved futile that members of the Welsh Language Society started taking signs down or defacing them.[55] The really committed took signs down and then delivered them personally to police stations, inviting arrest in the process. They would then refuse to respond to summonses to appear in court unless they received them in Welsh, demand that their case should be heard in Welsh, and refuse to pay fines unless the demand was in Welsh.

---

[55] I did make a cowardly contribution to this cause by removing a particularly offensive sign on the way to meet someone from the Irish ferry in Holyhead in the middle of the night.

Many served prison terms and in the process generated a lot of support for the cause.

It needs to be emphasised at this point that the Welsh Language Society was explicitly nonviolent from its foundation. It drew a lot of its inspiration from the Ghandian movement for independence in India and the civil rights movement led by Martin Luther King in the USA.[56] Several of its leading activists have been very committed Christians, with one of them becoming General Secretary of the Evangelical Alliance in Wales once his intense campaigning days were over. I am convinced that it was this Christian and pacifist influence that saved us in Wales from the sort of violence that has blighted so many lives in Ireland.

Another major campaign was for bilingual official forms. This campaign was focused on the post office because of its responsibility for driving licences, television licences, and other official documents. This was the one campaign in which I got involved briefly by joining a sit-down protest outside the main post office in Aberyswyth. I was certainly not perceived as one of the leaders of the protest, who were roughly removed from the scene by the police. But I was committed to the cause and felt strongly that government in Wales should accord equal status to the Welsh language in its official documents.

Supporting the demand for theological education through the medium of Welsh and a sit-down protest outside the post office in Aberystwyth was the sum total of my active involvement in the Welsh language struggle in the 1960s. My marriage in 1967 was destined to lead to a more significant involvement. Our first child, a daughter, was born in 1969, to be followed by three more, two sons and one daughter, in the 1970s, and a fifth, another daughter,

---

[56] In 1966 the Society officially dissociated itself from the Free Wales Army and in 1979 was the first to condemn the campaign to burn down holiday cottages in rural Wales. For those who can read Welsh, a scholarly history of the Welsh Language Society has been published: Dylan Phillips, *Trwy Ddulliau Chwyldro...? Hanes Cymdeithas yr Iaith Gymraeg 1962–92* (Llandysul, Wales: Gomer, 1998). Pages 237–241 deal with the influence of Gandhi, Martin Luther King, and Christian nonviolence.

in 1984. When the time came in 1972 for us as parents to decide where our eldest daughter was to be educated, we were faced with the choice of either an English- or Welsh-medium school.

The Option of Education in the Welsh Language

The fact that there was a Welsh-medium school in Bangor was due to a movement for Welsh-medium education that had began with the establishment of the first Welsh-medium primary school in 1947. As stated in the last chapter, the state came to dominate education in Wales in the last quarter of the nineteenth century. That this state education was aggressively committed to anglicisation was one of the main factors in the decline of Welsh. Those who pushed for Welsh-medium education had the vision to see what was happening and took the first significant step in stemming the tide. The growth of this movement was slow at first, but it gathered momentum in the 1960s. In the Welsh-medium schools a child's education is through the medium of Welsh, and English is taught as a subject. The aim is that children should be thoroughly bilingual by the end of their primary education.

My wife is English, so the possibility that our children could be educated through the medium of Welsh became a matter of some discussion. This discussion, which is not uncommon in interethnic marriages, ended with the agreement that our children should be educated through the medium of Welsh. This was the alternative most consistent with our decision to raise our children bilingually from the beginning. For me the thought that my own children would not be able to communicate in Welsh with my family and me was inconceivable, so I determined to always speak Welsh to them. Since their mother was English, their mother tongue would be English. We have found that this policy works well, and the children developed bilingually very early and very naturally. But even in Bangor the whole cultural atmosphere has been deeply influenced by English, so I was very glad that a school was available where the children could experience a community functioning entirely in

Welsh. This became even more essential when we moved to South Wales in 1975.

In Bangor most of the children who attended the Welsh school came from homes where at least one of the parents was Welsh-speaking. Most were from Welsh-speaking homes, so it was not at all difficult to create a school with a totally Welsh ethos. In South Wales things were very different. Anglicisation had proceeded much further, and the percentage of Welsh speakers had become minute. Yet the valleys branching out from Pontypridd, where we settled in 1975, was the area in which the Welsh schools movement was growing most rapidly in the 1970s. Our children now attended a Welsh-medium school where more than 90 percent of the pupils came from homes where no Welsh was spoken at all.

I was puzzled as to why parents should want to send their children to a school where their children would be educated in a language they could not understand. The fact that the Welsh schools were building a reputation for being good schools undoubtedly influenced parents. However, in talking with parents, I discovered that many of them had a real sense of loss at having lost touch with their cultural roots. Many have told me that some of their grandparents could speak Welsh, but because of the heavy cultural and social pressure on them, they failed to pass on the language to their children. As the grandchildren of Welsh speakers, they regretted this failure and were keen that their own children should have the opportunity to reengage with their cultural roots.

For whatever reason, the demand for places in the Welsh schools in our area was growing, and the school that our children attended was very full. In the summer term of 1980 I was elected as the chairman of the Parents and Teachers Association (PTA) of the school for the following year. The normal task of the PTA was to hold social gatherings and raise extra funds for the school, and I looked forward to being involved with such activities. I never imagined that, from the first day of my chairmanship, most of my year would be taken up with protesting, campaigning, and negotiating with the authorities.

The Political Context of the Conflict in Pontypridd

In the UK, responsibility for education has been devolved to local authorities. In our case, in 1980 the authority in charge of education was Mid Glamorgan County Council. The pressure for the provision of Welsh-medium education was coming from parents, and the council had been responding rather slowly and grudgingly. There was a complex knot of reasons for this reluctance. An obvious reason was political. The political party that was most vigorous in its support of Welsh-medium education was the Welsh nationalist party, Plaid Cymru (the Party of Wales). The Labour Party had been the dominant political party in Mid Glamorgan for fifty years, but Plaid Cymru was beginning to provide something of a challenge. If the Labour Party really supported Welsh-medium education, it could appear as if they were giving in to Plaid's demands.

There were some on both sides of the fence, including myself, who were eager to uncouple the issue from politics and to make it a matter of human rights in general, but there was strong emotional resistance to this on both sides of the political divide. Many Labour Party supporters also feared that the growth of Welsh-medium education would lead to the growth of a consciousness of separate identity that could lead to a politically separatist identity from which they would be excluded as non-Welsh speakers. Those supporters of the Welsh language movement who undoubtedly gave the impression that only Welsh speakers were genuinely and fully Welsh fed this fear. Probably more than half of the population of Mid Glamorgan were the descendants of fairly recent immigrants from England, Ireland, and other countries whose families had never been Welsh-speaking. Yet as they shared their life with migrants from rural Wales, in what was often the harsh and exploitative conditions of the coalfields, they came to think of themselves as Welsh. This new ethnic identity that had been carved out of the coal face was never a Welsh-speaking identity, so it is not surprising that those who owned it should feel threatened by an increasing demand for Welsh-medium education.[57]

Our situation in the South Wales valleys is an excellent illustration of the complexity of the whole issue of ethnic identity. Our mixed community of people from mainly Welsh, English, and Irish extraction has unquestionably developed an identity of its own. Even the majority language is a form of English that has been so influenced by Welsh syntax that some call it Wenglish! But I believe that most of the immigrants into this area have changed enough to become a part of the long history of the territory that is Wales as a whole. However, to do so fully they need the memory that has been preserved primarily by the Welsh speakers. Together we could become a fully fledged "nation." I believe that the movement for Welsh education is an important step in this direction.

The Conflict

I was conscious earlier in 1980 that the growth of the demand for Welsh education in our area was becoming a problem for Mid Glamorgan County Council. The Union of Parents Associations of the Welsh Schools had been warning them for some time that there was urgent need for greater provision in the Pontypridd area. The solution favoured by the Council was the establishment of small Welsh-medium infant units in a number of English-medium schools that would then feed into the primary school that our children attended. The parents did not consider this a satisfactory solution and made their views known in no uncertain terms. Our school year starts at the beginning of September, but by the end of the previous term, in July, the matter had not been resolved.

When negotiations began, there were seventeen children eligible to start school in September 1980 that could not be admitted into the Welsh school because the school was already full. The parents of these children were told that they would have to attend a Welsh unit

---

[57] I believe that this fear was one of the key factors that drove most of the leaders of the Labour Party in Wales to campaign against their own party's policy of devolving government to Wales in a referendum in 1979 and ensured that the measure was comprehensively defeated.

in an English school that was being opened to accommodate them. By August parents of nine of these children had decided to wait a year before sending their children to school in the hope that the situation would be more satisfactory in a year's time. That left eight children to attend the proposed unit. For a variety of reasons, the headmistress of the Welsh school decided during August that she could accommodate the eight and informed the parents that there was room for their children at the school. So on the first day of term their proud parents brought the children fully kitted out in their pristine uniforms to begin their Welsh education. They were met by an officer of the council who refused them entrance to their classroom and insisted that they should go to the Welsh unit in an English school instead. Not surprisingly, a heated debate ensued, which ended with the parents saying that they had no intention of leaving the school premises until the authorities allowed their children to start school. They occupied the music room in the school and prepared to stay there. Some of them were to remain there on a rota basis night and day for two months. This was my first day as chairman of the PTA, and I was plunged into a situation of intense conflict!

I found myself in the forefront of negotiations with the authorities on behalf of the parents. Getting a County Council to change its mind and admit that it had taken a wrong decision is not easy, and we were asking them to take two steps back by allowing the eight children entrance into the Welsh school and to abandon their plan to open Welsh-medium units. The two issues were inextricably linked in the mind of the council, so after weeks of protests, legal threats from the council, and a lot of media exposure, it became clear that the only way to get the children into the school was to appear to compromise on the matter of the Welsh unit. The sit-in begun on September 1, 1980, and eventually came to an end on November 2 when the council agreed that the eight children could go to the Welsh school since the parents of the children who were due to start school in September 1981 had agreed for their children to go to the proposed Welsh unit. This agreement was achieved on a Sunday afternoon at the school where it was proposed to open the unit. The parents were in one room and senior representatives of the council in another, with myself and the secretary of the Union of Parents Associations acting as the negotiators. It was not easy to get the parents to agree, but we were able to convince them that with strong opposition the plan to open a Welsh unit could still be abandoned. An alliance was formed with the parents of the children in the English-medium school where the Welsh-medium unit was to be placed to oppose its establishment. In a very stormy meeting with councillors and officers early in 1981, it was made very clear that no one wanted Welsh units in English schools. As it turned out, that was the last anyone heard of units from the council. In just a few years another Welsh school was opened in the town. This is now the largest Welsh-medium primary school in Pontypridd, and the Welsh schools movement continues to grow.

The Conflict from a Christian Perspective

The story of the growth of the movement for Welsh-medium education and especially of the conflict in which I became involved may not be that significant in world history, but it is an example of a struggle for the right of a minority ethnic identity to survive and flourish. I also believe that my involvement in such a conflict was not inconsistent with my Christian profession.

As Christians we are called to serve God in Christ through the power of the Spirit with what we are and have. My whole being in its unique historical context is marred by sin, but it is that being that God redeems by his grace. My genetic endowment marks me out as a human being, but it also marks me out as a person with particular human and cultural characteristics at a specific time. My salvation is not only the salvation of my human nature but of my unique character that can only be expressed in my time and my place. I was born and raised in the cultural and religious context of Welsh-speaking Wales. I was converted in a Welsh-speaking evangelical youth camp. I had the privilege of becoming familiar with my very rich cultural and religious Welsh-language heritage through my study of Welsh literature, church history, and theology. It so happens that this was happening at the time when many of my fellow Welsh speakers were realising that this heritage was in mortal danger. What could I do as a Christian but support the struggle to preserve the language? How could I stand to one side and be content with the thought that the rich heritage that I was able to enjoy would soon perish from the earth? God has not redeemed me *from* but *in* my Welshness. I believe that I would have failed in my calling if as a result of my Christian life I allowed the Welshness that I inherited to diminish before God.

UNITY IN CHRIST AND ETHNIC DIVERSITY: GALATIANS 3:28 AND COLOSSIANS 3:11

In my experience many non-Welsh-speaking Welsh, English, and Northern Irish Christians find this Christian love of a separate identity very difficult to comprehend. Because all Welsh speakers are now bilingual, all they can see are Christians who are well able to worship in English but who want to be awkward and divisive by insisting on doing things in a language that the English speakers cannot understand. They even appeal to verses such as Galatians 3:28 or Colossians 3:11 to try to convict us of our sin of division. I would say that their rebuke is based on a profound misunderstanding of Paul in these passages.

When Paul says in Galatians that "there is neither Jew nor Greek, slave nor free, male nor female, for you are all one in Christ Jesus" (Gal 3:28), he was thinking of equal access to God through Christ. It would be ridiculous to suggest that he was thinking of the dissolution of all difference. He did not envisage women ceasing to be women and men ceasing to be men! It is also significant that each pair in Paul's list expresses an unequal power relationship. Women were demeaned and dominated by men, who more often than not treated them as mere chattels. The free owned slaves in the same way as they owned animals or furniture and had the power to dispose of them in the same way. In the case of the Jew and the Greek, both considered themselves superior to the other in different ways. The Jews claimed spiritual and the Greeks cultural superiority. It was probably the Jewish sense of spiritual superiority that was in Paul's mind, although as a diaspora Jew he was also very familiar with the fact that Greek culture was dominant in the Eastern Roman Empire, so that familiarity with it was essential to political or economic success. As such it was corrosive of other identities including the Jewish. The gospel according to Paul introduces equality into unequal power relationships. Males must think of females, the free must think of slaves, and Jews must think of Greeks as their equals before God. The tragedy of church history is that Christians have more often than not failed to work out the implications of this radical transformation in their social relationships. Many Christian men continued to treat women as inferior and subservient, defended the institution of slavery, and colluded with cultural and spiritual superiority and oppression. Equality in Christ should have eroded these oppressions much sooner than it did in many cases. Galatians 3:28 is not about the destruction of difference but mutual respect.

Colossians 3:11 proclaims essentially the same message. When Paul says that "here there is no Greek or Jew, circumcised or uncircumcised, barbarian, Scythian, slave or free, but Christ is all, and is in all" (Col 3:11), he is saying that no one begins from a superior position in their approach to God. The Jew with his circumcision has no advantage over a Greek. The Greeks with all their cultural refinement have no advantage over non-Greek-speaking peoples (barbarians), and the free have no advantage over the Scythians or slaves. The Scythians were a people that lived in the Caucasus to the north and east of the Black Sea. They were intermediaries in trade between what is now Turkey and Russia and provided many slaves for the Turkish market. The Colossians probably called the slaves that had come to their community through Scythian hands "Scythians" and viewed them as the lowest of the low. Even they, according to Paul, were equal to Jews and Greeks in Christ. Immediately after this statement Paul encourages these Christians from different ethnic backgrounds and social positions to compassion, kindness, humility, gentleness, patience, forgiveness and, above all, love. I find it impossible to believe that trampling on another person's identity could be consistent with these virtues. To object to a fellow Christian's desire to worship and serve God within their cultural heritage is the exact opposite of what Paul is saying. It is to say that I must jettison what I am in order to be united with another in Christ, while Paul is saying that we are already one as Greeks, Jews, barbarians—those who speak other languages—Scythians, slaves, and free. This unity that we have is to be expressed in mutual love and respect and not in destroying each other's identity.[58]

THE OBLIGATION TO RESPECT THE IDENTITY OF OTHERS

If it is an obligation of our union with Christ to love as equals those who differ from us, then those who differ have a right to our love. That in no way annuls the obligation to love in return. What is being underlined here is that there would be no obligation without a right. The radical nature of Christianity is seen in the fact that any right we may have does not flow from some inherent righteousness or justice but from grace. Mercy by definition is undeserved. It is helpless need, not self-righteous demand, that invites grace. The evangelical Protestant missionary strategy of Bible translation is a wonderful example of this grace at work with reference to ethnic identity. Thousands of able missionaries and their local helpers have spent themselves in making it clear that God loves people as they are within their own cultural and historical context. The people with their language and traditions may be insignificant in terms of world

---

[58] In the case of slaves, the recognition of equality in Christ should have led to recognition of equal human identity and so to the freeing of the slave. It is one of the great tragedies of Christian history that this obvious implication of Christian teaching was ignored for so long.

power and influence, but making the Bible available to them in their own language says that their identity matters to God. People's need of God's grace as understood in the evangelical Protestant tradition creates an obligation to respect their identity.

If this principle of respect, especially for the weak and vulnerable, is good for the church, then it must also be good for humanity as a whole. So, from within a Christian framework of thought, it could be legitimate to charge government with the obligation in their jurisdiction to respect the difference of Welsh speakers or those parents who wanted their children to be Welsh speakers. From my point of view I cannot claim that I saw this clearly at the time of the struggle, but I can remember feeling strongly at the time that we had the right to ask for Welsh-medium education and that the local authority was under an obligation to provide it. I certainly felt no contradiction whatsoever between my Christian faith and the principle that we were trying to establish.

BEING CHRISTIAN IN A CONFLICT SITUATION

If my conscience was clear on the principle of the struggle, it was also vital that it was kept clear in the conduct of the campaign. This is not easy in the heat of a conflict. I had to chair packed meetings of parents whose temper was up and try to direct their energy into ways of bringing pressure on politicians that was consistent with grace. This was not always easy, and I can think of at least one suggestion that was accepted that I should have opposed strongly. I also struggled to love the senior councillor who rang me and in no uncertain terms threatened to undermine my employment as a college teacher if I persisted in the struggle. However, by God's grace, when the conflict over the eight children was resolved, I am confident that I was viewed as someone that had helped the authorities to get out of a difficult situation with some honour intact. I learnt that even in the political world resolving a conflict must contain a strong element of reconciliation and that both the opposing parties need to be able to leave the negotiating table feeling that something has been gained.

CONFLICT OVER ETHNIC IDENTITY IN A WIDER CONTEXT

With the undoubted heightening of consciousness of ethnic identity in many parts of the world, it may be helpful to think of the struggle in which I became involved in a wider context. The situation in which we found ourselves in the valleys of South Wales was the result of extended colonial rule and industrialisation. But these are two factors that impact a very large proportion of the earth's peoples. Colonialism means the imposition of an alien culture, and industrialisation attracts alien peoples. In the case of Wales the inward migration into the industrial areas was so great and so English that when the majority of the immigrants' descendants became wedded to the English-dominated Labour Party the industrialised parts of Wales were in great danger of being assimilated into England. As a result the battle for Welsh identity has been mainly with the authorities in Wales rather than in England. Although the story of every country is unique, colonialism and industrialism seems generally to make peoples divided against themselves. For economic and political reasons some become assimilated into the culture and values of the ruling power while others cling to their traditional identity. Even after independence from the ruling power, its culture and values continue to threaten ethnic identity in many countries.

From a Christian perspective it is crucial that we understand the underlying principles that drove colonialism and industrialism and the struggle for independence in the modern period. Some English colonial theorists, for example, may have attempted to justify colonialism in terms of trusteeship or even God's providence, but there can be little doubt that it was the desire for wealth and power that really drove empire building. The fact that just about every country that had been incorporated into the British Empire had to struggle for its independence proves this beyond doubt. If empire was really established for the good of the ruled, then the rulers would not have been quite so reluctant to relinquish the benefits of power and wealth that they gained from it. Sadly, those who led the struggle for independence, in most cases, adopted the political philosophy of their oppressors.

Independence from colonial oppression was sought on the basis of the European model of the nation-state that had made individualistic, political, and economic values supreme. Independence was sought on the assumption that applying modernist political and economic strategies to the area of colonial administration by local rather than imperial politicians and administrators would lead to equality and prosperity for all. The fact that scant attention was paid to the significance of ethnic identity is proof that the whole movement was driven by materialist values. Multiethnic states were formed within the boundaries set by colonial administration on the assumption that gaining democratic rights and the freedom to develop a modernised economy would make ethnic difference irrelevant. It was assumed that people in modernised nation-states are not concerned about their ethnic identity. This policy has proved utterly disastrous for Africa in particular and continues to cause problems in many other former colonial countries.[59]

As Christians we should not be surprised that the worship of the individual and mammon has not proved a blessing to humanity. We should also be suspicious of the corrosive influence that this worship has on ethnic identity. In practice, as evangelical Christians, we have done much to counter the effect of modernisation on ethnic identity in the postcolonial world. Through its translation work in particular, evangelical missionary activity empowers and affirms ethnic identity. The question we now need to face is whether we are content as evangelicals to provide the means for ethnic groups to develop their identity in the direction of nationhood while being disinterested in what that might mean in terms of the relationship

---

[59] This matter will be discussed further in chapter 8.

of the group to the state and the wider church? I suspect that very little thought has been given to this important question.

I suspect that many translators did not look beyond the horizon of individualistic evangelisation. Bible translation was seen as simply an evangelistic tool; a means to get people saved. The preservation of a people's identity as bound up with their language was not part of the agenda. Respecting ethnic identity was simply a means to an end. Once they had become Christian, it would not be that much of a loss for them to be assimilated with another identity. The general approach to evangelisation was modernist in its individualism and took no account of the fact that each individual belongs to a variety of social groups that give meaning to their life and are the context in which salvation becomes a reality.

A more realistic and Christian approach to Bible translation would be to assume that by ennobling a people with God's word we are helping them to value what they are, and are giving them a much better chance of survival. Since the Bible can become a living reality within any ethnic identity and sanctify their life, it would make more sense to continue to defend a people's right to exist than to abandon them to the forces of modernisation with its worship of mammon. To do so would be simply to help an ethnic group to walk after helping them to their feet. The aim of evangelical mission to translate the Bible into every language should include a commitment to defend the right of those ethnic groups that receive God's word from our hands to exist and flourish.

I can imagine some Christians I know interpreting the statement that we have an obligation to promote ethnic identity as a mandate to support nationalist movements all over the world—and Welsh nationalism in particular! To do so is to fail to grasp that recognising and defending the value of this type of collective human identity is not the same as making ethnic identity into an idol, as happens in ideological nationalism. What I am advocating is much more consistent with the central biblical theme of defending the weak and marginalised than with the bluster and violence of ideological nationalism. It also needs to be emphasised that it is the oppression of ethnic difference by modern nation-states that has bred ideological nationalism by fostering monoethnic domination as a fundamental characteristic of a state. Oppression breeds oppression. It is now so very obvious that the modernist political experiment has failed and that ethnic identity is here to stay and that its oppression is a sure recipe for violence and disruption. What I am advocating, as a biblical and Christian approach, is the fostering of ethnic identity as a way of peace within and between nation-states.

This does not mean denying that the ultimate fate of all ethnic groups is in God's hands. I fully recognise that ethnic identities are not ultimate realities within history. They have their time and place and can come to an end (Acts 17:26). During their "time" they can build eternal capital, but there is no guarantee of historical survival. But that does not give us permission to destroy ethnic identities. God only is the judge. Our task as Christians is to do everything in our power to build up and realise the eternal potential of every ethnic group.

THE UNITED NATIONS AND THE RIGHTS OF ETHNIC IDENTITIES

Christians are not alone in fostering ethnic identity so we can now turn to the world of human rights and international law. The story of how the United Nations (UN) has moved towards the recognition of the rights of ethnic identities is the story of a struggle to find a place for something that really goes against the grain of the very foundations of the modern movement for international peace and justice focused on the UN. After all, the UN is an assembly of "nations" as defined by modernist political philosophy. The emphasis in this philosophy is very much on individual rather than collective rights. As long as citizens can eat, vote, and enjoy the benefits of modern industrialism, then that is all that is required of a nation-state. Ethnic difference was considered irrelevant to nation building and would melt away in the warmth of democratic freedom and the material prosperity generated in an industrialised society.

However, at the point when the UN was being born in the late 1940s, with the aim of avoiding another world war, the push for independence for the colonies of the great European empires was beginning in earnest. It is not surprising that the Charter of the United Nations approved in 1945 stated that one of its aims is "to develop friendly relations among nations based on the principle of equal rights and self-determination for all peoples."[60] It may be possible to interpret "self-determination for all peoples" as a statement supporting political autonomy for all ethnic groups, but it is very doubtful whether this was the intention of those who drafted the UN Charter. This statement was not meant to pledge support for ethnic autonomy or nationalism but for the struggle of the colonies to gain independence from imperial thralldom. It is also conditioned by what is almost a standard clause in UN instruments forbidding interference in the internal affairs of any nation-state. Since almost all the struggles of ethnic groups for recognition, autonomy, or independence are struggles within nation-states, even if the clause about self-determination indicated support for such struggles, this clause would render it toothless. Again, in the UN Universal Declaration of Human Rights (UDHR), agreed in 1948, there is no mention of self-determination for all peoples. Despite this, there was a promise in the "self-determination" clause of the UN Charter that could become more significant in due course.

Building on its foundation instruments, the UN set about drafting treaties that would spell out their implications in more detail and be ratified by its member states. The first treaty that is relevant to ethnicity is the International Covenant on Civil and Political Rights that was finally passed by the General Assembly of the UN in 1966. By 1976 enough individual states had ratified it for it to become international law. The first article of this covenant again states that "all peoples have the right to self-determination," but Article 27 fleshes out the relevance of this statement to the topic of ethnic identity:

---

60 Charter of the United Nations, ch. 1, par. 2.

In those States in which ethnic, religious or linguistic minorities exist, persons belonging to such minorities shall not be denied the right, in community with the other members of their group, to enjoy their own culture, to profess and practise their own religion, or to use their own language.[61]

There is a move towards collective rights in this article, although the emphasis is still individualistic; it is "persons belonging to... minorities" that are in view, although their rights concern things which they can only enjoy "in community with the other members of their group." This issue of minority ethnic identity that is becoming more and more of a reality as globalisation has led to the biggest movements of population in history deserves a whole chapter to itself.

CONCLUSION

This chapter has been a reflection on defending the right of an ethnic identity to exist and flourish from a Christian perspective. While recognising that it would be quite impossible for me to be objective on this issue, I have argued that defending ethnic rights are consistent with the spirit of grace manifested in the gospel. Furthermore, since evangelical missionary strategy has fostered ethnic identity, there is no reason why it should not continue to defend it. In fact the flourishing of a multiplicity of ethnic identities would seem to be more consistent with the spirit of the gospel than the monoethnic spread of Western modernisation with its devotion to mammon.

But modernisation has become globalisation, so that in the ethnic mixing bowl of our contemporary world, ethnic identity has become a matter of choice to a much greater extent than it has ever been. Together with the rights of ethnic minorities, what this may mean for the future of ethnic identity is the subject of the next chapter.

---

[61] Henry P. Steiner and Philip Alston, eds., *International Human Rights in Context: Law, Politics, Morals* (Oxford: Clarendon, 1996), 992. Much of the material on UN legislation in the section on ethnic minorities is drawn from this volume.

6

THE ETHNIC CAULDRON OF THE CONTEMPORARY WORLD

FILLING AND REFILLING THE EARTH

People have been on the move ever since Babel. At first they moved into empty places, but for most of prehistory and all of history they almost invariably followed earlier migrations to places that were already populated. The outworking of God's command to fill the earth has been more of a process of refilling or filling more intensively. The process has also been linked with fulfilling the original divine mandate given to human beings to subdue the natural world. Those peoples who have discovered smarter ways of harnessing nature and developed better agriculture, social organisation and, most significantly, weaponry have gone on to fill places that were partially occupied by others.

Interestingly, the occupation of Canaan by Israel stands out as an exception to this rule. The Canaanites had the superior weapons, and even some of the people who wielded them were bigger and more powerful. When the slaves that had just been freed from slavery in Egypt first realised this, they refused to fight and to trust God for a victory by means other than the superiority of human weapons. Forty years later they did possess the land with divine help and in the process exacted severe divine judgement on the ungodliness and barbarity of the Canaanite peoples (Deut 9:4,5). This divine paradigm for filling the earth is rare if not unique. The norm is for the strong to supplant the weak by superior military might.

Scholars are divided in their opinion as to when the Celts, my probable ancestors, came to the British Isles. One opinion is that they arrived between 2000–1000 BC so that the furthest western advance of the Celtic peoples from the Russian Caucasus was happening around the same time as their furthest eastern advance as Aryans into North India. It would be nice to think that my forefathers have been in Wales for up to 4,000 years! Most scholars now believe that the Celts came to Britain after 600 BC and that they came in relatively small numbers. Because of their superior military capability they were able to dominate the indigenous people who quickly became assimilated into their Celtic ways and language. By the time the Romans arrived in 55 BC, Britain was a Celtic land and was part of the Celtic world that covered a substantial part of Europe to the west of Italy and north of Greece and then beyond Europe to the east.

It has been well said of the Celts that:

> their descendants in Galatia received a letter from Paul; Jerome knew of them at Trier, as did Martin at Tours. They left a deep mark on the toponomy of Europe. The names of the rivers Rhone, Rhine and Danube are Celtic, as are those of the cities of London, Paris and Vienna; Gallipoli is the city of the Celts or Gauls, and the town of Bala was built on the banks of a lake in Anatolia centuries before the building of Bala, Penllyn.[62]

Apart from a remnant in Galicia in Spain and Brittany in France, the Celts have disappeared from mainland Europe. Their most vigorous descendants now live on the Celtic fringe of Europe in Ireland, Scotland, and Wales. Bala, Penllyn, my hometown, might have been built centuries after Bala in Anatolia, but it remains a Celtic town.

I am in danger of going astray here as I think of my Celtic ancestry. The point I want to make is not that my ethnic ancestry is ancient or noble but that most of it has been swept away by other peoples on the move. So effective has been the movement of other peoples that the once-powerful Celts have either disappeared altogether or remain as small minorities in the countries where they were once dominant.

---

[62] J. Davies, *A History of Wales* (London: Allen Lane, 1990), 23.

The Germanic peoples that supplanted the Celts in Britain, France, and Spain, as the Roman Empire collapsed, themselves came under heavy pressure from other peoples on the move in due course. A substantial part of Britain was occupied by Vikings and Danes,[63] Spain fell into the hands of Muslim Saracens, and much of France was ravaged by Slavic Magyars between the ninth and twelfth centuries. One legacy of this movement was the establishment of the Danish/Viking duchy of Normandy in northern France when Rollo was made duke in 911. William the Conqueror, who became king of England in 1066, was duke of Normandy. The kings of England did not finally abandon all claims to Normandy until 1450. Then from 1499 until 1789 Normandy had its own parliament in Rouen, which though without much power, remained as a focus of Norman identity. The dissolution of this parliament by the revolutionary government led to the Chouan[64] rebellion of 1793 that was brutally crushed. Some contemporary Normans refer to its crushing as the first modern genocide. Even today there is a separatist movement in Normandy campaigning for independence from France.

> The survival of the declining Norman dialect has become a major nationalist issue in the 1990s. For the small, but growing, number of pro-European separatists, the survival of the Norman culture and dialect depends on achieving Norman sovereignty in a united, federal Europe of regions.[65]

CRISES CAUSED BY PEOPLE MOVEMENTS

Stories of people movements leading eventually to identity crises abound from all over the world. A few examples will suffice:

---

[63] Known as Norsemen (North-men).
[64] *Chouan* means "owl" in the Norman dialect. This rebellion has been immortalised in Balzac's novel *The Chouans,* although the Chouans on which he focused were Bretons. Norman and Breton royalists were allies in the rebellion.
[65] Minahan, *Nations without States,* 403.

1. Mosquitia is a region along the Caribbean coast of Nicaragua and Honduras comprising about a third of the former and a quarter of the latter's land. The bulk of the population are descended from Chibchan migrants from what is now Colombia that had settled along the Caribbean coast some time before the sixteenth century. Columbus spotted them on his fourth visit in 1502, but the Spanish failed to establish themselves on the coast because of fierce opposition from the Moskitu. Dutch pirates used the Mosquitia coast as a base from which to plunder Spanish shipping in the early seventeenth century, and then in 1630 English Puritans established a colony on Providence Island off the coast and developed excellent relationships with the Moskitu. The colony was destroyed by the Spanish in 1641, but many English people continued to live on the coast. The area was eventually proclaimed an English protectorate in 1844, opening the door to missions. German Moravians were successful in converting almost the whole population to Protestant Christianity. With support from the United States, Nicaragua and Honduras—who both became independent from Spain in 1835—claimed the Mosquitia region between them, with the bulk going to Nicaragua. Even so, the area retained its autonomy and anglicised character until after the Sandinista revolution in 1979, when an attempt was made to integrate it into Nicaragua. Moskitu leaders rebelled against this in 1981 and formed an alliance with the contras that led to Sandinista forces attacking Mosquitia, burning towns and villages and creating eighty-five thousand refugees in the process. A movement for independence continues in the Nicaraguan Mosquitia.[66]

2. The Uighur of the Xinjiang-Uijgur Autonomous Region of the People's Republic of China are a Turkic people that have populated the northwest region of China between Kazakhstan and Mongolia since the eighth century AD. Having been militarily absorbed by

---

[66] Ibid., 377–79.

the Mongols, they contributed to the vast expansion of the Mongol Empire that was pioneered under the leadership of Genghis Khan. In modern times China has attempted to dilute Uighur identity by colonisation. Between 1950 and 1975 the Chinese proportion of the population went up from 3 percent to nearly 50 percent. Uighur language and customs were severely suppressed, especially during the Cultural Revolution of 1966–76. Since 1981 the non-Chinese languages of the area have received official recognition, and the Uighur proportion of the population is rising again. The discovery of an ancient mummified female by a Chinese archaeologist in Xingjiang in 1980 illustrates the current revival of Uighur identity. The mummy was a beautiful Caucasian woman who lived in Xingjiang long before the appearance of Han Chinese in the area.

> When the Loulan beauty was put on exhibition, Uygurs took her to their hearts and claimed her as "the mother of our nation." Her face, re-created by an artist, adorns a poster advertising a cassette in tribute to her. In a song on the cassette she is called Kiruran Guzali, "the beauty of Kiruran." That phrase makes her a citizen of Kiruran, the Uygur name for Loulan.[67]

3. Darfur in Western Sudan. The majority ethnic group in this area is the Fur, probably descended from North African Berbers that were driven south by the advance of Muslim Arabs in the seventh and eighth centuries AD. They remained Christian until the thirteenth century when they converted to Islam. The Muslim kingdom of Darfur was the last independent Muslim state in Africa to succumb to European rule when it was incorporated by the British into Anglo-Egyptian Sudan. When Sudan became independent in 1956 under Arab domination, a separatist movement was formed in Darfur. In consequence Darfur experienced severe repression by the Arab government of Sudan.

---

[67] Thomas B. Allen, "Xingjang Province," *National Geographic* 189, no. 3 (1996): 50–51.

THE IMPERIAL LEGACY

The case of Darfur is a very good example of the way the postimperial organisation of many states led to the creation—and often the suppression—of ethnic minorities. By definition, empire means the imposition of an alien culture upon a conquered people. What followed empire was the imposition of a Western modernist view of the nation-state that also involves the imposition of an alien culture that had no regard for ethnic identity. The jurisdiction of the newly independent countries was coterminous with the imperial jurisdiction. Belgian Rwanda became independent Rwanda. The fact that Rwandans also lived in Congo (formerly Zaire) and Uganda did not seem to matter. They had to be content with becoming minorities in states created as a result of French and English imperial rule. In most cases the areas of imperial administration were very multiethnic, and the states that were established on modernist lines were made up of ethnic minorities. In many cases the new states retained the language and culture of the imperial power for its administration as the only way to preserve the artificial unity of the state. So English remains as the language of administration in a number of postcolonial states such as India, Nigeria, Uganda, and Papua New Guinea; Portuguese is the official language of Brazil, Angola, Guinea-Bissau, and Mozambique; French is the official language of Côte d'Ivoire, Gambia, and Senegal; Spanish is the official language of almost all the Latin American countries except Brazil. Some postimperial states such as Myanmar (Burma) had one dominant ethnic group that has been able to impose its will on other ethnic groups. The Burmese (Bama) have severely oppressed the Arakanese and are being charged with the attempted genocide of the Karen.

THE LEGACY OF INDUSTRIALISM

Today industrialism is probably the most significant cause of people movements that leads to the creation of ethnic minorities. In the twentieth century, economic migration within multiethnic states and internationally reached unprecedented levels. The movement of people from rural areas to urban administrative and industrial centres, that accelerated through the twentieth century and is still ongoing, is the biggest people movement in history. In multiethnic states this leads to the creation of urban ethnic minorities. India's capital Delhi is a microcosm of India as a whole with its significant ethnic communities from most of the states. A big industrial city like Bombay has communities from Andhra Pradesh, Karnataka, and Tamil Nadu that are large enough to preserve their own identity. Some peoples such as the Chinese and Indians took advantage of the imperial era to establish themselves in many countries. The Chinese in particular are very widely spread and are also very good at retaining their identity.

In the postimperial era, many from former colonies have been able to seek their fortune in the countries of their former colonisers. There was a shortage of labour in the former colonial powers as they recovered economically after the Second World War, so they welcomed workers from former colonies. The United Kingdom encouraged the migration of significant numbers of Afro-Caribbeans in the 1950s. By now there are also large communities of Asians concentrated in cities such as London, Birmingham, Bradford, and Leicester. Some of these people, such as the Pakistanis and Bangladeshis, are clinging resolutely to their culture and traditions and offering a challenge to the state as to how to accommodate them. Other former colonial powers such as France, Holland, and Belgium are facing the same problem.

THE USA: THE SUPREME EXAMPLE OF ETHNIC MIXING?

The USA is the state that has witnessed the greatest mixing of ethnic identities in modern times, so it is impossible to talk about such mixing without saying something about its unique experience. Israel Zangwill's play *The Melting Pot*, first performed in New

York in 1908, expresses the idea that an "American" is the result of the fusion of many identities, but the truth is that for most of its history the official policy of the state has been the assimilation of all its people into a dominant white, English culture. The Declaration of Independence may have proclaimed the equality of all men and the inalienable right to life, liberty, and the pursuit of happiness to all, but in reality those blessings were only available within the framework of an English state. Native Americans were granted none of these rights, because they refused to be assimilated into the white, English state. Even the strong desire of large immigrant groups, such as the Germans in the nineteenth century, to retain their identity was treated with suspicion and eventually totally scuppered.[68] Interestingly, there have been some successes in the twentieth century in resisting the relentless pressure of assimilation into English culture. One example is the resistance of the Amish to the consolidation of education and compulsory high schooling. In a struggle lasting from 1938–72 that saw many Amish fathers imprisoned, the right of Amish parents to control their children's education was eventually granted in a Supreme Court decision. The language of instruction in Amish one-room schools may be English, but the culture of the schools is such as to tie the pupils in to the German ethnic-religious past of the community.[69] However, the Amish are a small, eccentric community that can be accommodated without any great impact on American society as a whole. For the future, what the very large Hispanic population of the United States may demand by way of recognition of their identity may be far more significant.

---

[68] In Stephen Cornell and Douglas Hartmann, *Ethnicity and Race: Making Identities in a Changing World* (Thousand Oaks, CA / London: Pine Forge, 1998), 121–30, there is an interesting account of the attempt by Germans to preserve their identity and their eventual failure to do so.

[69] For a detailed account of the Amish struggle over education, see Donald B. Kraybill, *The Riddle of Amish Culture* (Baltimore: Johns Hopkins Univ. Press, 1989), 119–38.

THE UN DECLARATION ON THE RIGHTS OF ETHNIC MINORITIES

It was probably the unprecedented mixing of peoples in the twentieth century that led to a proposal being put to the UN Commission on Human Rights in 1978 for drafting a declaration on minorities. This began a process lasting for fourteen years which culminated in acceptance by the General Assembly in 1992 of the Declaration on the Rights of Persons Belonging to National or Ethnic, Religious or Linguistic Minorities. It is ironic that it was Yugoslavia that moved the original proposal, because by 1992 it was falling apart in ethnic conflict. This declaration is the first UN instrument that clearly advocates collective rights. It recognises that certain groups of people, "minorities," have rights which are corporately and not individually owned, although after Article 1 the declaration returns to an individualistic emphasis with its oft-repeated key phrase "persons belonging to minorities." However, the declaration affirms in no uncertain terms that ethnic identity is positive and that states have a duty to protect and promote such identities: "States shall protect the existence and the national or ethnic, cultural, religious and linguistic identity of minorities within their respective territories and shall encourage conditions for the promotion of that identity."[70]

This declaration would have been very useful in the struggle with Mid Glamorgan County Council in the autumn of 1980, but it is comforting to know that the international community has since recognised that right was on our side. As the declaration says:

Article 2

1. Persons belonging to national or ethnic, religious and linguistic minorities (hereinafter referred to as persons belonging to minorities) have the right to enjoy their own culture, to profess and practise their own religion, and to use their own language, in private and in public, freely and without interference or any form of discrimination.

---

[70] Declaration on the Rights of Persons Belonging to National or Ethnic, Religious or Linguistic Minorities, Article 1, par. 1.

Article 4

2. States shall take measures to create favourable conditions to enable persons belonging to minorities to express their characteristics and to develop their culture, language, religion, traditions and customs, except where specific practices are in violation of national law and contrary to international standards.

3. States should take appropriate measures so that, wherever possible, persons belonging to minorities may have adequate opportunities to learn their mother tongue or to have instruction in their mother tongue.

There is one important difference between what the UN determined and our situation in Wales. Whereas the UN legislates against the erosion of identity in the Welsh schools movement, we are attempting to regain elements of our identity that have been lost. We were not defending the right to education in our mother tongue but in our grandmother tongue. What we are calling for is the right to claim back what was taken away from us by force in a previous generation.

The UN declaration is probably formulated in the way it is because what is primarily in view is the fate of those who become ethnic minorities by moving away from their ancestral homeland. By choosing, for whatever reason, to leave their ancestral territory for a new place, which in the modern world usually means the industrial city, people are really saying that they are prepared to seek a new identity in cooperation with many others who have taken the same step.[71] That is not to say that, at first, they will not try to preserve their ethnic identity. In fact, historically, people who migrate into the city begin by recreating something of their own community within it. However, as time goes on, the ethnic dividing

---

[71] Will Kymlicka, "Modernity and National Identity," in *Ethnic Challenges to the Modern Nation State,* ed. S. Ben-Ami, Y. Peled, and A. Spektorowski (London: Macmillan, 2000), 19.

lines become weaker as a new identity is fashioned in the context of the city. What the UN declaration asserts is that such people have a right to have their identity respected as they come to terms with their host country.

THE BIBLE AND MINORITIES

The Bible also has some significant things to say about the treatment of minorities. While the UN mixes the rights of minorities and the obligations of the majority, the biblical emphasis is on the obligations of the majority. What is in view here in particular is the Old Testament legislation concerning the stranger ("alien"). The strangers in view in the law were not just people passing through but those who seemed to have every intention of staying. They could be the remnant of conquered peoples or immigrants that had come to seek refuge from elsewhere.[72]

The theological foundation of this legislation can be seen in Deuteronomy 10:14–19.[73] This beautiful passage is a good summary of Old Testament theology as a whole:

> [14]To the LORD your God belong the heavens, even the highest heavens, the earth and everything in it. [15]Yet the LORD set his affection on your forefathers and loved them, and he chose you, their descendants, above all the nations, as it is today. [16]Circumcise your hearts, therefore, and do not be stiff-necked any longer. [17]For the LORD your God is God of gods and Lord of lords, the great God, mighty and awesome, who shows no partiality and accepts no bribes. [18]He defends the cause of the fatherless and the widow, and loves the alien, giving him food and clothing. [19]And you are to love those who are aliens, for you yourselves were aliens in Egypt.

---

[72] The most common Hebrew term for stranger/alien is *gēr*, translated as *proselutos* most frequently in the Septuagint. In later Judaism, *gēr* came to mean "proselyte." Full discussion of this topic is beyond the scope of this chapter, but there is no reason for identifying the Old Testament "strangers" exclusively with proselytes.
[73] This passage was brought to my attention by Vinoth Ramachandra. My understanding of it is shaped by his powerful exposition.

This passage divides naturally into two groups of three verses (14–16 and 17–19), which follow the same conceptual rhythm. The first verse in each group (14 and 17) says something about the character of God, the second (15 and 18), something about God's action, and the third (16 and 19), something about what God requires from his people in response. The first group of three verses (14–16) focuses on God's electing grace towards Israel. God is the sovereign Lord of the whole cosmos, including the earth and all its peoples, but he has chosen Israel to be his own in a unique way and expects them to respond to him with love and obedience.

The focus in the second group (17–19) is wider. The universal greatness of God's character is again emphasised. He is sovereign Lord over all authorities and powers in heaven and earth. However, as universal Lord he "shows no partiality and accepts no bribes." It is a difficult concept for our finite human mind to grasp, but God's election is not favouritism (cf. Deut 7:7; 9:4,5). He owns the whole earth including its peoples (14) and is impartial (17). The idea that God can have favourite nations or ethnic identities is excluded here. The description of what God does in verse 18, in this second group of verses, is just as remarkable. Coupled with the universal tendency among nations and ethnic identities to see themselves as the favourites of their god has been the tendency to focus that favouritism in the rulers. The God of gods and Lord of lords, the mighty and awesome One, in contrast, is concerned about the fatherless, the widow, and the alien/stranger (18). His great power is focused not on the mighty of this world but on the marginalised, the weak, and the vulnerable, although here again his action does not flow from partiality but from grace.

It is particularly relevant in the context of this chapter that God is said to love strangers and provide for their physical needs. I believe that Christopher Wright's comment on this verse gets to the heart of what is being revealed here:

This singling out of Yahweh's love for the alien must have a bearing on the meaning of his impartiality . . . God's electing love for Israel has been affirmed to be free of sheer favouritism and so not in conflict with the affirmation that God **shows no partiality**. That point is now expressed in a converse way. The impartiality of Yahweh is seen in that he not only **loved** Israel's forebears but he also **loves** the alien. The same word is used, and the additional phrase, that Yahweh feeds and clothes the alien, undoubtedly echoes that particular token of his loving grace experienced by Israel in the wilderness (8:3,4). Granted all the redemptive, covenantal uniqueness of Yahweh's action on Israel's behalf, it remains true that what Yahweh did for them was...typical of him. Yahweh is the God who loves the aliens and feeds and clothes them...Once again we find this remarkable balance-in-tension between the particularism of Yahweh's action for Israel in redemption and covenant and the universality of his character on which that behavior is based. His action for Israel was paradigmatic *for them*, but it was also paradigmatic *of God*.[74]

Having been described as someone who loves the stranger, it is not surprising that God commands his people to love them as well (19). God gives a similar command in Leviticus 19:34, but there it is preceded by the general command to the Israelites to love their neighbours as themselves (19:18). It is possible that the focus in Deuteronomy is on loving the stranger, because this is the point at which loving our neighbour meets its greatest test. Especially when things are not going very well for a country or a community, it is often the strangers that become the scapegoats. The Jews were blamed for all of Germany's ills in the Nazi period, and neo-Nazis today in Germany and the United Kingdom vent their frustrations on immigrants. Strangers are also much more likely to be treated with suspicion if they look different. Blacks in white societies, whites in black societies, both whites and blacks in Asian societies, and Asians in both black and white societies struggle to find acceptance, but God commands his people to love strangers.

---

[74] Christopher Wright, *New International Biblical Commentary: Deuteronomy* (Peabody MA: Hendrickson, 1996), 149–50 (bolding and italics by Wright).

The reason Israel is given for loving strangers is that they were themselves at one time strangers in Egypt (19).[75] Jacob/Israel had moved to Egypt with his large extended family and settled there with the Pharaoh's permission because of Joseph's influence. Even though their trade as shepherds was considered detestable by the Egyptians, they were welcomed and given a place because of their potential usefulness to the Pharaoh in looking after his livestock (Gen 46:1–7; 26–34; 47:1–5). So it seems that from the start the Israelites were kept at arm's length by the Egyptians but tolerated because of Joseph and their useful skills. As God had promised, the Israelites eventually grew dramatically in numbers in their host country, and the initial suspicion turned to fear and hostility. Suspicion of, and hostility towards, strangers is much more likely when they become numerous. The Egyptians were caught in a dilemma. They did not want to lose the Israelites, who had proved themselves very useful to them. Yet they were afraid that because of their large numbers they could take sides with an enemy, fight against them, and leave the country (Ex 1:10). The Egyptians attempted to solve their dilemma through violent oppression; they forced the Israelites into slave labour, thus retaining their usefulness, and tried to limit their population growth through infanticide. In commanding his people to love the strangers, God reminds them of the very bitter experience of their forefathers in Egypt. They knew what it meant to be treated cruelly as strangers. The impartial God saw their oppression and came to their rescue. He sees the oppression of other strangers too and wants his people to be compassionate towards them.

God must have known that, just as in the case of his own people when they were treated kindly at first in Egypt, strangers in Israel could multiply and prosper. In fact this happened; when Solomon took a census when he was making final preparations to build the

---

[75] This is also the reason given for loving strangers in Leviticus 19:34, and for leaving gleanings for them in Deuteronomy 24:22—"Remember that you were slaves in Egypt. That is why I command you to do this."

temple, he found that there were 153,600 people of non-Israelite origin living in Israel (2 Chr 2:17).[76] Contrary to God's will, Solomon utilised them as forced labour in temple construction which, ironically, is reminiscent of the way the Pharaoh also used Israelites as forced labour in major construction works. God did not approve of the oppression of one ethnic group by another in Egypt, and neither did he approve the same action by his own people. "Do not ill-treat an alien or oppress him, for you were aliens in Egypt" (Ex 22:21). Love is the only way to treat strangers from the divine perspective, even if showing love seems to threaten the position of my own ethnic group.

This command is also very interesting when put side by side with other commands that clearly imply that Israelites were to keep themselves separate from other ethnic groups. What God warns his people against very strongly was adopting the ungodly religious practices of strangers with their disastrous moral implications. But warning against the possible negative influence of strangers on Israelites does not in any way annul the command to the Israelites to exercise a positive influence on strangers by loving them. This command to love the stranger has not been annulled by the coming of Christ, and in a world that is creating more and more communities of strangers, it is more needed than ever. As an example of the outworking of this law, it is imperative that as Christians we love our Pakistani Muslim neighbours in the United States or any other country where they may be a minority. This will mean protecting them from abuse and discrimination, respecting their culture, and granting them freedom to practise their religion, which is possible without adopting Muslim beliefs and practices.

Building on the theological foundations summarised in Deuteronomy 10, a number of laws were revealed to Moses that dealt directly with the treatment of strangers. They were to enjoy the Sabbath rest (Ex 20:10; 23:12; Deut 4:14) and the annual festi-

---

[76] Although it seems that it was David's idea (1 Chr 22:2).

vals (Deut 16:9–14) with everyone else in Israel.[77] In the first case, they were to be allowed to enjoy the rhythm of work and rest which was divinely instituted at creation for all humanity. In the second case, they could enjoy the divinely instituted parties that God had ordained for his chosen people. Love gives permission to join in the feasting while not belonging to the community for which the feast was meant. Strangers as well as native-born Israelites were commanded not to work on the Day of Atonement (Lev 16:29,30). The implication in this passage is that both the stranger and the native-born Israelite could be cleansed from their sin on the Day of Atonement. Strangers could participate in fasting as well as feasting. In fact the frequent coupling of strangers with Israelites in Leviticus 16–18 suggests strongly that they could participate fully in the blessings and responsibilities of Israelite religion (cf. Lev 17:8,10,12,13; 18:26; 22:18; Num 15:14–29).[78] Gleanings were to be left for them as well as for the fatherless and the widow if they were poor (Lev 19:10; Deut 24:19–21). The fact that they were often included with the fatherless and widows suggests that it was envisaged that most strangers would be poor. The triennial tithe was to be shared with the poor stranger as well as the Levites, the fatherless, and the widows (Deut 26:1–13). Judges were to make no distinction between hearing a case between two Israelites or between an Israelite and a stranger (Deut 1:16; 24:17; 27:19—"Cursed is the man who withholds justice from the alien, the fatherless or the widow"). When hiring a stranger or a fellow Israelite to do some work, they were to be treated justly in exactly the same way, by being paid promptly (Deut 24:14,15).[79]

---

[77] To join in the Passover celebration, male strangers had to be circumcised, although as long as they were circumcised they could take part like any other Israelite (Ex 12:48,49; Num 9:14).
[78] One difference is that the stranger could eat an animal that had been found already dead (Deut 14:21).
[79] One of Ezekiel's charges against the rulers of Israel was that they had treated strangers unjustly (Ezek 22:7,29; cf. Zech 7:10).

In view of the very exclusivist nature of Judaism for much of its history, the openheartedness of the Torah towards strangers is remarkable. The motive for such openheartedness was God's love for them that was to be expressed in a very high level of inclusiveness in the religious, legal, and economic realms.

There remains the issue of how to view this Old Testament legislation from the perspective of the New Testament. That Jesus reasserted the obligation of the second great commandment to love our neighbour as ourselves is unquestionable. If anything he expanded and universalised the command so that our enemies and anyone in need with whom we come into contact becomes a neighbour. Such a broad understanding of "neighbour" must include those from other ethnic groups who have come to live near us.

WELCOMING THE STRANGER: PRACTICAL IMPLICATIONS

The "missionary" intent of the Old prevails in the New Testament, though with obvious differences. Under the New Testament God's people are not one nation or ethnic group living in a specific territory but a worshipping people drawn from every nation or ethnic group. In the Old Testament era, to become a full member of God's people meant moving to live in Israel, being circumcised if male, and joining in the worship that was centred on the temple. In the New Testament era, one identifies with God's people through repentance, faith in Christ, and baptism, wherever God's people are found. In both eras a welcoming and inclusive attitude towards the stranger should characterise God's people, but in the New Testament era there is no ethnic qualification. Anyone can come as they are. That is why missionaries learn the language of people unfamiliar with the gospel and make a great effort to translate the Bible into their language. They do not have to forsake their ethnic identity to belong to God's people. But what if the strangers come to live near us, rather than us sending missionaries across the sea to them? What difference does that make? None whatsoever in certain respects.

Some of the strangers, usually the wives, may not be able to speak our language, so we should make an effort to learn theirs as we help them in every way we can to learn ours. If the Bible has been translated into the strangers' language, we should make it available to them. Evangelistic efforts should be culturally and linguistically appropriate, and every encouragement should be given if they want to worship in their own language. If we have a missionary heart, then we will affirm the ethnic identity of the strangers.

In other respects, welcoming the stranger will inevitably undermine their identity. While valuing their place of origin and their ethnic inheritance, strangers have decided to leave and seek safety or economic well-being somewhere else. They must realise that familiarity with the ways of their host people is essential if their enterprise is to succeed. From this perspective their position is similar to the strangers who came to live in ancient Israel. In this context our responsibility as Christians is to help the stranger to get a foothold and become established in our community. We should reject utterly the sort of xenophobic attitude which is so common today, especially in the West, as more and more people come seeking asylum. Old Testament legislation points in the direction of a generous legal immigration policy with impartiality before the law, workers' rights, and welfare benefits. Added to this we should help strangers with language, employment, and understanding the way our bureaucracy and government works so that they can claim their rights and become established in our community. This type of welcome works more towards integration and assimilation than affirmation of identity, which is fine because since the stranger has come to our place there is nothing wrong in their assimilating with our identity or us together moving in the direction of a new identity.

As Christian hosts we may not only need a missionary heart and a welcoming spirit but a tolerant attitude towards the strangers as well. Many reject our faith and choose rather to cling to their faith and identity. They prefer to be a colony or a diaspora, a people continuing to look to their ancestral roots for spiritual, moral, and social sustenance. It is such people that are primarily in view in the UN declaration on minorities. I also believe that God's law as fulfilled in Jesus would have us respect the strangers' desire to remain different. The key question in the context of this chapter is whether our neighbourly love of the ethnic strangers implies respecting their insistence on clinging to their separate identity. It seems to me that it would be very difficult to claim to love them without doing so.

There are often good reasons why strangers cling to their identity. The official stance towards immigrants in host countries sometimes forces them to retain their own identity. In Germany, for example, strangers are denied citizenship. The official stance in other countries is that they should become assimilated as soon as possible for their own good. This was the accepted approach in the United Kingdom until 1966 when Roy Jenkins as home secretary established cultural pluralism as government policy.[80] Of course official policy and popular opinion are not always the same, and there remains a strong resistance in much of the population of the United Kingdom to accepting that foreigners belong at all. Foreigners are just not welcome, period. Then there is resistance to assimilation among immigrants themselves. They may be attracted by the economic benefits of their host country but appalled by its lax morality, godlessness, and indifference to respect for the family. It is not surprising that they want to hang on to those things that are bound up with their ethnic identity.

Christian love has an assimilative effect, but such love is rarely the predominant attitude to strangers in any society. So, while reaching out to the strangers, we must also respect their right to be what they want to be. They must be granted the freedom to reject our Christian overtures and make their own overtures to us if they

---

[80] Jenkins described his new approach as "integration," which he defined "not as a flattening process of assimilation but as equal opportunity, coupled with cultural diversity, in an atmosphere of mutual tolerance." This has been the official line of every administration since then in the United Kingdom. See Sebastian Poulter, *Ethnicity, Law and Human Rights: The English Experience* (Oxford Univ. Press, 1998), 15–18.

so desire; and even if they welcome our Christianity, they must be given the freedom to be Christian within the context of their own identity.[81] From my perspective as a Christian who is also a member of a minority ethnic group, I have a Christian responsibility to defend and foster the identity of strangers that have come to live in my community.

MIXED IDENTITIES: WHERE DO I BELONG?

There is one important topic that needs to be addressed in this chapter on the ethnic cauldron of our contemporary world and that is the radical mixing that leaves an increasing number of people wondering whether they have an ethnic identity at all. With the increasing ease of communication that is leading to an unprecedented movement of people, often across very large distances, there are a growing number of people in the world who find it difficult to identify with any of the key characteristics of ethnic identity. How can they name the people to whom they belong if their parents and grandparents are from different ethnic roots? Which history is their history? The situation for people of mixed parentage can be further complicated if they are brought up in a country in which neither their parents nor grandparents were brought up. If this is the case, even language and custom become problematic. They may feel that they belong to the country in which they were brought up, although their mother tongue may not be the language of that country. To further complicate matters, some people spend a considerable period of their life in more than one country. It is not surprising that which ethnic group they should feel solidarity with becomes a problem.

---

[81] I am very conscious that big questions arise here. Should we allow Muslims the freedom to preach Islam freely while knowing that where Islam is dominant other points of view are severely suppressed? Should non-Christian communities be allowed to establish their own schools? I would say yes to both these questions, but since there is no space to justify my answer without wandering too far from the purpose of the book, I have relegated mentioning them to a footnote.

Some people in this situation have come to the conclusion that they have no ethnic identity; that they are citizens of the world; that it is enough to have the name of human being.

To claim to have no ethnic identity or to be multiethnic does not annul the fact that such people often live among those who do have a sense of ethnic identity. Living among such people, especially if they have a strong sense of ethnic identity, complicates life for those who may want to be multiethnic. Those with a sense of ethnic identity will either expect those who want to be multiethnic to adopt one ethnic identity or they will give them an identity. Multiethnicity occurs as a result of interethnic marriage following migration. Such marriages are more common today than they have ever been. Interestingly, in the USA the progeny of such marriages are increasingly resistant to being categorised into one of the five official categories of racial origin: Euro-American, Asian American, African American, Hispanic, and Native American. They want to be Pakistani/African American; Colombian/Scottish/Irish American; Filipino/Italian/Russian American, etc.[82] From a biblical perspective this is not at all surprising, because migration into a new place is one of the key reasons for the development of new identities. The picture that we have of people scattering in the early history of humanity was more a case of families, clans, or tribes moving and growing a different identity, but in a world with a vastly bigger population, there is no reason why people from different families, clans, and tribes should not gather to the same place to establish a new identity. It is such a process that can be observed happening in the United States, although the dominant identity, what defines "American," is an English culture. The United States remains more of an assimilationist than a culturally pluralist state.

---

[82] These are real examples. See Cornell and Hartmann, *Ethnicity and Race,* 240.

THE POWER OF THE MEMORY OF AN ETHNIC ORIGIN

The last point of the previous paragraph seems to confirm the constructivist view of ethnic identity discussed earlier. As already stated, this view is consistent with biblical truth to a certain extent. On the other hand, the long hand of ethnic history continues to have quite a hold over a great many in countries such as the United States that is characterised by intense ethnic mixture. Many Americans make the pilgrimage to Europe and Africa every year in search of their roots and rejoice when they find them. In fact it can be argued that ethnic memory has a significant impact in many of the trouble spots in the world.

I hope that it is not a case of spurious psychologising to suggest that a significant number of people who have migrated and their descendants, and who have no intention of returning to their country of origin, compensate for their "betrayal" by supporting "nationalist" movements. So Americans of Irish extraction provided substantial support for the IRA, Americans of Asian Indian extraction are generous supporters of the Indian People's Party (BJP) in India, the Sikh separatist movement is largely funded by Sikhs living in Europe, etc.[83] That this happens is evidence of the more primordial reality of ethnic identity. The ethnic past is not something that is easy to deny. Of course this can be used to a beneficial as well as to a maleficent end as witnessed by the resources that are released by Christian and non-Christian "strangers" to bring blessing to their country of origin.[84]

CONCLUSION

Mobility is a characteristic of humanity. Ever since Babel people have been on the move, so the ethnic claim to have been the first

---

[83] I am grateful to Ian Wallace for this suggestion. I have not followed up the suggestion with any research—a good MA or PhD topic for someone.
[84] Though I did not use it in writing this section, parts of the following volume cover the same ground and come to similar conclusions: Stephen Castles, *Ethnicity and Globalization: From Migrant Worker to Transnational Citizen* (London: Sage, 2000).

anywhere is hardly ever true. The norm is that our ancestors supplanted or were supplanted by someone else. Often the supplanters become the supplanted. This was certainly true of the Celts who stamped their identity on the inhabitants of Britain before the appearance of the Romans or the English. In modern times, as a result of imperialism and industrialism an expanding world population has been moving about as never before. The result is the creation of more and more ethnic minorities, particularly in cities, all over the world.

This is the reality that is recognised in the UN Declaration on the Rights of Persons Belonging to National or Ethnic, Religious or Linguistic Minorities that was adopted by the General Assembly in 1992. It is undeniable that the whole idea of international law on human rights is an expression of Western humanism to a great extent. But a good case could be made that many humanist values are really Christian values without their supernatural foundations. As Christians we have every right to claim back our own principles. Where human rights law is consistent with biblical principles, then we are at liberty to appeal to it in the interest of truth and justice. This declaration on the rights of minorities contains a lot that we can and should endorse as Christians. The Old Testament legislation concerning the "stranger" provides a good biblical foundation for a Christian approach to treatment of ethnic minorities. The keynote of the biblical material is risky generosity.

Increasing mobility is also leading to more mixing of ethnic identities than ever before. This means that there is an increasing number of people that find it difficult to identify with any one ethnic group because of their multiethnic origins. They are probably on the way to developing a new identity but may insist that they have no ethnic identity. Such people may have a valuable contribution to make in countering the excesses of those who idolise their identity, but they may also experience crises of identity since they live in a world where most of the people around them know to whom they belong. A danger for such people is that their ethnic history can come to wield too great a power over them, so that whatever is done in their ancestral home to secure their identity will be supported. This has led to substantial support for violent ideological nationalism in many places. However, this does not have to follow. Love for the ancestral home can also lead to generous support for beneficial movements including Christian mission.

NOT JUST A MINORITY: THE CASE OF INDIGENOUS PEOPLES

NOT all ethnic minorities are the same. This became clear to me when I was thinking about minority rights and the conflict I became involved with in Pontypridd. There is a difference between our claim in Wales that the state should provide education in our ancestral language and the claim for such education, for example, by a recently arrived Asian minority in an English city. My ancestors were living in Wales long before the English came and took their land by force and imposed their culture on them. I accept that there is no such thing as an autochthonous people and that there can be no absolute claim by a people to any piece of earth on the grounds of having been in possession for a long time, but length of possession must confer some rights. The fact that my ancestors may have been living in Wales for more than 2,500 years must put my people in a different category than those minorities that have settled in a strange country in the last fifty years. The Welsh may not be autochthonous, but we are certainly indigenous to this piece of earth called Wales. Together with many other indigenous peoples, we feel that this ancient indigeneity deserves some respect at least.

Even when the UN Commission on Human Rights was thinking about formulating a declaration on the rights of minorities, representatives of indigenous peoples objected to their inclusion as just one type of "minority." Representatives of indigenous peoples in the Americas actually started work on a declaration, which would be relevant to their particular situation, in 1977, which was the year before the UN Commission on Human Rights officially decided to formulate a declaration on minority rights. This effort was eventually officially recognised by the UN, and after a decade of work a Draft Declaration on the Rights of Indigenous Peoples was presented for consideration to the UN Commission on Human Rights in 1995. This declaration was adopted with some amendments by the General Assembly in September 2007.[85]

DEFINITION

Unfortunately there is no generally accepted definition of indigenous peoples. One key characteristic is that they are "communities or nations that inhabited the same general territory and that predated colonization or invasion by other peoples."[86] They are generally the dispossessed remnants of conquered peoples who have been subjected to sustained oppression but have refused to die out.

> The history of indigenous peoples has universally included exploitation by other groups, often in the form of harsh colonization, and generally involving one or another degree of dispossession of hereditary lands and destruction of native culture. Such peoples—referred to in different cultures or states in different ways, including Indians, nations, aboriginals, natives, tribes or bands—have long been plagued by the sense of inferiority imposed upon them by the dominant culture. They have rarely participated in a serious way in governance or decision-making in their states of residence on matters of vital interest to them.[87]

In my opinion indigenous people are what Wil Kymlicka calls "national minorities."

A much narrower definition has been formulated when indigenous peoples are viewed from a development or anthropological perspective. In this context emphasis is laid on the sustainable way

---

[85] For a selection of the key statements from the declaration, see the appendix.
[86] Steiner and Alston, *International Human Rights,* 1006.
[87] Ibid., 1007.

they use natural resources, their communal use of land, the practice of the equal sharing of wealth, their organisation of society on the basis of kinship, and their intense vulnerability when they come into contact with modern society.[88] This definition does reflect development experience in many countries, especially in Latin America, but it is too narrow because it excludes a host of indigenous peoples such as the Basques, Catalans, Bretons, Irish, Scots, Welsh, etc. What this definition highlights, however, is the fact that by helping to ensure that indigenous peoples survive much wisdom may be preserved that could be of great benefit to a world dominated by the Western way of doing things. Some indigenous peoples at least provide us with a living model of a nonindustrial way of life that could be of benefit for us.

The Welsh, in contrast, were at the forefront of the Industrial Revolution, with Merthyr Tudful in South Wales being one of the earliest centres of the industrialised production of iron. The first steam train in the world ran from Merthyr to Cardiff. Most of those who were driving the industrial development were English, but the Welsh are unquestionably an example of an indigenous people who were among the first people anywhere to experience the full impact of industrialisation and modernisation. As a result the industrial parts of Wales became much anglicised, while the rural areas retained more of their Welsh-speaking culture. There have been some movements in Wales that have implied that the rural areas, where Welsh prevails, are the areas where true indigeneity prevails, so that any "nationalist" effort should be focused on them. Others, including myself, believe that indigeneity also belongs to the mixed population of the industrial belt. In an international context the people of industrialised Wales could be classified as *mestizo*. What I am claiming is that *mestizos* can be indigenous, so that indigeneity can also be a characteristic of industrialised and urban peoples. The

---

88 John Beauclerk and Jeremy Narby, *Indigenous Peoples: A Field Guide for Development*, with J. Townsend, Development Guidelines 2 (Oxford: Oxfam, 1988), 4–6.

fact that many of the people who live in industrial Wales think of themselves as Welsh is evidence for this claim, although I accept that a lot of work needs to be done to construct a stronger sense of ethnic identity among them. I believe that the success of such an effort in Wales or anywhere else is crucial for the future well-being of indigenous peoples, because the alternative is either to be able to live in a modernised world or die.

The motivation to preserve the uniqueness of indigenous peoples in their premodern state is driven by a demeaning museum mentality or by a romantic attitude. Museums are places for displaying dead things, and cultures by definition are living, changing things. The cultures of even indigenous peoples are in a state of flux. The origin of the romantic attitude goes back as far as the eighteenth-century idea of the "noble savage," and there is more than an echo of it in Beauclerk and Narby's definition mentioned above. It is a reflection of the hankering of the modern mind, maybe of the human mind and heart, for a lifestyle that is close to and in tune with nature, where life is a much more communal affair. It is an attitude which has gained currency among some anthropologists. Their criticism of some Christian missions among indigenous peoples may have some validity, but they are extremely naive to think that such people can now be insulated from the rest of the world. Even their so-called objective study is very much a Western intrusion. The issue is not if such peoples are going to be influenced by the outside world but how.

A DESTRUCTIVE CHRISTIAN APPROACH TO INDIGENOUS PEOPLES

For us the key question is what part we should play as Christians in the process of change that is inevitable for indigenous peoples. In the first place, should we be interested in their survival? Many Christians in the past believed that the destruction of a weaker people by a stronger, especially if the stronger had been impacted by Christianity, was a good thing—it was a case of civilisation and Christianity sweeping superstition and barbarity to one side.

What happened in Latin America with the expansion of Roman Catholic empire after Columbus' discovery in 1492 is a shameful example of the spread of so-called Christian civilisation. It is not surprising that the indigenous peoples of the Andes wrote to the Pope as they did when he visited Peru in the early 1990s:

> We peoples of the Andean countries of America decided to avail of your visit in order to give back your Bible because in five centuries it has brought neither love, nor peace, nor justice. Please take your Bible and give it back to our oppressors because they clearly need its moral precepts more than we do.[89]

We are also far from guiltless as Protestants. We may try to hide behind the Protestant division of church and state and claim that it was the secular authorities that perpetrated atrocities against indigenous peoples, but very often evil is only possible when "good" people say and do nothing to condemn and resist it. "Good" Christian people have even been complicit in oppression and murder.

What happened to Native Americans in Canada and the United States, to Aborigines in Australia, and to Maoris in New Zealand was primarily the work of people from Protestant countries. The idea of Manifest Destiny, advocated by many Christians in North America in the nineteenth century, is a case in point. It was believed that it was God's will that the Christian civilisation of the European immigrants to North America should replace what was considered the savage and unchristian society of the indigenous Indian tribes that were there before. Native Americans were given few options by the increasing flood of Europeans invading their lands; they had to get out of the way or die if they desired to preserve their identity. Another option was to embrace Christianity, but that was no real option, because conversion to Christianity was understood in terms of assimilation into European ways. "Samuel Worcester, in

---

[89] Quoted by Gearóid Ó Fatharta in "Good News to the Poor," *Vocation for Justice 9*, no. 3 (Autumn 1995): 2.

1816 described the objectives of the American Board [of Mission] with respect to American Indians as making 'the whole tribe English in their language, civilized in their habits, and Christian in their religion.'"[90]

The story of Little Crow, a chief of the Mdewkantons that was a subgroup of the Sioux, illustrates the impossible dilemmas faced by so many Native Americans in the nineteenth century. It seems that Little Crow realised that it was impossible for his people to resist the coming of the white people. The only alternative, as he saw it, was to negotiate favourable terms that would ensure the survival of his people. So in return for giving up much of their ancestral land, he signed treaties securing annual annuities for his people payable by the federal government in Washington. To prove his peaceable intentions, he also adopted a white man's lifestyle. He built a house, started farming, adopted Western clothes, and became a member of the Episcopal Church. Little Crow was moving in the direction of Worcester's ideal of being English in his language, civilised in his habits, and Christian in his religion. However, by the summer of 1862 things were not going well for his people. Denied the right to hunt in their traditional hunting grounds that had been ceded to settlers, and having experienced a poor harvest, they were very dependent on the annual annuity from Washington. Unfortunately, because of the demands of the Civil War, the annuity did not come on time, and the traders who were commissioned by the state to deal with the natives refused to release supplies from their full warehouses until the money arrived. One trader responded to the desperate entreaty of the natives by telling them to go and "eat grass or their own dung." By this time some were blaming Little Crow for his people's suffering, which they attributed to trusting the word of the whites. Then in their half-starved frustration a group of young

---

[90] David J. Bosch, *Transforming Mission: Paradigm Shifts in Theology of Mission* (Maryknoll, NY: Orbis Books, 1991), 292. Cf. Bosch's reference to Cotton Mather's opinion expressed around a hundred years earlier: "The best thing we can do for our Indians is to Anglicize them" (ibid., 260).

Sioux men murdered five white settlers including two women. Little Crow knew that the retribution for this crime would be dreadful and that the whites would not be satisfied with bringing the perpetrators to justice. What was he to do? He could stand by and watch his people being brutally humiliated or he could act like a chief and lead his people in their resistance to white oppression. He decided to lead his people into war in the full knowledge that it was futile and that it would lead to his own death and the decimation of his people. Little Crow was eventually killed by a settler in July 1863, and the settler was paid $25 by the state of Minnesota for his scalp. By that time the war was over, and the remnants of his people were being shipped away to reservation land that was considered good enough for "Indians" if no good for whites.[91]

This is just one example of what indigenous peoples had to face at the hands of invaders who called themselves Christians. The story could probably be repeated thousands of times. I realise fully that the story of Little Crow, typical of so many other stories, has been told from the perspective of the "little people" that were being overwhelmed. Whether it is something instinctive in me or not, I cannot tell, but from childhood I have always been on the side of the Indian. Much of my childhood was spent playing in fields and forests and, like most children of my generation, "cowboys and Indians" often featured in my play. I always played the part of the Indian in this game and considered him to be the "goody." The reason for my settled childhood preference is a mystery. It could have been the influence of adults like my uncle Bob, something I read, or just the fact that it was simpler to construct a tepee than a log cabin! With age this childhood preference has become a settled conviction reflecting what has happened, and is still happening, to my own people.

---

[91] For the story of Little Crow, see Brown, *Bury My Heart,* 39–65. A brief account of the historical background and bibliography can be found in Minahan, *Nations without States,* 325–27.

Imperial Evangelicalism

My evangelical faith at first threatened to undermine this childhood conviction as I became impressed with what may be called "imperial" evangelicalism. This is the evangelicalism that sees ethnic diversity as a nuisance and a hindrance to quick church growth. It says that the faster differences disappear the more efficient Christian mission will be. In a sense it is the modernist version of mission strategy. Modernism says that ethnic diversity will inevitably melt away in the heat of industrialism. Modernist mission strategy says that the adoption of Anglo-American culture will enhance the success of the gospel and the universal expression of the unity of the people of God. History as well as the Bible has taught me that neither secular nor evangelical modernism can be right in God's eyes. I cannot believe that the terrible effect of the oppression of ethnic identity can be consistent with the gospel.

The positive face of evangelical mission with regard to ethnic identity is seen in the noble and continuing story of Bible translation, but there is a negative face as well. This was most in evidence from around 1850–1950 when mission and empire were very closely allied. It is true that many great missionaries in this period were not entirely happy with the fact that they were often identified with fellow countrymen who came to rule and exploit, but they were convinced that their Western culture and civilisation was a fruit of the gospel and an integral part of their message. With such a conviction they were often happy to support the expansion of empire and to shelter under the protection of imperial power. It is not surprising to find in missionary biography from this period that something good is hardly ever said about native culture. The overwhelming impression is that the sooner people forget about their own customs and traditions and become Westernised the better. This is not to deny that some aspects of native customs and culture were and are evil. It is not surprising, either, that the missionaries focused on the evil which would be undone if the gospel was welcomed. What is surprising is the sense of superiority. The missionaries of this period give the impression at least that they were superior to the people they had come to serve. Their housing, tools, arts, clothing, manners, ideas of governance, religion, and so on were all better than what was possessed by the natives. So British missionaries set out to make English people of the natives, German missionaries set out to make German people, North Americans North American people, and so on.

The case of the prevailing approach among North Americans in the same period of 1850–1950 is interesting because, while being proud of the fact that they were not guilty of empire building like England, Holland, and others, their missionary strategy was just as oppressive of indigenous culture. They were also guilty of being unable to dissociate the gospel from the North American way of life. The gospel and North American culture came as a single package. This became very apparent to me while in Quito, Ecuador, for the Latin American Congress for Evangelisation in 1992. I was having breakfast one morning with a Baptist pastor from Cuba. He told me that he had gone to a school run by missionaries from North America. The policy of the school was to eradicate every vestige of Cuban culture from its pupils. As an example, he told me how he was severely punished after he was caught singing a Cuban folk song! I went to a Baptist church in Quito for Sunday worship that was the fruit of a North American mission. Apart from the language, which was Spanish, everything from architecture to liturgy was North American. Even the hymnbook was a North American Baptist hymnbook translated into Spanish. A group did sing a Latin American song in the service to the accompaniment of Latin American instruments, but I was told that this was a recent innovation that was seen as a radical break with the church's tradition![92]

---

[92] This section on mission and cultural superiority is based on the biographies of missionaries like George Grenfell, Alexander Mackay, David Livingstone, Roger Price (a Welshman), and others; and Bosch, *Transforming Mission*, 298–313.

Rediscovering a Better Way

Since the end of the Second World War and the collapse of empire, we in the West have been slowly learning a bit of humility. We are not at all sure anymore that our Western civilisation and Christianity are identical. What happened to the natives in North America, particularly in the nineteenth century, is now seen by some evangelical Christians as a terrible injustice which calls for repentance. Some Australian evangelicals are expressing remorse because of the terribly unjust treatment of the Aborigines.[93] Even in the United Kingdom some are learning to value the remnant of the indigenous peoples that have survived in these islands.

Evangelical missionary theology and strategy have also changed. Since the collapse of empire, at least in theory, the equation of Christianity and Western civilisation has been widely rejected, even though in many cases the Western evangelical church still continues to impose its vision and methods on the rest of the evangelical world. More significantly, mission theology has come to understand that mission is most effective when the Christian message comes to possess those elements in a culture that are not inherently antipathetic to it. This is what is now called the process of contextualisation. This was always a part of evangelical mission strategy because Bible translation is by definition an exercise in contextualisation. If the gospel can be made to speak my language, then it already belongs in a very profound way. But it can also take possession of much more of any culture. In this context those elements of the developmental definition of indigenous peoples can be seen as positively Christian. It is a good and Christian thing to respect the natural world, to share possessions, and to have a strong sense of family solidarity. This is not a naive and romantic view but an affirmation of values in an indigenous culture that are consistent with biblical principles. Whether such values can survive the transition

---

[93] E.g., John Smith, *Advance Australia Where?* (Homebush West, Australia: Anzea, 1989), 117–31.

to a more Western type of economic activity, which may be essential to ensure the survival of an indigenous people, is another matter, even if the transition is driven by the values of Christian development. In the West, increasing wealth has generally accompanied an increasing indifference to God and neighbour. Western Christians are generally very reluctant to share their wealth.

In its relationship with the powers of this world, the church has swung between the poles of rejection and acceptance. The period when Christianity was identified with Western civilisation is an example of acceptance. The evangelical movement represented by Pietism in Germany, the Methodist Revival in the United Kingdom, and the Great Awakening in the United States began in the eighteenth century as a marginal movement that was despised and rejected by church authorities. By the middle of the nineteenth century, especially in the United States and the United Kingdom, it had grown into a very large and influential movement that included a significant number of the great of this world in its ranks. This is always a very dangerous moment for the Christian faith, because it is the moment when worldly power becomes available for promoting the faith and when the church is most likely to fail to distinguish between the essence of faith and its cultural clothing. This is the mistake that was made in the nineteenth century. In the United States, Christianity and North American culture were identified and had a tremendous impact on mission simply because of the sheer size of its missionary community. In the United Kingdom the same identification had far-reaching consequences because of the further link with the most extensive empire that the world had ever seen.

By the middle of the twentieth century the British Empire was falling apart and evangelicalism had returned to the status of a despised minority once again. Riding the tiger of worldly power was not an option anymore as evangelicals had to relearn what it means to be Christ's little flock. When the church is close to worldly power, it is much more likely to act like it and be dismissive of diversity. When the church is small and despised, it is more able to empathise with small, oppressed peoples. I believe that this is what is happening in mission theology in Western Europe at the moment, where there is a much greater readiness to respect ethnic diversity than there was during the period of empire. There is now a possibility that Bible translation can come into its own as a means of ennobling ethnic identities, because the agenda of empire is not present anymore. During the time of empire, Bible translation was often viewed as a necessary step in the direction of literacy, that was a step in the direction of acquiring a European language, that was believed to be essential for assimilation into civilisation, that was in turn equated with Christianity.

In many cases the problem has now moved to within many of the nation-states that were formed as a result of the collapse of empire. The church is strong in many African countries, for example, and liable to be tempted to attempt to ride the tiger of worldly power. Since these countries have retained a European language as the language of power, Christians in postcolonial countries are now in greater danger of failing to appreciate the value of ethnic diversity.

The United States is a different case. Compared with Europe, the church remains very strong, and the influence that the country is able to have because of its immense economic and military power is greater than ever. There is a great temptation to believe that Christians from the US have discovered the formula for success in faith and every other aspect of life and to impose it on others. The economic success of the United States is undoubtedly the key factor in the contemporary universal rush to learn English, and this could be of great benefit to the spread of the gospel. But not all the values that come from the US are Christian by any means, and we must remember that the cross as the central symbol of our faith is a symbol of powerlessness. It may be more consistent with our faith to focus on the plight of the powerless little peoples of the earth than attempt to hang on to the coattails of the powerful.

There is another argument for the preservation of indigenous peoples that has some merit that is used by the Wycliffe Bible

Translators / SIL. Just as we should be concerned to preserve the diversity of the natural world because of the potential benefit to humanity that could be lost with the loss of any species, so we must make every effort to preserve indigenous cultures and the wisdom that they embody. As applied to peoples / ethnic identities, this argument has no biblical foundation in the way it does when applied to the nonhuman world. God's command to the original human beings to take care of the earth surely means that they were not to exploit the earth's resources to destruction. Specific ethnic identities, of which indigenous peoples are types, though founded in nature, are largely human creations, so they cannot be the objects of perpetually valid divine commands. Ethnic identities have a time allocated to them. However, though not necessarily biblical wisdom, the desire to preserve the culture of indigenous peoples may still be a wise thing to do.

INDIGENOUS PEOPLES AND POVERTY

There is also a clear link between being an indigenous people and poverty. What is in view here is not only cultural impoverishment as a result of oppression but also physical poverty. The idea of the nation-state that developed in Europe after the French Revolution encouraged the domination of its life and administration by a dominant ethnic identity. The outworking of this political philosophy meant that in France, for example, the French dominated and the Bretons and Corsicans were oppressed. Since ethnic groups such as these were territorially as well as culturally marginal, they are also often physically poorer than the majority ethnic identity. In countries with a more recent history of colonisation, indigenous peoples have been discriminated against on racial grounds. The result is that many of the indigenous peoples that have survived (though a great many have not) belong to the margins of the social, cultural, and economic life of the countries where they live. Good examples are the indigenous peoples of Latin America and the "tribal" peoples of

India. They are literally as well as socially, economically, and politically poor.[94] Even the Welsh live on the margins of an economy that is dominated by the South East of England, and as a result have much lower average incomes and all the relative deprivation that flows from that.

As poor and marginalised, the survival and blessing of indigenous people should be a particular concern of Christians. We should be concerned to counter those forces that are destroying their identity and strengthen those aspects of their corporate life that will make their survival more likely. As already pointed out, giving a people a Bible in their own language is one important contribution that we can make as Christians. This gives an indigenous people the possibility of developing a literary tradition that will give them a much better chance of survival.

The direction that development thinking has taken recently is also encouraging for indigenous peoples and much closer to a biblical perspective. Since the publication of Schumacher's famous work entitled *Small Is Beautiful*,[95] the emphasis has shifted from a modernist view of development by means of large-scale investment to enabling those outside the globalised economic system to help themselves with their own resources. Development orthodoxy now speaks of empowering those on the margins of the world economy and building up their capacity to participate in their own uplift. That is not to say that development has forsaken its Western agenda. In reality the participatory approach still involves the inculcation of a whole range of Western attitudes such as democratic representation, recognition of women's rights, and the raising of cash crops so that indigenous peoples can be plugged into the international economy. What is dif-

---

[94] I have to admit that the claim made in this paragraph is impressionistic and not founded on solid research. Roger Riddell in *Minorities, Minority Rights and Development: An Issues Paper* (London: Minority Rights Group, 1998), 10, maintains that this research has not been done, so I have some excuse!
[95] E. F. Schumacher, *Small is Beautiful: Economics as if People Mattered*, 2nd ed., (New York: Harper Collins, 1989).

ferent is the respect that is shown to the poor in the development process. This is what we would expect as Christians. It is also interesting that in their discussion on training indigenous people in marketing that Beauclerk and Narby list problems such as dissension, lack of participation, and dishonesty among the major hindrances to success.[96] This is what we as Christians call sin, and the gospel message which we bear deals directly with such problems.

Land is also a crucial issue for many indigenous peoples. They have survived in many cases because they live in remote and inaccessible places, but with the exploitation of resources, the creation of infrastructure, and the growing demand for land, the places where they have been able to practise their environmentally friendly lifestyle are being whittled away. In some way it is ironic that their way of using natural resources has come to be valued; not because it sustains human beings, but because it is good for preserving the forest. Preserving forests has come to be a good in the West. Yet we rejoice that this attitude does give us a good foundation to struggle for the protection and preservation of indigenous peoples, because it makes it easier to secure land rights for them.

THE CRUCIAL ROLE OF MOTHER TONGUE EDUCATION

Education is a key factor in any survival strategy for an indigenous people, because by definition they represent a minority culture that has been overshadowed by a majority culture. All indigenous peoples are linked to states that are dominated at their centre by an alien people and culture. As people of the periphery their only route to full enjoyment of the social, political, and economic benefits of the state is, more often than not, to become fully integrated into the culture of the dominant people. Historically states have set up educational systems to enable everyone to do this. So in France Bretons went through a French system of education, in the United

---

[96] Beauclerk and Narby, *Indigenous Peoples*, 84.

Kingdom the Welsh and Irish went through an English system, in Bolivia Quechua and Aymara went through a Spanish system, and so on. The consequences of this approach for indigenous peoples are devastating. Morally it is a continual reminder that their ethnic identity and heritage have a second-class status in their own country. Educationally and economically it puts them at a disadvantage from the beginning. A child from a Quechua home in Bolivia whose whole life has been lived within Quechua language and culture up to the point when she goes to school is then expected to learn through Spanish, which is a totally alien language. It is not surprising that most Quechua have made very slow progress educationally and that they are stigmatised as slow and unprogressive. The folly of this approach is being recognised, and it is now commonly accepted that children learn a lot better and quicker in their mother tongue. Catalonia in Spain is a very good example of a very successful and effective bilingual education policy, and Wales is also encouraging. Even countries like Bolivia have recognised the problem and begun to make some provision, but there is a long way to go.

We must also recognise that some indigenous people will be fearful of bilingual education, because they will see it as a means of alienating them even more from the benefits of being familiar with the dominant culture. They need to be reassured that such fears are not well founded. To the contrary, beginning to learn in a mother tongue ensures greater progress in a second language and gives the opportunity to enter the dominant culture from a position of strength rather than weakness.

In October 1998 I had the privilege of visiting Bolivia on behalf of Tearfund to accompany the staff of the San Juanillo Bible Institute in Sucre through part of their process of strategic planning. The college was established as a result of the work of a Western mission agency but is now in Bolivian hands, although expatriate missionaries still have a part to play in its operation. I met the principal, Juan Carlos de la Fuente, in a conference near Sao Paulo, Brazil, en route to Sucre. Talking to him during the conference gave me a lot of insight into what is happening to indigenous people in Bolivia that provides the context for the work of the college in Sucre.

Juan Carlos is a Quechua who was not encouraged by his Quechua-speaking parents to value his cultural heritage. As a result he is unable to speak the language, although he understands a fair amount when he hears it spoken. I was sad when I learnt this, because my own people went through the same stage a couple of generations ago, and we are now struggling to regain the ground that was lost. By now Juan Carlos is the only member of the family that is based in the Quechua heartland of the Andes. The rest of the family are now in the bustling lowland industrial city of Santa Cruz. I met most of them on my way to Sucre with him. Most are committed Christians who are upwardly mobile in the Westernised, Spanish-dominated culture of the city. Their Quechua identity is disappearing very fast. For the grandchildren of Juan Carlos' parents, their Quechua origin is but a faint memory that could return to haunt them.

Sucre is a world away from Santa Cruz. Arriving by plane is an exciting experience. With the plane obviously descending, one wonders where it will find a runway in the middle of the mountains! The top of a hill has had to be levelled so that planes can land, and the runway is just long enough for landing and takeoff on a dry day. Sucre has the feel of a provincial town, even though it is the legal capital of Bolivia. Its major "industry" is law and education and, unlike Santa Cruz, many of the people seen on the streets are very obviously indigenous.

My translator and guide during my time in Sucre was Ann Matthews, an SIM missionary who hails from Penybont ar Ogwr,[97] which is twenty-five miles west of Pontypridd, where I live. Ann was educated in Welsh-medium schools and attended the secondary school that my children attended. By the time I met her, she had added Spanish and a considerable amount of Quechua to her linguistic repertoire, but since she had very little opportunity to use

---

[97] Bridgend in English.

her Welsh, I enjoyed the confusion of Spanish and Welsh that came out when I insisted on speaking Welsh to her! I felt that her home background was a wonderful preparation for understanding the plight of the Quechua people that she had been called to serve.

At the time of my visit she was living in a Quechua village on the outskirts of Sucre so that she could improve her Quechua and attend a Quechua-speaking church. On the Sunday evening she took me to church in her village. The people met in a plain, rectangular building lit by gas lamps, because it had not yet been linked to an electricity supply. The worship was warm, and the music was excellent and very indigenous. There was sharing of needs and ardent prayer. All this was in Quechua. Then the preacher delivered a Spanish sermon which, as Ann explained, was hardly intelligible to many in the congregation. The reason for this was the fact that preachers received their theological education entirely in Spanish, so that when they came out of college to serve their people they were unable to preach in their own heart language. This was the best possible preparation that Ann could have given me for the strategic planning meetings that began on the following Monday morning.

As it transpired we did not get to the issue of language until the Tuesday morning. That seemed to me the appropriate point at which to share something of our experience in Wales. I told them something of our story beginning with Griffith Jones of Llanddowror and ending with the flourishing of Welsh-medium education in the anglicised valleys of South Wales. I shared with them the sense of being inferior and excluded that I had felt as a child because I did not belong to the dominant culture and the difference it has made to have Welsh as an official language. There is still plenty of prejudice, but we are not ignorant Welsh anymore, and I would hope that the day would come when the indigenous in Sucre would not be called "dirty Indians," and that they would lose the sense of inferiority that was written on their faces. I explained that it is possible to be bilingual, to enjoy the dignity of our traditional cultural heritage, and to have full access to the benefits that come from being familiar with the dominant culture. The reason for saying these things was to underline the fact that, in order to fulfil its aim of preparing church leaders to serve the churches in the Quechua-speaking communities of the area, the college needed to begin teaching through the medium of Quechua. As I was saying these things the feeling of approval, especially from the Quechua speakers, was almost tangible. Since my visit a start has been made with short Quechua theological training courses in various districts, which I hope is a first step towards some teaching through Quechua in the college. Hopefully this is the beginning of a process that will lead to qualifying and not disqualifying leaders for service in their communities. There was a teacher from a college in Oruro present at the meetings in Sucre as well, and I was glad to hear that his college has also started moving in the same direction as San Juanillo. I believe that this is one area where we could make a very significant contribution as evangelicals to empowering and building the capacity of indigenous peoples.

WHY NOT SELF-DETERMINATION?

States have been very reluctant to go down the route of bolstering the culture of indigenous peoples, because it makes central control of a country more difficult. To allow a people to develop a culture that is different to the dominant culture is to allow a measure of self-determination that means a loss of control. Politically the encouraging of diversity will probably lead to a more federal system of government, and that is a path that many of the nation-states established on modernist lines are reluctant to take. Interestingly, in the age of globalisation the UN is committing itself more and more to the recognition of diversity. In this it is probably responding to the reawakening of ethnic consciousness that is happening all over the world. From a Christian perspective we should rejoice at this development, because our biblical instinct should drive us to stand alongside the weak and the marginalised.

Since support of indigenous peoples does involve giving them more autonomy, this may be a good point at which to say something more about "nationalism." Some will view encouraging the preservation of language and culture and territorial rights as moving in a "nationalist" direction. For many evangelicals nationalism is evil by definition and is identified with what happened in Nazi Germany, South Africa under apartheid, or contemporary Serbia. These "nations" emphasised the virtue of their own ethnic identity to the point of excluding others by genocide, repressive law, or ethnic cleansing. But what they were doing in fact was only a more extreme version of what had been done by all the "civilised" European nation-states since at least the end of the eighteenth century if not before. The Basques and Catalans were severely oppressed by the Spaniards, the Bretons by the French, the Irish and Welsh by the English, Native Americans by Europeans, Aborigines by Europeans, and so on. The justification for repression might have differed, but in most cases the idea of ethnic or national superiority was crucial. Nationalism in this sense is unquestionably an ungodly ideology that sets up the nation or an ethnic identity as an idol, and it is regrettable that many ethnic groups that have sought political freedom from such ideological nation-states have done so in the name of the same ungodly ideology. Violence breeds violence.

In advocating greater self-determination for indigenous peoples, we must be careful to inculcate a different vision of the significance of ethnic identity, of what it means to be a nation. As Christians we are not in the business of making people think that they are superior to others. It is a part of our sinful nature to judge the value of something by comparing it with the value of something else. In the context of ethnic identity in its ideological nationalist form, the value of an ethnic identity is judged by its superiority in relation to other ethnic identities. This may be fairly innocent in the context of sport, but it can have a much more sinister manifestation. From a Christian perspective we say that ethnic identity has value in and of itself because it is God-given. We do not value our identity because it is better than the identity of others, but because it is a gift of God. Any gift from God is also a responsibility. It is not something to hide in the ground while waiting for the Master's return. When he comes he will expect me to have made capital for him with all that he has given me, including my ethnic identity. Our aim with indigenous peoples should be to empower them to make capital for God with their ethnic heritage. This may lead to greater autonomy, federal status, or even independence, but it should not lead to violent conflict, at least from the side of the indigenous people.

The testimony of Artidoro Tuanama, the director of AIKSEL (Association of Quechua Evangelical Churches of the Jungle) in northeast Peru, is a good example of what is meant by a Christian development of the ethnic identity of an indigenous people. With support from Tearfund, AIKSEL has been training leaders in Quechua in order to encourage the development of native liturgy and to help the community rediscover its culture. Artidoro says:

> We simply want to take our place as indigenous and native Quechua people, understanding and living out the gospel. We assume our identity without shame, retaliation or indignation against those who have caused harm to our past and castrated our culture.[98]

CONCLUSION

The case that indigenous peoples have made to be treated as a special category of minority or ethnic group is persuasive. They have not chosen to be marginalised but are communities or nations that existed before colonization or invasion by other people and that have survived despite terrible oppression in most cases. In the development community other qualities are added to the historical definition such as a sustainable use of natural resources, equal sharing of wealth, a society based on kinship, and extreme vulnerability

---

[98] "Christ among the Quechua," Tearfund Media Release, April 1996.

when impacted by the modern world. These are really mainly characteristics of preindustrial societies that have come to be appreciated with greater awareness of the damage that industrialism is doing to the earth and community. While the characteristics defined by the development community are clearly applicable to some indigenous peoples, they are clearly not applicable to all and are not, therefore, of the essence of indigeneity.

While modernism in its liberal or socialist manifestations laid little value on the survival of indigenous peoples, the failures of Western civilisation in the twentieth century has been humbling enough to cause a reassessment of their value. There is now a greater readiness to support survival strategies often tinged with a strong dash of romanticism.

Evangelical missionary strategy past and present, as well as the rediscovery of the social implications of the Bible's teaching, is continuing to create a bias among many Western Christians in favour of the weak and vulnerable, which includes indigenous peoples. We are now moving from the "accidental" to a more deliberate policy of support for such national minorities. Wisdom also suggests that just as it is good to preserve plant and animal species, it may be of benefit to humanity to preserve ethnic "species."

There may be a need for greater realism in the so-called participative approach to the preservation of indigenous peoples. Whatever is done by Western NGOs, Christian or otherwise, is largely driven by a Western agenda. As Christians we have the advantage of being subject, like those whom we seek to serve, to a higher authority. That is why the most significant developmental action we can take is to give the Bible and its gospel to indigenous peoples.

Land and education are crucial factors for the survival of indigenous peoples. Their right to territory needs to be protected. Education means education in their own language and culture first, and in the dominant state culture second. To survive, indigenous peoples need to have the dignity and authenticity of their own identity affirmed as well as to be equipped to competently inhabit the majority culture.

But we need to recognise that if we encourage the survival of indigenous peoples through such means as participative development, the protection of land rights, and bilingual education, we are encouraging them to move in the direction of self-determination and autonomy. We should be concerned that the move in this direction should be in a Christian rather than ideological nationalist direction.

8

BEYOND ETHNIC CONFLICT

WE come finally to what immediately springs to mind for most people when ethnicity is mentioned—conflict. This is understandable because a number of very vicious conflicts that have had a high media profile in recent years have been described as "ethnic" conflicts. The collapse of Yugoslavia and the genocide in Rwanda are the most vicious examples. It was during the conflict in Yugoslavia that the chilling phrase "ethnic cleansing" was coined, although the phenomenon is not new. After all, the Celtic peoples of what became known as England were ethnically cleansed by Anglo-Saxons, as were the overwhelming majority of the native peoples of the United States, Tasmania, Australia, and New Zealand. And then there is the continuing saga of the destruction of South American peoples at the hands of Europeans of mainly Portuguese and Spanish descent.

The fact that ethnic identity has been and continues to be a significant factor in human conflict is undeniable. But whether ethnic identity is actually the root cause of conflict is debatable. Firstly, it is not legitimate to condemn an institution simply because a lot of problems may be associated with that institution. The family is a good example. It is a known fact that a large proportion of murders or child sexual abuse happens within the family, but that does not mean that we condemn the institution of the family. We may, however, criticise a particular cultural manifestation of the institution. The sort of fluid or unstable families that are now common in the West, it can be argued, are much more likely to lead to violence and abuse. If, as has been argued, ethnic identity, like the family, is a part of the created order, then however much it might have been abused because of human sin, ethnic identity can be a blessing and not a curse.

It may be helpful at this point to underline what is meant by saying that ethnic identity, like the family, is a part of the created order. By saying that it is a part of God's purpose that human beings should have a family "home" or an ethnic "home," I am not saying that either have an absolute claim on any individual or that they are historically or culturally unchangeable. What I am saying is that in God's providence human beings need a good ethnic "home" in order to function at their best. To ignore this need is to invite disaster. Even "secular" opinion is now beginning to recognise that this has been a factor in the many disasters that have befallen postcolonial Africa.

THE LEGACY OF EMPIRE IN AFRICA

Modernism was the dominant ideology that drove the independence struggle in Africa. The leaders of liberation movements adopted the modernist concept of the nation-state. According to this political philosophy the state exists to uphold democratic, political, and judicial rights and to foster the development of industrialism. Success would mean dignity, prosperity, and the disappearance of ethnic diversity. Any attempt to highlight ethnic diversity or to use the political process to gain advantage for a particular ethnic group was condemned as "tribalism." Given the political philosophy on which they were founded, it is not surprising that "tribalism" came to be viewed as one of the key hindrances to the success of the new independent nation-states of Africa. But despite the condemnation, power has often been used in African countries for tribal ends. This is not surprising, because the very common colonial policy of "divide and rule" fostered tribal rivalries.

During the last twenty years or so "tribalism," which had become a very pejorative term, has been replaced by "ethnicity" or "ethnic identity." To an extent this shift has marked a move to a more positive evaluation of ethnic diversity. From one perspective it is a move to realism. After all, the modernist position was never sound. The assumption was that ethnic diversity would disappear in industrialised democracies that were more often than not built around the imposition of the culture of a dominant majority on all the citizens of a state. However, the European nation-states did not become monoethnic, despite democratisation, industrialisation, and the oppression of ethnic minorities. Even in Britain, the prototype modernist nation-state, the Scots, Irish, and Welsh have doggedly refused to disappear. In fact their claim to be different is getting stronger. Realism is now dictating that just government of a nation-state needs to recognise ethnic diversity and allow for its expression even in the way a country is governed. This type of realism is now embodied in UN declarations on minorities and indigenous peoples.

There is evidence that this type of realism is beginning to take hold in Africa. Sam G. Amoo from Ghana, writing as senior adviser at the Emergency Response Division of the United Nations Development Programme, says:

> The fundamental challenge Africa faces as it strives to eliminate ethnic conflicts is to change the popular mindset which views ethnicity as some pathological societal condition with backward atavistic roots, to be cured with an enlightened dosage from the medicine cabinet of modernisation.[99]

Amoo argues that an ethnic identity is a basic human need so that the "critical salience of ethnicity in African conflicts is not a pathological condition but a challenge to governance."[100] He believes that the answer is to be found in decentralisation, benign integration, and electoral arrangements that hinder the tyranny of the majority. Amoo is on the side of those in the human rights movement who believe

---

99 Sam G. Amoo, *The Challenge of Ethnicity and Conflict in Africa: The Need for a New Paradigm* (New York: Emergency Response Division, UN Development Programme, 1997), 22.
100 Ibid., 14.

that there are collective rights that need to be protected if there is to be true democracy and justice. Positive discrimination in favour of the weak may sometimes be necessary in order to secure equality. Within Western political philosophy the idea that inequality may be needed to ensure equality is not an easy concept, but in a biblical context where there seems to be a distinct bias in favour of the weak and marginalised, the concept is perfectly understandable.

A paper prepared for a meeting on "The Economics of Civil Conflicts in Africa" confirms Amoo's thesis.[101] The authors argue that ethnic or religious diversity is not the cause of civil war in Africa as is commonly believed. According to them the key causes are poverty and political institutions that have failed the people. Like Amoo they advocate reform of political structures to better reflect the fact of ethnic diversity. They argue that, given appropriate political institutions, ethnic diversity could enhance development and lessen the likelihood of civil war.

> Taking the view that civil wars are the extreme case of non-co-operation among social groups, this paper argues that under the right conditions, Africa's ethnic diversity would actually enhance development...provided that "appropriate" democratic institutions embody the principles of participation, inclusion and consensus-building among social groups and that these social (especially ethnic) groups be explicitly recognized as legitimate partners in the bargaining process.[102]

Sadly, many evangelical Christians in Africa are still firmly wedded to the modernisation model of government that has caused such devastation on their continent. In a recent paper entitled "Ethnicity: Identity and Christian Community in Crisis," Professor Prince Vuyani Ntintili from South Africa writes of the universal scourge,

---

[101] P. Collier, I. Elbadawi, and N. Sambanis, "Why Are There So Many Civil Wars in Africa? Prevention of Future Conflicts and Promotion of Inter-group Cooperation." Paper presented at the UNCEA Ad Hoc Experts Group Meeting, Addis Ababa, April 7–8, 2000.
[102] Ibid., 22.

curse, and problem of ethnicity and couples ethnicity and racism.[103] Likewise Robert Abogaye-Mensah, in a paper entitled "The Church, Ethnicity and Democracy," says that it is wrong to use ethnicity "as a basis for creating democratic culture. Anyone who receives or is denied a political or religious appointment simply on the basis of ethnic identity loses his or her true humanity."[104] This is the classical voice of modernism speaking here. Surely from a Christian perspective it could be profoundly democratic and just, and thus truly human, for a strong ethnic group to give a voice to a weak ethnic group by means of a policy of positive discrimination.

The problem for many Christians generally is that the very word "ethnic" or "ethnicity" has acquired such a bad image by being associated with terrible cruelty, such as in Rwanda, that it has become very difficult to think of it as a positive thing. Responding to this dilemma, a recent Bible study booklet on the topic published by the Fellowship of Christian Unions (FOCUS) in Africa helpfully distinguishes between ethnocentrism and ethnicity. Ethnocentrism is evil but, as the booklet states, "We should not deny our ethnic backgrounds. They are God given and should be used for God's glory."[105]

Rwanda: An Ethnic Conflict?

As we would expect, a great deal of work has been done on the Rwandan genocide since 1994 so that the role of ethnicity in that terrible event is now very clear. A very brief account of the main conclusions of the research will be helpful. It is now generally held that ethnicity was not driving but being driven in the genocide. The population of Rwanda is made up of three groups—the Twa[106]

---

103 Paper delivered at an IFES consultation on ethnicity in Africa.
104 David A. Dortey and Vesta Nyarko-Mensah, eds., *The Church, Ethnicity and Democracy* (Accra: Christian Council of Ghana, 1995), 27.
105 Fellowship of Christian Unions, *The Bible in Focus: The Challenge of Ethnicity* (Nairobi: Fellowship of Christian Unions, 1999), 39.
106 The Twa are ignored in the following discussion because the Hutu and Tutsi were the main players in the genocide and not because the Twa are not significant.

(1 percent), who had probably arrived by AD 1000; the Hutu (85–90 percent), who had arrived by AD 1500; and the Tutsi, who moved in from around AD 1600–1900. The Tutsi became the ruling class in a society that shared the same language, religion, and customs. The fact that being a Tutsi was becoming a matter of class is proved by the fact that rich Hutus could become Tutsis. Before colonisation there is no evidence of systematic violence between the two groups. To the contrary there was considerable intermarriage, and they fought aggressors side by side. This is not to deny that Tutsis had a mythology that bolstered their supremacy. The point is that that supremacy was coming to be seen not as ethnic but political. There is every reason to believe that the Tutsi-Hutu population of Rwanda would have developed into a single ethnic identity if it had been left alone, although class conflict could not be ruled out.

Colonialism put a stop to such a development. The zenith of colonialism at the beginning of the twentieth century coincided with the ascendancy of an anthropology dominated by social Darwinism. Peoples were classified according to an evolutionary scale. With these anthropological tools Belgian colonial administrators created the ethnic identities of Tutsi and Hutu. According to their ethnic definitions, the Tutsi were superior in all ways and destined to rule, while the Hutu were backward and destined to serve. The introduction of identity cards for the two groups confirmed this ethnic distinction that had been created for them. Having bolstered Tutsi supremacy for forty years, the Belgian authorities then changed policy when in 1959 they opted for democracy. The result of this shift was that when independence came in 1962 the Hutu majority were handed the reins of power for the first time. It is not at all surprising that some Hutus were keen to avenge the injustices of the past Tutsi domination. This led to conflict. Thousands of Tutsis were killed, and a large Tutsi community living as refugees outside Rwanda was created.

The second president of independent Rwanda, Juvenal Habyarimana,[107] came to power in 1973 preaching a message of ethnic pacification. However, like many administrations his came more and more to serve the interests of a faction who in his case was dominated by his wife's family and their associates. Faced with growing disaffection because of the economic decline of the country, it was this faction that planned and executed the genocide so that they could maintain their hold on power. This was the direct cause of the genocide in 1994 and not ethnic hatred. That a particular political faction was able to foment ethnic hatred was the direct result of the way in which ethnic identity had been defined and solidified in Rwanda by colonial administrators influenced by Darwinist anthropological theories. The tragedy of Rwanda is that there were very few Christian leaders in either the Catholic or Protestant churches, that most Rwandans joined in due course, which had the vision to challenge the ungodly policies of the colonial and postcolonial administrations.[108]

If it has taught us nothing else, Rwanda has taught us that to limit the meaning of the gospel to prayer, Bible study, and private morality while leaving the world to define the social and political meaning of life is a recipe for disaster. In the context of this book, it highlights the need for a Christian understanding of ethnic identity which appreciates that, though often implicated in conflict, it is very rarely, if ever, the simple cause of conflict. In a fallen world, what is essentially good in God's creation is often used to serve evil ends. Rwanda is also a warning that we need to be very careful in the the-

---

107 He ruled from 1973–94. His death when the plane he was travelling in was shot down as it came in to land in Kigali airport sparked the beginning of the genocide.
108 The section on Rwanda is based on: G. Prunier, *The Rwanda Crisis: History of a Genocide* (London: Hurst, 1995); D. Waller, *Rwanda: Which Way Now?* rev. ed. (Oxford: Oxfam, 1996); Steering Committee of the Joint Evaluation of Emergency Assistance to Rwanda, *Joint Evaluation of Emergency Assistance to Rwanda, Study 1*, 1996. See www.ess.uwe.ac.uk/Rwanda/Rwanda4a.htm and Fergal Keane, *Season of Blood: A Rwandan Journey* (London: Penguin, 1996). Also see D. Hughes, *God of the Poor* (Carlisle, England: OM Publishing, 1998), 228–33.

ory of ethnic identity that we advocate as Christians. While wanting to affirm diversity, we must be very careful not to contribute to the creation of conditions in which hatred and conflict can flourish.

HEALING THE WOUND OF ETHNIC CONFLICT

At its heart the tension between Hutu and Tutsi in Rwanda that led to the genocide was a class conflict that had been redefined as an ethnic conflict by colonial administrators. However, to say that what happened in Rwanda was not really an ethnic conflict does not annul the suspicion and hatred that many Hutus and Tutsis still feel towards each other. Discovering the real cause of the conflict may not be that significant in dealing with the feelings that one group may have towards another. The same is true in other centres of conflict. Much of the responsibility for the conflict in what was once Yugoslavia can be laid at the feet of Miloševic's lust for power, but that does not do away with the fact that it has left a legacy of ethnic hatred and suspicion in the area. The great need is for people to be able to move away from hatred and suspicion in the direction of reconciliation. The remainder of this chapter will look first at a theological approach, and second, at a practical approach to this issue.

A Theological Foundation

The theological approach comes from the Croat Miroslav Volf. The problem that he faces as a Croat is put very graphically in the preface to his book Exclusion and Embrace:

> After I finished my lecture Professor Jürgen Moltmann stood up and asked one of his typical questions . . .: "But can you embrace a *četnik*?" It was the winter of 1993. For months now the notorious Serbian fighters called "*četnik*" had been sowing desolation in my native country, herding people into concentration camps, raping women, burning down churches, and destroying cities. I had just

argued that we ought to embrace our enemies as God has embraced us in Christ. Can I embrace a četnik—the ultimate other, so to speak, the evil other? What would justify the embrace? Where would I draw the strength for it? What would it do to my identity as a human being and a Croat? It took me a while to answer, though I immediately knew what I wanted to say. "No, I cannot—but as a follower of Christ I think I should be able to."[109]

Volf recognises that the upsurge of ethnic consciousness in Yugoslavia reflects, or maybe is reflected in, a change in emphasis that is happening in political philosophy. The modernist political philosophy that was built on the concept of sameness is giving way to an emphasis on difference. While the emphasis on sameness prevailed, the question of identity had little significance. It was assumed that the modernist tide would inevitably sweep away difference as people came to enjoy the material fruits of industrialism. But contrary to modernist expectations, the end of the twentieth century witnessed a strong rediscovery of difference. Identity has become a significant issue. What happened in Yugoslavia after the collapse of communism was that people came to see themselves in terms of their history, territory, customs, language, and religion rather than in terms of a modernist, materialist, economic, and political philosophy. The result was a rediscovery of what distinguished one group from another, with the resultant awareness of historic injustices that may have been perpetrated by one group against another. It is this rediscovery that fuels the conflict in the area. Volf believes that this new emphasis on difference and identity is a reality of contemporary life that is likely to persist and must be taken seriously by theologians.

While believing that the Christian faith has something to say about social arrangements, Volf believes that the role of the theologian is to "explore *what kind of selves we need to be* in order to live

---

[109] Miroslav Volf, *Exclusion and Embrace: A Theological Exploration of Identity, Otherness, and Reconciliation* (Nashville: Abingdon, 1996), 9.

in harmony with others."[110] In this context his central concern is the place of the cross of Christ in shaping the way we relate to the "other," including the ultimate other, the enemy. The glory of the cross is not only its witness to Christ's solidarity with the victim but also the fact that he gave up his life for his enemies that they too can be reconciled to God. As the only way to reconciliation with God, the cross highlights the sin of the victim and the perpetrator in a situation of ethnic conflict. If the situation is one of oppression of one ethnic group by another, as in the case of most indigenous peoples, in the light of the cross, freedom can never be the ultimate goal. It is never a case of the whiter than white oppressed gaining their liberation from the blacker than black oppressors. The oppressed also need to change, to repent of their sin. The failure to recognise this has led so often to the liberated oppressed becoming the oppressors. Oppressors are regularly "recruited among the martyrs not quite beheaded."[111]

To illustrate his point, Volf focuses on the case of a Bosnian Muslim woman who was treated with horrifying cruelty by Serbs. In her testimony she states that she had named her newborn son Jihad and that she had vowed to raise him to hate Serbs and to seek revenge for the cruelty that she had suffered. She blamed the Serbs for having taught her to hate.[112] Without diminishing the horrors of her torture, for which her torturers need to repent, this poor mother, if she persisted in her hatred would, if given the opportunity, become like her torturers. She even wanted her son to grow up prepared to treat a Serb woman like she had been treated. What she was doing was adopting the values of the oppressor that promises nothing but an unbroken cycle of violence and disharmony. If Jesus commands that we should love our enemies, then hatred of enemies is a sin from which we need to repent. This seems a hard thing to say to the Bosnian woman, but without repentance her life would be

---

[110] Ibid., 21; Volf's italics.
[111] Ibid., 104; quoting E. M. Cioran.
[112] Ibid., 111.

destroyed by bitterness, and if she ever got to the position of being able to exact revenge on her oppressors, she would only multiply her sins and further deface her humanity.

The cross represents God's refusal to answer hatred in kind. By accepting rather than combatting the hatred of his enemies, Jesus makes it possible for God's enemies to find reconciliation with him. An opening is created through which enemies can find a way to the very heart of God. Volf argues that entering through this opening into God's heart is inextricably linked with the creation of an opening in our human hearts through which the enemy can come in, and reconciliation, even communion, becomes a possibility. Our forgiveness must be reflected in our forgiving. He does not pretend that being reconciled with our enemies is an easy task, nor does he avoid the difficult questions that the grace of forgiveness poses for justice and truth, but he insists that the cross of Christ makes grace primary. It is grace that opens the door to reconciliation, and justice has to be viewed from the perspective of that glorious reality. Volf recognises that this grace that can make room even for the enemy is a divine gift. It is not something that we can do in our own strength. This is why Volf wanted to say that he could not love the *četnik* but that as a follower of Jesus Christ he should be able to do so.

Practically Outworking Theological Principles

In just a few paragraphs I have tried to convey something of the heart of Volf's rich and often profound volume on issues that he had to face as a Croat in a situation of intense ethnic conflict. As a theologian he found the route to peace and reconciliation in the cross of Christ. I discovered that the cross was also central in the seminar on "Healing the Wounds of Ethnic Conflict" led by Rhiannon Lloyd that I attended in KwaZulu Natal in September 2000. In many ways what I witnessed in the seminar was the practical application of the principles expounded in Volf's book.

I travelled to South Africa with the sole purpose of attending one of Rhiannon's seminars because, having become familiar with her work in Rwanda and South Africa as one of her prayer partners, I wanted to be an eyewitness of what she did so that I could finish my work on ethnicity on a positive note. I was not disappointed.

Rhiannon hails from a little village near Bangor in North Wales, which is forty miles from my hometown of Bala, and like myself was raised in a Welsh-speaking home and community. We were both converted around the same time in the 1960s and got to know each other through Evangelical Movement of Wales circles. Our paths have crossed now and again ever since. She became a medical doctor. Her testimony is that, after ministering to people's bodies for some time, she decided that she should minister to people's minds, so she trained and practised as a psychiatrist. Finally, she was drawn to focus on people's souls as she came to realise more profoundly that Jesus knows above any other how to heal bruised hearts.

Her first experience of Africa was in Liberia, after the civil war in 1992, where she went to do some posttrauma counselling. Then in December 1994 the leader of the Christian group that she had worked with in Liberia rang her from Rwanda inviting her to join him there. He believed that she had a contribution to make in a country that had been totally traumatised by the genocide earlier in 1994. Arriving in Rwanda she came face to face with immense suffering. The stories she was told were terrible. All she could do was weep before God, asking whether it was possible for hope to be reborn in such a situation. All she could see all around her was despair. However, God assured her that there was hope.[113] There were many in Rwanda that had remained faithful. She felt God telling her to go and tell his faithful ones that he still loves them. There was one brother who believed that the church could be healed, and through the church the nation as a whole. Together they started dreaming about gathering church leaders together to begin this process of healing. So the first seminar was held with prayer that God would do something remarkable among them. Remarkable things

---

[113] The passage she was given at this time was Romans 15:13.

did indeed happen. They saw reconciliation. They saw Hutu and Tutsi embracing each other. This was the beginning of a process that lasted for eighteen months, in which they held a seminar and established a group committed to reconciliation in every main town in Rwanda.

Then many of the Hutus who had been in the refugee camps in Tanzania and Zaire came back to reclaim their houses and land. Many had said in the seminars that they were prepared to forgive, but that was when their enemies were far away in the camps. Now they were nearby once again. Would the determination to forgive withstand the pressure? Rhiannon and her friends began to hear of amazing things happening. The work has now been in the hands of Rwandans for some time, with the seminar being taught jointly by a Tutsi and a Hutu. They are also training teams who can teach the seminar so that the impact can be multiplied.

After the work had been progressing for some time in Rwanda, she met Michael Cassidy there who encouraged her very strongly to take the seminar to South Africa. She responded to the call and with support from South Africans has been holding seminars in different parts of the country since 1997. The seminar I attended was held in an Afrikaner farm that is also a small conference centre some forty kilometres outside Newcastle, halfway between Johannesburg and Durban.

I had noticed on my way down by coach from Johannesburg to Newcastle that as soon as we got out from the industrialised area the countryside was very sparsely populated. Small clumps of trees now and again broke up the stark, shrivelled countryside and more often than not marked the presence of a farmhouse. A little distance from each farmhouse there was usually a little group of what can only be described as shacks that I gathered were the homes of the farm workers. The scenery between Newcastle and Horseshoe Farm was no different. About ten kilometres from the farm we turned onto a dirt track and eventually came through a small pass and dropped down into an extensive plain surrounded by mountains and called the Ark. Horseshoe Farm is nestled into the hillside on the northern side of the plain in a slightly elevated position. From the front of the house, that faces south, the whole plain is visible and the lovely Drakensburg hills beyond. A little distance from the farm, the workers live in brick houses.

To this beautiful place six Afrikans, five English, two Indians, one Swazi, and a dozen Zulus had gathered to spend three days thinking about healing the wounds of ethnic conflict under the direction of "a little lady from Wales," as Rhiannon calls herself. Most of the participants were church leaders. What follows is a brief account of what was taught and done in the seminar.[114]

Rhiannon said that her aim in the seminar was to build a house whose foundation was knowing the heart of God, the walls were healing our pain at the foot of the cross, the ceiling was forgiveness and repentance, and the roof was reconciliation.

The eternal being of God in the Trinity is the ultimate foundation of everything—Father, Son, and Holy Spirit in total unity, existing eternally in an amazing circle of relationships. There is one God in three Persons with each Person in no way threatening another. What we have in the Godhead is unity in diversity. There is difference, yet there is perfect love. It is an indestructible "team." Being different has not been a problem in eternity.

This triune God is love, and love wants to share. So God opened the circle and created the earth and its creatures in order to multiply the love and the beauty. As he created, God expressed his feelings by declaring that what he had created was good. When he came to the creation of human beings, he declared that what he had made was very good (Gen 1:9,12,18,25,31; cf. Prov 8:30,31). Human beings are all individually designed by God. Each individual is a unique work of art.

But what about ethnic groups? Are they also a part of God's design? Acts 17:26 is a key text which asserts that ethnic groups are

---

[114] Rhiannon Lloyd, and Joseph Nyamutera, *Healing the Wounds of Ethnic Conflict*, Geneva: Mercy Ministries International, 2010. Available at www.ess.uwe.ac.uk/Rwanda/Rwanda4a.htm.

God's idea. Now anything that is a part of God's design must be a blessing. The whole creation witnesses to the fact that God enjoys diversity, and different ethnic groups are but one expression of this divine joy. To say this is not to deny the unity of the human race. Every human being may be unique, and ethnic groups are all different, but there is only *one* human race. Racism is nonsense. There is unity in diversity here too.

Why does God desire ethnic diversity? One ethnic group could not possibly adequately express the glory of God. The beauty of a diamond consists in the number of facets that it has. The greater the number of facets, the greater the glory of an individual diamond; ethnic diversity is meant to express the glory of God in different ways. God expects the glory, honour, and wealth of all ethnic groups to be brought into his kingdom (Rev 21:24). It is for people's well-being that they should belong to an ethnic group, because "authentic living is only found in corporate connectedness."[115] God believes in groups—family, clan, ethnic group. The need to belong to a group is deeply ingrained in our human nature as created by God.

What was God's intention for the relationships between different ethnic groups? We should be excited about getting to know the "other." It is an opportunity to expand our limited world and to enrich our lives. Space must be made to let the "other" enter our lives. Sadly, what we do as human beings all too often is reject the "other," build a wall around ourselves, and then claim that we are superior. The result is oppression and conflict and the inflicting of deep wounds that need healing.

The next step in the process was to look at the possible reasons for excluding the "other" from our lives and even treating them as enemies, especially when the "other" belongs to another ethnic group. Our fears, prejudices, and enmities are rooted in our experience of corporate identity on every level, beginning with our im-

---

[115] Quotation from notes taken by the author during his attendance at Rhiannon Lloyd's workshop.

mediate family and going down into our family history, religion, ethnic and political identity, and finally the original source of our humanity in Adam. Where there is enmity and hatred, these roots have become bitter and need to be healed. Rhiannon illustrates how bitterness may be healed by telling her own story.

She grew up hating the English. It is undeniable that the Welsh have suffered a lot of injustice at the hands of the English, so much so that many Welsh people came to think of themselves as inferior. The "Welsh Not," referred to earlier in this volume, is a good example of oppression that has sunk deep into the Welsh psyche. In Rhiannon's case a close relative had worn the Welsh Not with pride, had refused to pass it on to anyone else, and suffered the consequent beatings. This bravery in the face of English cruelty had become a *cause celebre* in her family. In school she remembers English fellow pupils telling her that the Welsh were inferior. On her side of the fence Rhiannon's father made it very clear to her that he disliked the English intensely. Her reaction to this sense of oppression was to become a fighter. She remembers writing a play about the Welsh Not while in school. When the play was performed, she played the part of the child that suffered because of the Welsh Not. Her performance was not just an act but an expression of emotions that were very real to her. She was the one suffering injustice and not some historical character. Not surprisingly, she was an ardent nationalist by the time she was a teenager.

Then at sixteen she became a Christian and was filled with enthusiasm for evangelism, while her friends became involved with the Welsh Language Society. Many things changed, but her prejudice against the English remained. She had intended to study medicine in the University of Wales Cardiff, but she failed to get a place and found herself going to Leeds instead. In a big English city all her feelings of inferiority came flooding in as she thought that someone like her from a little village in Wales could not possibly fit in. In this crisis of identity she would most probably have abandoned ship and gone home had it not been for the fellowship that she found in the Christian Union. At first she made friends with international students, but she soon had very good English friends as well. This is when she realised that not all English people are the same.

Despite this the bitter roots went very deep. After a long process it was eventually dealt with in an intercessory prayer group. She came to understand that it was the bruising of her identity that was the cause of her anger. Like many of her contemporaries, the realisation that their identity was under threat had led her to exalt her Welsh identity to the point of making it an idol. So the group engaged in intercession against the idol of nationalism. Then someone said that something else needed to be dealt with first. The Englishwoman who said this got up and knelt at Rhiannon's feet and offered her heart to her as a servant's heart. Rhiannon began to weep as her English friend went on to apologise for all the English oppression of the Welsh. The apology was accepted, and in response Rhiannon forgave the English for the oppression and unjust treatment of the Welsh. She also repented of her hardness of heart and unforgiving nature. This act of forgiveness led to losing friends who came to see her as a traitor to the Welsh cause. However, to forgive the English was not the same as saying that everything they had done to the Welsh in the past was fine. The injustice remains as injustice in the sight of God. The significant change had happened not to historical reality but in her heart. The bitter root had been removed.

What happened in the intercessory prayer group was a step on the way to realising that Jesus bore our pain as well as our sin in his death on the cross. The problem is that we often uncouple sin and pain, and while claiming that God has forgiven our sin we continue to carry our pain. However, to do so is to fail to appreciate who God is and to distance ourselves from the Father's embrace. For example, she was surprised to find Tutsi Christians very soon after the genocide in Rwanda praising God as if nothing had happened. But when she started probing beneath the surface, she found that many were very bitter against God and saying that he belonged to the Hutu militia. So she had to get them to face the difficult questions in order to bring them back to believe God, despite the terrible things that had happened to them and their families. This has now become an integral part of the seminar process, and we were asked to consider the following questions: Is God just? If he is, why is there so much injustice? Is everything that happens God's will? If God is omnipotent, why does he not stop people doing evil? If God is a God of love, why does he allow the innocent to suffer? The purpose of the exercise is to encourage a deeper understanding of who God is and to strengthen faith in him, despite the ultimately insoluble mystery of pain and suffering. God is never the author of our pain and suffering although, to achieve an end that is often beyond our understanding, he allows us to pass through very deep waters. If he is not the cause of our suffering, then we can always look to him for relief and help in our pain.

John the Baptist had lost sight of this when he was in prison and sent some of his disciples to ask Jesus if he was the Messiah. Jesus told John's disciples to go and tell him what he already knew about the miracles and the fact that the good news was being preached to the poor. Then he added a warning: "Blessed is the man who does not fall away on account of me" (Matt 11:6). It seems that John's faith was wavering in the face of neglect by the one whom he had declared as Messiah. John knew that Jesus was performing miracles, but had Jesus not also proclaimed that he would release those that were imprisoned. Why then was John forgotten and left to languish in prison? We may wonder what passed through John's mind when he faced his executioner shortly after but he had been told to trust the Messiah even when it seemed to him that he had been left in the darkness.

Any attempt to accuse God of indifference or to blame him for our pain becomes impossible at the foot of the cross. In a sense, in Jesus' trial, humanity was putting God on trial. But Jesus made no attempt to defend himself. He accepted the charge of guilty, even though it was totally unjust. He was prepared to take the blame for all the sin and suffering in the world, even though he was totally blameless. If we have any understanding of who it was who hung on the cross, we cannot say that it was his guilt that took him there. The sin and pain in the world was not his fault. It was not his sin and grief that he bore but ours.

What we bring to the cross is our brokenness, and rejection is a major cause of the pain of a broken heart. However sinful we may be, God values us so much that he sent his Son to die for us. It is people that devalue and demean each other. This is what happens so often among ethnic groups. One group rejects another simply because of what they are supposed to be. So for the Hutu the Tutsi were *inienzi* ("cockroaches"); in South Africa all whites are racists, all Zulus are corrupt, all Indians are liars and cheats, and all coloureds are drunkards. In the United Kingdom all the Irish and Welsh are stupid, all the Scots are mean, and all the English are haughty. This type of ethnic stereotyping is often expressed in humour, but it is not really funny, because as an attack on an ethnic group's character it leaves them helpless. In fact this very common characteristic of ethnic groups is an expression of the vicious circle of claim and counterclaim in which ethnic groups are engaged in the process of establishing and preserving their identity in a fallen world.

Rejection causes a whole range of responses in individuals and also among ethnic groups. Competitiveness, exclusiveness, anger, a sense of national superiority, apathy, and escapism are some of the effects of ethnic rejection. Escapism, for example, is very common among indigenous peoples whose ethnic identity has been so deeply wounded that alcohol and drugs are resorted to in order to dull the pain.[116] To experience the love and acceptance of God in Christ is the only way out of these consequences of rejection.

In Christ, because what we are, which includes our ethnic identity, is valued so greatly by God, we have an escape route from the vicious circle of rejection. There is no need to react in any of the destructive ways listed in the previous paragraph. Beginning from

---

[116] I fear that the rise of alcoholism in rural Wales is symptomatic of this.

the confidence that our heavenly Father values our identity, we can reclaim what has been stolen from us. At this point Rhiannon contrasted the work of Satan the great "thief" who comes "to steal and kill and destroy" and the Good Shepherd who has come to give abundant life (John 10:10,11). The different ethnic groups in the seminar were then invited to make a list of the things Satan had taken from them. Each group came up with a long list.

The Zulu and Indian lists were the same, although the Indians felt that they had suffered less than the Zulus. Interestingly, the first item on each of their lists was a right conception of God. They had come to believe that God was the God of the whites, that Jesus was white, and that spiritual and moral darkness is black. It was this God that had been used to rob them of everything else—their wealth, culture, and dignity. The Afrikaners had lost the opportunity to grow numerically as a people because of the many deaths in English concentration camps during the Boer war. They also had been robbed of their wealth when they lost the gold and diamond mines to the English. Their culture had also been oppressed in the past and is again under threat in the new South Africa. Now that they are being branded as the oppressor, they are losing their dignity and self-respect. The English also were robbed of their culture, especially during the apartheid years. Now they are losing some of their wealth as well. They have also been robbed of meaningful contact with other peoples in South Africa because of their deep sense of superiority.

It was striking that there was a significant overlap in what the different groups had lost. At the end of this exercise we were encouraged to go to the enemy's house and take back what he had robbed from us all. Obviously this can only happen when the different ethnic groups are able to look to the needs of others as well as to their own needs. This is the great challenge facing the church in South Africa. It must model mutual respect and begin to address the issue of redistribution of wealth if there is to be any real hope of peace in the country's future. To claim this destiny in God, South

African Christians must express their oneness in Christ as well as their ethnic diversity.

By this point in the seminar Rhiannon believes that the time has come to give the participants an opportunity to bring their pain to the cross. First of all, we were encouraged to write down what had caused us pain. These could be things that were caused by living in South Africa or personal things. Then in mixed ethnic groups of two or three we were asked to share as much of what we had written as we could, so that we could hear what was in each other's hearts. When this was done we were invited to go to a room where a large, wooden cross had been placed in the middle of the floor with a hammer and some nails next to it. We were then invited to nail our lists of pain to the cross to symbolise our belief that Jesus has already suffered it on our behalf. When this was done the pieces of paper were then taken off the cross and burnt to symbolise the completeness of the transaction.

When this workshop was over, it was recognised that not everything may have been dealt with in this one workshop. The key point was to experience the healing that comes from taking our pain to the cross as the door to forgiveness, repentance, and reconciliation. Again and again in Rwanda Rhiannon has seen Tutsis and Hutus being released to forgive each other once their pain, which was often very intense, had been taken to the cross. She has witnessed people being forgiven unspeakable crimes. But does this mean that sin and wickedness are not to be taken seriously? The authorities in Rwanda certainly believed that this was the case when Rhiannon began her work there. They did not want Christians coming and proclaiming forgiveness when what was needed was for the perpetrators of the evil to be brought face to face with the terrible evil that they had done. They saw forgiveness as a way of denying that evil is evil. This was a misunderstanding of forgiveness.

Forgiveness is a legal term for freeing someone who is guilty. It assumes an admission of guilt. Where the victim is concerned, forgiveness means dissociating the evil and pain that has been caused us from those who caused it and finding relief in Christ as our pain bearer. We are then free from the evil that has been caused us and are able to view our tormentor(s) with mercy. But while forgiveness marks a significant change in the victim, it does not necessarily mark any change in the perpetrator of the crime who remains guilty before God and the law of the land. In Romans, having encouraged Christians to show a loving and forgiving spirit towards their enemies, Paul goes on immediately to talk about the governing authorities whose task is to punish the evildoer (Rom 12:17–13:5). An interesting discussion developed at this point about what a Christian should do if they discovered that someone was guilty of murder. One Zulu pastor thought that the murderer should first be encouraged to repent and brought face to face with the family of the victim in the hope that there could be reconciliation. Only after this had been attempted should the matter be brought before the court. Another Zulu leader talked of an actual case of a man who had struck a child who was caught stealing fruit so hard that the child had died. The family of the child requested that the murderer should not be sent to prison, because that would cause unnecessary suffering to his family and contribute nothing to alleviating the pain of the family that had lost a child. It seems that the Zulus could teach the rest of the world a lot about the relationship between forgiveness and justice.

The role of Christians as a "royal priesthood" (1 Pet 2:9) is crucial if there is to be a significant move towards reconciliation in a situation of ethnic conflict. According to Deuteronomy 10:8 the priests had three main functions. Firstly, as bearers of the ark they carried the visible presence of God among the people. Secondly, they proclaimed blessing in God's name. This is a marvellous antidote to judgement and enmity. We can bless ethnic groups when others mock and demean. Thirdly, they engaged in intercession that could be both personal and corporate. Rhiannon believes that it is possible for us as a royal priesthood to repent on behalf of a community that has wronged others. She herself was saved from her bitterness towards the English when an Englishwoman who had not sinned against her repented on behalf of her people. An ethnic identity that is a system of relationships, customs, and history cannot repent. It is only people that can repent, and sometimes a breakthrough can happen when someone who may not be in need of repentance is prepared to repent on behalf of others.

Rhiannon was stunned in one of her seminars in Rwanda when a woman started screaming at her that she was responsible for the genocide. She eventually discovered that the woman was blaming the genocide on the Belgians who came from Europe. To her Rhiannon represented European people whom she rightly discerned as having played a crucial role in creating the circumstances that led to the genocide. Rhiannon's response was to repent on behalf of Europeans. The Rwandans were stunned at first, because they had never heard a European expressing sorrow for what Europeans had done to them. Then they began repenting of their hatred of Europeans. Finally the Hutus and Tutsis decided that if Europeans and Rwandans could say sorry to each other, they could do the same. She has found that one of the most effective things that she does in Rwanda is give the Rwandans an opportunity to see a European repenting!

Having been to the cross with our pain and talked about forgiveness and repentance, we were then given an opportunity to apply the lesson. Sitting in a circle with water and a towel available, representatives of the different ethnic groups began to forgive and ask for forgiveness. Afrikaners washed the feet of Zulus and English. Zulus did the same to English and Afrikaners. Even the Welsh washed the feet of a Zulu to express their sorrow for the many Zulus that had been killed by the Welsh regiment in the siege of Roark's Drift. Many kind words were said and tears shed in this precious time.

After this we were ready to go together to the King's table as his holy nation. Early in the seminar Rhiannon had shared with us the tremendous significance of being God's "holy nation" as Christians drawn from different ethnic groups. For us our unity in Christ is the overarching reality, and our diversity, which remains precious and significant, is subsumed within our oneness. We had experienced this as we sought forgiveness and forgave each other. We could now celebrate it around the banqueting table of our King. A banqueting table was laid in the middle of the room laden with good things. As we entered we were all given a crown to wear and invited to take someone from a different ethnic group to the table where we could serve them and pray together. Having done this we all sat round the table, and each ethnic group was asked to stand in a group in their turn. While they were standing, the rest of us affirmed them and told them what we appreciated in them. We then shared scriptures with them, prayed for them and finally, embraced them. This time was unquestionably a little foretaste of heaven and, if repeated often enough, could have a tremendous impact on the future of South Africa as a whole. It was at the King's table that the rainbow nation became a reality.

CONCLUSION

Ethnicity may have become associated with conflict in the popular mind but if, as has been argued in this volume, ethnic identity is a part of God's purpose for humanity, then there is a need to examine the link between ethnicity and conflict very carefully. We must avoid jumping to the conclusion that ethnicity is bad simply because it is sometimes, even often, put to bad use. In the case of Africa in particular, the common colonial policy of "divide and rule" highlighted ethnic difference, while the postcolonial states were established on modernist principles that are essentially antiethnic. That conflict ensued is not surprising. Even the international community is now beginning to realise that the modernist agenda is unrealistic, and that ethnic diversity is not going to disappear with modernisation, as was once assumed. In the African context, some are calling for political structures that will recognise and empower ethnic identities. Some believe that to do this could diminish rather than increase the number of so-called ethnic conflicts.

Many evangelical Christian have sadly been wedded to the modernist model of the state, which is much more likely to increase rather than diminish ethnic tensions. There is some evidence of a move to a more positive appreciation of ethnic identity, with ethnocentrism being distinguished from God given-ethnic identity. Rwanda is a good example of the way ethnicity has been blamed for conflict. However, it is now commonly agreed that the fault for the genocide lies with patterns of thinking and behaviour that were established by the Belgian colonial administration, coupled with the lust for power and wealth. A political faction in a desperate bid to retain power used an ethnic consciousness institutionalised by colonialism. The colonial history also provides a clear warning against accentuating diversity unnecessarily.

As Christians we have considerable responsibility as to how ethnic identity is perceived, so that people will be encouraged to walk the narrow path between the twin evils of the oppression of ethnic identity and destructive ethnocentrism. In Christ we are able to affirm our unity and diversity as I experienced in the seminar in South Africa. However, before we can do this, we may have to face up to the violence that has been done to our ethnic identity, take the pain to the cross, and forgive our enemies. It is only then that reconciliation and mutual respect becomes possible.

APPENDIX

UN documents that are particularly relevant to the issue of minority ethnic identity

CHARTER OF THE UNITED NATIONS (1945)
Chapter 1. Purposes and Principles
The Purposes of the United Nations are:...

Article 1.2

To develop friendly relations among nations based on respect for the principles of equal rights and *self-determination of peoples*,...

[There is no mention of "the self-determination of peoples" or minority rights in the Universal Declaration of Human Rights.]

INTERNATIONAL COVENANT ON CIVIL AND POLITICAL RIGHTS (1966)
Part 1

Article 1.1

All peoples have the right of self-determination. By virtue of that right they freely determine their political status and freely pursue their economic, social and cultural development.

Article 27

In those States in which ethnic, religious or linguistic minorities exist, persons belonging to such minorities shall not be denied the right, in community with the other members of their group, to enjoy their own culture, to profess and practise their own religion, or to use their own language.

DECLARATION ON THE RIGHTS OF PERSONS BELONGING TO NATIONAL OR ETHNIC, RELIGIOUS AND LINGUISTIC MINORITIES (1992)[117]

The General Assembly,...

Inspired by the provisions of article 27 of the International Covenant on Civil and Political Rights concerning the rights of persons belonging to ethnic, religious or linguistic minorities,...

Proclaims this Declaration on the Rights of Persons Belonging to National or Ethnic, Religious and Linguistic Minorities:

Article 1

1. States shall protect the existence and the national or ethnic, cultural, religious and linguistic identity of minorities within their respective territories and shall encourage conditions for the promotion of that identity...

Article 2

1. Persons belonging to national or ethnic, religious and linguistic minorities (hereinafter referred to as persons belonging to minorities) have the right to enjoy their own culture, to profess and practise their own religion, and to use their own language, in private and in public, freely and without interference or any form of discrimination...

---

[117] See www.ohchr.org/Documents/Publications/GuideMinoritiesDeclarationen.pdf. The whole of the following declarations are relevant, but they have been abbreviated because the purpose of the appendix is to indicate how human rights law is moving towards the protection of minority ethnic identities.

3. Persons belonging to minorities have the right to participate effectively in decisions on the national and, where appropriate, regional level concerning the minority to which they belong or the regions in which they live, in a manner not incompatible with national legislation...

5. Persons belonging to minorities have the right to establish and maintain, without any discrimination, free and peaceful contacts with other members of their group and with persons belonging to other minorities, as well as contacts across frontiers with citizens of other States to whom they are related by national or ethnic, religious or linguistic ties.

Article 3

1. Persons belonging to minorities may exercise their rights, including those set forth in the present Declaration, individually as well as in community with other members of their group, without any discrimination...

Article 4

2. States shall take measures to create favourable conditions to enable persons belonging to minorities to express their characteristics and to develop their culture, language, religion, traditions and customs, except where specific practices are in violation of national law and contrary to international standards.

3. States should take appropriate measures so that, wherever possible, persons belonging to minorities may have adequate opportunities to learn their mother tongue or to have instruction in their mother tongue.

4. States should, where appropriate, take measures in the field of education, in order to encourage knowledge of the history, traditions, language and culture of the minorities existing within their territory. Persons belonging to minorities should have adequate opportunities to gain knowledge of the society as a whole...

Article 8

2. The exercise of the rights set forth in the present Declaration shall not prejudice the enjoyment by all persons of universally recognized human rights and fundamental freedoms...

UNITED NATIONS DECLARATION ON THE RIGHTS OF INDIGENOUS PEOPLES[118]
Adopted by General Assembly Resolution 61/295 on September 13, 2007

The General Assembly,...

Affirming that indigenous peoples are equal to all other peoples, while recognizing the right of all peoples to be different, to consider themselves different, and to be respected as such,

Affirming also that all peoples contribute to the diversity and richness of civilizations and cultures, which constitute the common heritage of humankind,

Affirming further that all doctrines, policies and practices based on or advocating superiority of peoples or individuals on the basis of national origin or racial, religious, ethnic or cultural differences are racist, scientifically false, legally invalid, morally condemnable and socially unjust,...

Concerned that indigenous peoples have suffered from historic injustices as a result of, inter alia, their colonization and dispossession of their lands, territories and resources, thus preventing them from exercising, in particular, their right to development in accordance with their own needs and interests,

Recognizing the urgent need to respect and promote the inherent

---

[118] See www.un.org/esa/socdev/unpfii/documents/DRIPS_en.pdf. When this book was first published in 2001, the UN only had a Draft Declaration on the Rights of Indigenous Peoples. This declaration that was adopted in 2007 does not seem to have weakened the draft declaration and could potentially be a powerful instrument to protect minority nations.

rights of indigenous peoples which derive from their political, economic and social structures and from their cultures, spiritual traditions, histories and philosophies, especially their rights to their lands, territories and resources,...

Convinced that control by indigenous peoples over developments affecting them and their lands, territories and resources will enable them to maintain and strengthen their institutions, cultures and traditions, and to promote their development in accordance with their aspirations and needs,

Recognizing that respect for indigenous knowledge, cultures and traditional practices contributes to sustainable and equitable development and proper management of the environment,...

Acknowledging that the Charter of the United Nations, the International Covenant on Economic, Social and Cultural Rights and the International Covenant on Civil and Political Rights, as well as the Vienna Declaration and Programme of Action, affirm the fundamental importance of the right to self-determination of all peoples, by virtue of which they freely determine their political status and freely pursue their economic, social and cultural development,...

Convinced that the recognition of the rights of indigenous peoples in this Declaration will enhance harmonious and cooperative relations between the State and indigenous peoples, based on principles of justice, democracy, respect for human rights, non-discrimination and good faith,...

Emphasizing that the United Nations has an important and continuing role to play in promoting and protecting the rights of indigenous peoples,

Believing that this Declaration is a further important step forward for the recognition, promotion and protection of the rights and freedoms of indigenous peoples and in the development of relevant activities of the United Nations system in this field,...

Solemnly proclaims the following United Nations Declaration on the Rights of Indigenous Peoples as a standard of achievement to be pursued in a spirit of partnership and mutual respect:…

Article 3

Indigenous peoples have the right to self-determination. By virtue of that right they freely determine their political status and freely pursue their economic, social and cultural development…

Article 5

Indigenous peoples have the right to maintain and strengthen their distinct political, legal, economic, social and cultural institutions, while retaining their right to participate fully, if they so choose, in the political, economic, social and cultural life of the State…

Article 8

1. Indigenous peoples and individuals have the right not to be subjected to forced assimilation or destruction of their culture.

2. States shall provide effective mechanisms for prevention of, and redress for:

    (a) Any action which has the aim or effect of depriving them of their integrity as distinct peoples, or of their cultural values or ethnic identities;
    (b) Any action which has the aim or effect of dispossessing them of their lands, territories or resources;…
    (d) Any form of forced assimilation or integration;…

Article 9

Indigenous peoples and individuals have the right to belong to an indigenous community or nation, in accordance with the traditions and customs of the community or nation concerned…

Article 10

Indigenous peoples shall not be forcibly removed from their lands or territories. No relocation shall take place without the free, prior and informed consent of the indigenous peoples concerned and after agreement on just and fair compensation and, where possible, with the option of return.

Article 11

1. Indigenous peoples have the right to practise and revitalize their cultural traditions and customs. This includes the right to maintain, protect and develop the past, present and future manifestations of their cultures, such as archaeological and historical sites, artefacts, designs, ceremonies, technologies and visual and performing arts and literature.

2. States shall provide redress through effective mechanisms, which may include restitution, developed in conjunction with indigenous peoples, with respect to their cultural, intellectual, religious and spiritual property taken without their free, prior and informed consent or in violation of their laws, traditions and customs.

Article 12

1. Indigenous peoples have the right to manifest, practise, develop and teach their spiritual and religious traditions, customs and ceremonies; the right to maintain, protect, and have access in privacy to their religious and cultural sites; the right to the use and control of their ceremonial objects; and the right to the repatriation of their human remains.

2. States shall seek to enable the access and/or repatriation of ceremonial objects and human remains in their possession through fair, transparent and effective mechanisms developed in conjunction with indigenous peoples concerned.

Article 13

1. Indigenous peoples have the right to revitalize, use, develop and transmit to future generations their histories, languages, oral traditions, philosophies, writing systems and literatures, and to designate and retain their own names for communities, places and persons.

2. States shall take effective measures to ensure that this right is protected and also to ensure that indigenous peoples can understand and be understood in political, legal and administrative proceedings, where necessary through the provision of interpretation or by other appropriate means.

Article 14

1. Indigenous peoples have the right to establish and control their educational systems and institutions providing education in their own languages, in a manner appropriate to their cultural methods of teaching and learning.

2. Indigenous individuals, particularly children, have the right to all levels and forms of education of the State without discrimination.

3. States shall, in conjunction with indigenous peoples, take effective measures, in order for indigenous individuals, particularly children, including those living outside their communities, to have access, when possible, to an education in their own culture and provided in their own language.

Article 15

1. Indigenous peoples have the right to the dignity and diversity of their cultures, traditions, histories and aspirations which shall be appropriately reflected in education and public information...

Article 16

1. Indigenous peoples have the right to establish their own media in their own languages and to have access to all forms of non-indigenous media without discrimination.

2. States shall take effective measures to ensure that State-owned media duly reflect indigenous cultural diversity…

Article 20

1. Indigenous peoples have the right to maintain and develop their political, economic and social systems…

Article 23

Indigenous peoples have the right to determine and develop priorities and strategies for exercising their right to development…

Article 24

1. Indigenous peoples have the right to their traditional medicines and to maintain their health practices, including the conservation of their vital medicinal plants, animals and minerals. Indigenous individuals also have the right to access, without any discrimination, to all social and health services.

2. Indigenous individuals have an equal right to the enjoyment of the highest attainable standard of physical and mental health…

Article 25

Indigenous peoples have the right to maintain and strengthen their distinctive spiritual relationship with their traditionally owned or otherwise occupied and used lands,…

Article 28

1. Indigenous peoples have the right to redress, by means that can include restitution or, when this is not possible, just, fair and equitable compensation, for the lands, territories and resources which they have traditionally owned or otherwise occupied or used, and which have been confiscated, taken, occupied, used or damaged without their free, prior and informed consent...

Article 31

1. Indigenous peoples have the right to maintain, control, protect and develop their cultural heritage, traditional knowledge and traditional cultural expressions, as well as the manifestations of their sciences, technologies and cultures, including human and genetic resources, seeds, medicines, knowledge of the properties of fauna and flora, oral traditions, literatures, designs, sports and traditional games and visual and performing arts. They also have the right to maintain, control, protect and develop their intellectual property over such cultural heritage, traditional knowledge, and traditional cultural expressions...

Article 33

1. Indigenous peoples have the right to determine their own identity or membership in accordance with their customs and traditions. This does not impair the right of indigenous individuals to obtain citizenship of the States in which they live...

Article 36

1. Indigenous peoples, in particular those divided by international borders, have the right to maintain and develop contacts, relations and cooperation, including activities for spiritual, cultural, political, economic and social purposes, with their own members as well as other peoples across borders...

Article 38

States in consultation and cooperation with indigenous peoples, shall take the appropriate measures, including legislative measures, to achieve the ends of this Declaration...

Article 43

The rights recognized herein constitute the minimum standards for the survival, dignity and well-being of the indigenous peoples of the world...

Article 45

Nothing in this Declaration may be construed as diminishing or extinguishing the rights indigenous peoples have now or may acquire in the future.

Article 46

1. Nothing in this Declaration may be interpreted as implying for any State, people, group or person any right to engage in any activity or to perform any act contrary to the Charter of the United Nations or construed as authorizing or encouraging any action which would dismember or impair, totally or in part, the territorial integrity or political unity of sovereign and independent States...

BIBLIOGRAPHY

Abogaye-Mensah, Robert. "The Church, Ethnicity and Democracy." In *The Church, Ethnicity and Democracy,* edited by David A. Dortey and Vesta Nyarko-Mensah. Accra: Christian Council of Ghana, 1995.

Agnew, John A. "The Geopolitical Context of Contemporary Ethnopolitiocal Conflict." In *Reconcilable Differences: Turning Points in Ethnopolitical Conflict,* edited by Sean Byrne and Cynthia L. Irvin, 3ff. West Hartford, CT: Kumarian, 2000.

Allen, Thomas B. "Xingjang Province," *National Geographic* 189, no. 3 (1996): 50–51.

Amoo, Sam G. *The Challenge of Ethnicity and Conflict in Africa: The Need for a New Paradigm.* New York: Emergency Response Division, UN Development Programme, 1997.

Bakke, Ray. *A Theology as Big as a City.* Downers Grove, IL: InterVarsity, 1997.

Banks, James A. "Race, Ethnicity and Schooling in the United States: Past, Present and Future." In *Multicultural Education in Western Societies,* edited by James A. Banks and James Lynch. London: Holt, Rinehart and Winston, 1986.

Barclay, O. *Evangelicalism in Britain 1935–1995.* Leicester, England: InterVarsity, 1997.

Bastian, Sunil, and Nicola Bastian. "Development NGOs Working in an Ethnic Conflict." *Appropriate Technology* 22, no. 4 (March 1996): 27–29.

Beauclerk, John, and Jeremy Narby. *Indigenous Peoples: A Field Guide for Development.* With Janet Townsend. Development Guidelines 2. Oxford: Oxfam, 1988.

Bediako, Kwame. *Christianity in Africa: A Renewal of a Non-Western Religion.* Edinburgh: Edinburgh Univ. Press; Maryknoll, NY: Orbis Books, 1995.

Ben-Ami, S., Y. Peled, and A. Spektorowski, eds. *Ethnic Challenges to the Modern Nation State.* London: Macmillan, 2000.

Bosch, David J. *Transforming Mission: Paradigm Shifts in Theology of Mission.* Maryknoll, NY: Orbis Books, 1991.

Bowen, Roger. "Revivalism and Ethnic Conflict: Questions from Rwanda." *Transformation* 12 (April–June 1995): 15–18.

Brown, Dee. *Bury My Heart at Wounded Knee: An Indian History of the American West.* London: Vintage, 1991. First published 1970.

Burnside, J. P. *The Status and Welfare of Immigrants: The Place of the Foreigner in Biblical Law and Its Relevance to Contemporary Society.* Cambridge: Jubilee Centre, 2000.

Byrne, Sean, and Cynthia L. Irvin, eds. *Reconcilable Differences: Turning Points in Ethnopolitical Conflict.* West Hartford, CT: Kumarian, 2000.

Carter, Isabel. *Locally Generated Printed Materials in Agriculture: Experience from Uganda and Ghana.* Education Research 31. London: Department for International Development, 1999.

Carter, Neal, and Sean Byrne. "The Dynamics of Social Cubism: A View from Northern Ireland and Quebec." In *Reconcilable Differences: Turning Points in Ethnopolitical Conflict*, edited by Sean Byrne and Cynthia L. Irvin, 42ff. West Hartford, CT: Kumarian, 2000.

Castellino, Joshua. *International Law and Self-determination: The Interplay of the Politics of Territorial Possession with Formulations of Post-colonial "National" Identity.* Developments in International Law 38. The Hague: Martinus Nijhoff, 2000.

Castles, Stephen. *Ethnicity and Globalization: From Migrant Worker to Transnational Citizen.* London: Sage, 2000.

Catherwood, Christopher. "Nationalism, Ethnicity and Tolerance: Some Historical, Political and Biblical Perspectives." *Transformation* 14, no. 1 (January–March 1997): 10–16.

Catherwood, Sir Fred. "Nationalism." *Christian Arena* 43, no. 3 (September 1990): 3–6.

———. *Pro-Europe*. London Lectures in Contemporary Christianity. Leicester, England: InterVarsity, 1991.

Cavanaugh, Kathleen A. "Understanding Protracted Social Conflicts: A Basic Needs Approach." In *Reconcilable Differences: Turning Points in Ethnopolitical Conflict,* edited by Sean Byrne and Cynthia L. Irvin, 65ff. West Hartford, CT: Kumarian, 2000.

Clements, P., and T. Spinks. *The Equal Opportunities Guide: How to Deal with Everyday Issues of Unfairness.* London: Kogan Page, 1994.

Collier, P., I. Elbadawi, and N. Sambanis. "Why Are There So Many Civil Wars in Africa? Prevention of Future Conflict and Promotion of Intergroup Cooperation." Paper presented at the UNCEA Ad Hoc Experts Group Meeting, Addis Ababa, April 7–8, 2000.

Cornell, Stephen, and Douglas Hartmann. *Ethnicity and Race: Making Identities in a Changing World.* Thousand Oaks, CA: Pine Forge, 1998.

Davies, J. *A History of Wales.* London: Allen Lane / Penguin, 1993. First Welsh edition 1990.

De Silva, K. M., and S. W. R. de A. Samarasinghe. *Peace Accords and Ethnic Conflict.* London / New York: International Centre for Ethnic Studies, 1993.

De Villiers, Marq. *White Tribe Dreaming.* Harmondsworth, England: Penguin, 1990.

Deng, F. M. "Negotiating Identity: Dishonoured Agreements in the Sudanese Conflict." In *Peace Accords and Ethnic Conflict,* edited by K. M. De Silva and S. W. R. de A. Samarasinghe, 60–82. London / New York: International Centre for Ethnic Studies, 1993.

Dwyer, D., and D. Drakakis-Smith, eds. *Ethnicity and Development: Geographical Perspectives.* Chichester, England: John Wiley, 1996.

Ebenezer, Reggie. "Reconciliation: The Church's Neglected Privilege." *Drishtikone: Evangelical Perspectives on Mission and Ethics* 1 (1998): 11–14.

Ellul, Jacques. *The Meaning of the City.* Grand Rapids: Eerdmans, 1970.

Escobar, Samuel. "A New Time for Mission." Paper delivered at the International Fellowship of Evangelical Students' World Assembly, Seoul, Korea, 1999.

Fellowship of Christian Unions. *The Bible in Focus: The Challenge of Ethnicity.* Nairobi: Fellowship of Christian Unions, 1999.

Fenton, Steve. "Ethnicity and Racism." *Echoes: Justice, Peace and Creation News* 17 (2000): 24–27.

Gatwa, Tharcisse. "Revivalism and Ethnicity: The Church in Rwanda." *Transformation* 12 (April–June 1995): 4–8.

Gellner, Ernest. *Nationalism.* London: Phoenix, 1998.

———. *Nations and Nationalism.* Oxford: Blackwell, 1983.

Goudzward, Bob. *Idols of Our Time.* Downers Grove, IL: InterVarsity, 1981.

Griffiths, Tudor. "Bishop A. R. Tucker of Uganda and the Implementation of an Evangelical Tradition of Mission." PhD thesis, Univ. of Leeds, 1999.

Gruber, Károly. "The Contemporary Ethnonationalist Renaissance in Europe and Its Implications for a Theory of Nationalism." *Nationalism and Ethnic Politics* 3 (Winter 1997): 128–51.

Harries, Patrick. "Exclusion, Classification and Internal Colonialism: The Emergence of Ethnicity among the Tsonga-speakers of South Africa." In *The Creation of Tribalism in Southern Africa,* edited by Leroy Vail, 82–117. London: James Currey, 1989.

———. "The Roots of Ethnicity: Discourse and the Politics of Language Construction in South-east Africa." *African Affairs* 87 (1988): 25–52.

Hastings, Adrian. *The Construction of Nationhood: Ethnicity, Religion and Nationalism.* Cambridge Univ. Press, 1997.

Hechter, Michael. *Containing Nationalism.* Oxford Univ. Press, 2000.

Hovil, Lucinda J. B. "An Exploration into the Relationship between Violence and Identity in KwaZulu and Natal, South Africa, 1990–1994." PhD thesis, Univ. of London, 1999.

Hutchinson, John, and Anthony D. Smith, eds. *Ethnicity.* Oxford Univ. Press, 1996.

Jaffrelot, Christophe. *The Hindu Nationalist Movement in Indian Politics: 1925 to the 1990s.* Delhi: Penguin Books, 1999.

Jenkins, D. E. *The Life of the Rev. Thomas Charles of Bala*, vol. 2. Denbigh, Wales: Llewelyn Jenkins, 1908.

Jenkins, Richard. *Rethinking Ethnicity: Arguments and Explorations.* London: Sage, 1997.

Jones, Bobi. *Crist a Chenedlaetholdeb*. Bridgend, Wales: Gwasg Efengylaidd Cymru, 1994.

Jones, R. M. "Language in God's Economy: A Welsh and International Perspective." *Themelios* 21, no. 3 (April 1996): 10–15.

Jones, R. Tudur. *The Desire of Nations*. Llandybie, Wales: Christopher Davies, 1974.

———. *Ffydd ac Argyfwng Cenedl: Cristionogaeth a Diwylliant yng Nghymru 1890–1914*, vol. 1. Swansea, Wales: Ty John Penry, 1981.

Jones, Robert Tudur, Sylvia Prys Jones, and Robert Pope, eds. *Faith and the Crisis of a Nation: Wales 1890-1914*. Cardiff: Univ. of Wales Press, 2004.

Jones, Watcyn L. *Cofio Tryweryn*. Llandysul, Wales: Gomer, 1988.

Keane, Fergal. *Season of Blood: A Rwandan Journey*. Harmondsworth, England: Penguin, 1996.

Kelly, Gerard. *Get a Grip on the Future without Losing Your Hold on the Past*. London: Monarch Books, 1999.

Kraybill, Donald B. *The Riddle of Amish Culture*. Baltimore: Johns Hopkins Univ. Press, 1989.

Kymlicka, Will. "Modernity and National Identity." In *Ethnic Challenges to the Modern Nation State*, edited by S. Ben-Ami, Y. Peled, and A. Spektorowski. London: Macmillan, 2000.

———. *Politics in the Vernacular: Nationalism, Multiculturalism, and Citizenship*. Oxford Univ. Press, 2001.

Levy, Jacob T. *The Multiculturalism of Fear*. Oxford Univ. Press, 2000.

Lloyd, Rhiannon. *Healing the Wounds of Ethnic Conflict: The Role of the Church in Healing, Forgiveness and Reconciliation*. With Kristine Bresser. 2000. Available from Mercy Ministries EMA (Youth With A Mission), Geneva.

MacFhionnlaigh, Fearghas. "Creative Tensions: Personal Reflections of an Evangelical Christian and Gaelic Poet." *Scottish Bulletin of Evangelical Theology* 14, no. 1 (1996): 37–50.

Malešević, Siniša. "Globalism and Nationalism: Which One Is Bad?" *Development in Practice* 9, no. 5 (November 1999): 579–83.

Metzger, Bruce M. *The Text of the New Testament.* Oxford: Clarendon, 1964.

Minahan, James. *Nations without States: A Historical Dictionary of Contemporary National Movements.* Westport, CT / London: Greenwood, 1996.

Minority Rights Group, ed. *World Directory of Minorities.* London: Minority Rights Group International, 1997.

Mompati, Tlamelo, and Gerard Prinsen. "Ethnicity and Participatory Development Methods in Botswana: Some Participants Are to Be Seen and Not Heard." *Development in Practice* 10, no. 5 (November 2000): 625–37.

Morgan, Prys. "From Long Knives to Blue Books." In *Welsh Society and Nationhood,* edited by R. R. Davies, R. A. Griffiths, I. G. Jones, and K. O. Morgan, 199–215. Cardiff: Univ. of Wales Press, 1984.

Neuberger, Benyamin. "Ethnic Groups and the State in Africa." In *Ethnic Challenges to the Modern Nation State,* edited by S. Ben-Ami, Y. Peled, and A. Spektorowski, 294–308. London: Macmillan, 2000.

Nichols, Alan. "Ethnicity and Conflict: Implications for Mission and Development." *Transformation* 12 (April–June 1995): 9–11.

Nnoli, Okwundiba. *Ethnicity and Development in Nigeria.* Aldershot, England: Avebury, 1995.

Ó Fatharta, Gearóid, *Vocation for Justice* 9, no. 3 (Autumn 1995): 2.

Papstein, Robert. "From Ethnic Identity to Tribalism: The Upper Zambesi Region of Zambia, 1830–1981." In *The Creation of Tribalism in Southern Africa,* edited by Leroy Vail, 372–94. London: James Currey, 1989.

Phillips, Dylan. *Trwy Ddulliau Chwyldro . . .? Hanes Cymdeithas yr Iaith Gymraeg 1962–92.* Llandysul, Wales: Gomer, 1998.

Poulter, Sebastian. *Ethnicity, Law and Human Rights: The English Experience*. Oxford Univ. Press, 1998.

Prunier, G. *The Rwanda Crisis: History of a Genocide*. London: Hurst, 1995.

Riddell, Roger. *Minorities, Minority Rights and Development: An Issues Paper*. London: Minority Rights Group, 1998.

Ringer, Terence. "Missionaries, Migrants and the Manyika: The Invention of Ethnicity in Zimbabwe." In *The Creation of Tribalism in Southern Africa*, edited by Leroy Vail, 118–50. London: James Currey, 1989.

Robinson, Clinton D. W. *Language Use in Rural Development*. New York: Mouton, 1996.

Rovillos, Raymundo. "Education in the International Decade of Indigenous Peoples: Bringing Education into the Mainstream of Indigenous Peoples' Lives." *Echoes: Justice, Peace and Creation News* 16 (1999): 4–7.

Samuel, C. B. "Building a Nation." *Transformation* 16, no. 4 (1999): 141–44.

Schumacher, E. F. *Small is Beautiful: Economics as if People Mattered*, 2nd ed., (New York: Harper Collins, 1989).

Senelin, Jessica. "Constructive Storytelling in Intercommunal Conflicts: Building Community, Building Peace." In *Reconcilable Differences: Turning Points in Ethnopolitical Conflict*, edited by Sean Byrne and Cynthia L. Irvin, 46ff. West Hartford, CT: Kumarian, 2000.

Seton, Kathy. "Fourth World Nations in an Era of Globalisation: An Introduction to Contemporary Theorizing Posed by Indigenous Nations." Center for World Indigenous Studies. www.cwis.org/fwj/41/fworld.html.

Silber, L., and A. Little. *The Death of Yugoslavia*. London: Penguin, 1995.

Smith, Anthony D. *Nations and Nationalism in a Global Era*. Cambridge: Polity, 1995.

Smith, John. *Advance Australia Where?* Homebush West, Australia: Anzea, 1989.

Stavenhagen, Rodolfo. *Ethnic Conflicts and the Nation-state*. London: Macmillan; New York: St. Martin's; in association with the United

Nations Research Institute for Social Development (UNRISD), 1996.

Steiner, Henry J., and Philip Alston, eds. *International Human Rights in Context: Law, Politics, Morals.* Oxford: Clarendon, 1996.

Steering Committee of the Joint Evaluation of Emergency Assistance to Rwanda. *Joint Evaluation of Emergency Assistance to Rwanda: Study 1.* Steering Committee of the Joint Evaluation of Emergency Assistance to Rwanda, 1996.

Storrar, William F. "The Modern Judas." *Christian Arena* 43, no. 3 (September 1990): 7–9.

———. "'Vertigo' or 'Imago'? Nations in the Divine Economy." *Themelios* 21, no. 3 (April 1996): 4–9.

Stuart, Morris. "Ethnicity and Race in Contextualisation." *World Evangelization* 80 (September–October 1997): 12–13.

Tschuy, Théo. *Ethnic Conflict and Religion: Challenge to the Churches.* Geneva: WCC Publications, 1997.

Vail, Leroy, ed. *The Creation of Tribalism in Southern Africa.* London: James Currey, 1989.

Volf, Miroslav. *Exclusion and Embrace: A Theological Exploration of Identity, Otherness, and Reconciliation.* Nashville: Abingdon, 1996.

———. "Exclusion and Embrace: Theological Reflections in the Wake of 'Ethnic Cleansing.'" In *Emerging Voices in Global Christian Theology,* edited by William A. Dyrness, 19–40. Grand Rapids: Zondervan, 1994.

———. "The social meaning of reconciliation." *Transformation* 16, no. 1 (1999): 7–12.

Wallace, Ian. "Post-conflict Reconstruction: Experiences in Rwanda." *Footsteps* 36 (September 1998): 4–5.

Waller, D. *Rwanda: Which Way Now?* rev. ed. Oxford: Oxfam, 1996.

Weller, R. Charles. *Rethinking Kazakh and Central Asian Nationhod: A Challenge to Prevailing Western Views,* Los Angeles: Asia Research Associates, 2006.

Wenham, Gordon J. "Genesis 1–15," *Word Biblical Commentary,* vol. 1. Waco: Word Publishers, 1987.

Williams, Glanmor. *The Welsh Church from Conquest to Reformation.* Cardiff: Univ. of Wales Press, 1962.

Williams, Gwyn A. *When Was Wales? A History of the Welsh.* London: Black Raven, 1985.

Wolterstorff, Nicholas. *Until Justice and Peace Embrace.* Grand Rapids: Eerdmans, 1983.

Wright, Christopher. *New International Biblical Commentary: Deuteronomy.* Peabody, MA: Paternoster, 1996.

Young, Elspeth. *Third World in the First: Development and Indigenous Peoples.* London / New York: Routledge, 1995.

INDEX

A

Aberyswyth, 91
Abogaye-Mensah, Robert, 161
Aborigines, 24, 137, 142, 152
Abraham, 40, 43–44, 46, 55
Acts of Union, 37
Adam, 31, 172
Africa, 78, 82, 103, 113, 130,
  158–61, 168, 180
African, 82
  conflicts. *See* conflict.
  countries, 144, 158
African American, 129
African-Caribbean, 6
Afro-Caribbeans, 115
Albania, 1
Albanian, 1
Alexandria, 41
Amazon basin, 3
America(n). *See* United States of
  America.
Amish, 116
Amoo, Sam G., 159–60
Anatolia, 110
ancestry, 110, 118, 126, 132–33,
  138
  common. *See* common.
Andes, 137, 149
Andhra Pradesh, 115
Anglican, 69–70, 75–76, 82
Anglo-American, 2, 50, 140
  magazines, 2
  music, 2
  television, 2
Anglo-Egyptian
  Sudan, 113
Anglo-Saxon, 27, 61, 64, 157
  race, 24
Angola, 114
Antioch, 41–42
apartheid, 152, 176
Arakanese, 114
Aramaic, 59
Ararat, 49
Armageddon, 54
Asia
  North, 51
Asia Minor, 44
Asian, 6, 115, 121, 133
Asian American, 129
Assembly of Evangelicals
  "National", 7
assimilation, 3, 15, 37, 39, 43,
  58, 74, 90, 102, 104, 110, 116,
  126–27, 129, 137, 144
Association of Quechua Evangelical
  Churches of the Jungle (AIKSEL),
  153
Assyrians, 48, 53
Australia, 27, 137, 157
Australian, 142
Aymara, 148

B

Babel, 2, 22, 51–52, 109, 130
　post-Babel world, 51
　Tower of, 49–50
Babylon, 48, 50
Babylonians, 50, 53
Baganda, 78, 80
Bala, 31, 33, 72, 110, 168
　Boys Grammar School, 12
Balkan, 30
Bangladeshis, 115
Bangor, 34–36, 38–39, 56–57, 66, 89, 92–93, 168
Bangor University, 38, 89
Baptist, 15, 32, 75, 141, 174
Baptist Missionary Society, 84
Barnabas, 41–42, 44, 60
Basque, 7, 135, 152
Beauclerk, 136, 147
Bede, 62, 82
Belarus, 4
Belgian, 114, 162, 179, 181
Belgium, 115
Berthoud, Henri, 79–81
Bethesda, 36
Bible, 31–32, 37, 39, 50, 52, 55, 58–59, 61–64, 66–74, 78–84, 101, 104, 119, 125–26, 137, 140, 146, 154
　biblical, 56, 87, 104–05, 119, 131, 145, 151, 160
　　justification, 54
　　knowledge, 68
　　nations, 52
　　perspective, 129, 146
　　principles, 131, 142
　　truth, 130
　　values, 73
　reading, 32
　Scripture, 52, 73, 180
　study, 161, 163
　　group, 36
　translation, 61, 78, 81, 83–85, 100, 104, 142, 144
Birmingham, 115
Bishop Parry, 68
Bishop Tucker, 80–81
Black Sea, 99
Boer war, 176
Bolivia, 148–49
Bombay, 115
Bosnia, 26
Bosnian, 26, 51
　Muslim woman, 166
Bradford, 115
Brazil, 114, 148
Breton, 22, 25, 135, 147, 152
Britain, 6, 13, 25–27, 29, 65, 74, 110–11, 131, 159
British, 28, 64, 66, 113, 141
　context, 27
　Empire, 25, 102, 143
　government, 75
　Isles, 109
　Labour Party, 14, 16
　militarism, 18
　rule, 25
British and Foreign Bible Society, 72–73
Brittany, 64, 110
Bryn y Groes, 31
Buchanan, George, 21
Buganda, 80–81
Burma, 114
Burmese, 114

C

Calvinistic Methodist, 15, 17, 75
　College, 72
Canaan, 109
Canaanite, 53, 109
Canada, 137
Canadian
　Aboriginals, 6

Canterbury, 62, 64–65
Capel Celyn, 33
Cardiff University, 36
Carlos, Juan, 149
Cassidy, Michael, 169
Catalans, 135, 152
Catalonia, 148
Celtic, 27, 62, 64–65, 110, 157
Celts, 109–11, 131
Central Asian Republics, 4
Charles, Thomas, 72–73, 75
Charles I, 21
Chechnya, 4
Cheyenne Daily Leader, 24
Chibchan migrants, 112
Children's Encyclopedia, 10
China, 3, 112–13
Chinese, 58, 113, 115
   Han, 113
Christian, 1, 28, 31, 34–35, 37,
   39–43, 50, 55–57, 59–64,
   72–73, 77–78, 82, 84, 87–89,
   91, 97–105, 107, 113, 123,
   126–28, 130–32, 136–40,
   142–44, 146–47, 149, 151–55,
   160–61, 163–65, 168, 172–73,
   177–79, 181
   heritage, 32
   responsibility, 87, 126, 128, 181
Christian Union, 35, 173
Christianity, 31, 51, 59–64, 82, 84,
   100, 112, 128, 136–37, 142–44
church, 15, 20, 32, 35–36, 40,
   55–57, 60, 62–70, 73, 83,
   98–99, 101, 104, 137, 140–44,
   150–51, 163–64, 168, 170, 176
   bilingual, 35–37, 39, 56–57
Church Missionary Society (CMS),
   80
Cilicia, 41
Ciltalgarth, 9–11
Ciltalgarth farm, 9–11

Cimmerians, 48
circumcision, 43–45, 99
Civil War, 21, 138, 160, 168
Coke, 2–3
Colombia, 112
Colombian, 129
Colonel Price, 33
colonization, 82, 113, 134, 145,
   153
   decolonization, 82
common
   ancestry, 6, 45, 48
   belief, 25
   culture, 6, 48
   language, 22, 49
   name, 52
   origin, 82
   past, 6, 48
   proper name, 6, 48
Communist, 4
   party, 4
community, 2, 5–6, 12, 22, 33–35,
   39, 56, 59–60, 82–83, 92, 95,
   99, 107, 116–18, 121, 124, 126,
   128, 143, 153–54, 162, 168,
   178, 180
conflict, 1, 30, 53, 78, 89, 94–97,
   101–02, 133, 153, 157, 159,
   162–65, 171, 180–81
   ethnic. *See* ethnic.
Congo, 114
Congregational, 15, 31–32, 36, 75
   chapel, 9, 66
Constitution of the Republic, 21
consumerism
   consumerist community, 2
conversion, 31–32, 68, 137
Cornelius, 42
Côte d'Ivoire, 114
Council of Arles, 64
Cowper, 66
Croats, 26, 51

Crowther, Samuel Ajayi, 82
Cuba, 141
culture, 3, 6, 12, 33–34, 37, 44–45, 48, 52, 60, 77, 99, 102, 107, 111, 114–18, 123, 129, 133–36, 140–43, 145, 147–54, 159, 161, 176
   cultural
      backgrounds, 39
      characteristics, 97
      community, 39
      differences, 14, 39
      effect, 77
      expression, 73
      heritage, 67, 98, 100, 149–50
      ideal, 2
      life, 17
      mandate, 51
      nuances, 14
      pluralism, 127
      power, 2
      pressure, 13
      roots, 93
      stereotype, 5
      superiority, 99
      values, 74
   dominant, 134, 147–48, 150–51, 154, 159
   shock, 13
Cush, 48
custom, 6, 42, 48, 52, 57, 80, 82, 113, 118, 128, 140, 162, 165, 179
Cwm Celyn, 33
Czech
   republic, 4
Czechoslovakia, 4

D

Darfur, 113–14
Darwinist, 162–63
Dda, Hywel, 65

de la Fuente, Juan Carlos, 148
Declaration of Independence, 21, 116
Dedan, 48
Delagoa Bay, 79
Delhi, 115
Depression, 17
discrimination, 5, 28, 117, 123, 160–61
diversity, 2–3, 25, 39, 47–48, 50–51, 57, 143, 145, 151, 160, 164, 170–71, 179, 181
   ethnic. *See* ethnic.
   linguistic, 50–51
Duke Rollo, 111
Durban, 169
Dutch
   pirates, 112

E

East, 3
East Africa, 80
Ebenezer Evangelical Church, 39
ecological, 3
   movement, 4
economics, 15, 20, 27, 29, 47, 79, 83, 102–03, 115, 125–26, 143–47, 163, 165
   free market, 14
Ecuador, 141
education, 1, 3, 11–12, 38, 69, 74–76, 88–89, 91–92, 94–96, 101, 116, 118, 133, 147–50, 154–55
Eglwys Efengylaidd Ebeneser, 39
Egypt, 41, 48, 59–60, 109, 113, 119, 122–23
eisteddfodau, 9
Eleven Plus, 12
Elizabeth I, 67
Encyclopedia, 10
England, 6–7, 10, 17, 19, 25, 27,

37, 61–67, 74, 84, 90, 94, 102, 111, 141, 146, 157
English, 6–7, 9–13, 15–16, 18–19, 21–22, 27–28, 32, 34–39, 50–52, 56–58, 61–69, 74–78, 82, 84, 89–90, 92, 95–98, 102, 112, 114, 116, 129, 131, 133, 135, 138, 141, 144, 148, 152, 170, 172–73, 175–76, 179
  Parliament, 37, 68
  schooling, 12
Enlightenment, 13, 20–23, 26, 29
Episcopal, 68, 138
Ethiopian, 78
ethne, 6, 18, 22–24, 26–27, 29–30
ethnic
  assimilation, 37
  cauldron of the contemporary world, 109, 128
  cleansing, 26, 30, 152, 157
  conflict, 1, 30, 51, 102, 117, 157, 161, 164, 166–67, 170, 178
    healing of, 164, 167, 170
  diversity, 3, 11, 22, 25, 27, 88, 98, 140, 144, 158–60, 171, 177, 180
  fences, 44
  folk memory, 38
  group, 3–6, 11, 14, 25–26, 43, 48, 51–52, 56, 58, 63, 79, 81, 83, 88, 103–06, 113–14, 123, 125, 128, 131, 145, 152–53, 158, 160–61, 166, 170–71, 175–80
  hostility, 14
  identity, 1, 4–6, 9, 14–16, 18–20, 22–23, 27–31, 43, 45, 48–49, 51–52, 56–57, 59, 61, 73–74, 77–80, 84–85, 87, 94–95, 97, 100, 102–07, 114, 117–18, 125–31, 136, 140, 145, 148, 152–53, 157–59, 161–64, 175, 179–81
    denial of, 1
    modern understanding, 9
    rights of, 105, 117
    suppression of, 1
  minorities, 6, 22, 27–28, 43, 97, 107, 114–15, 117–18, 128, 131, 133, 159
  mixing, 107, 115, 131
  origin, 22, 26, 37, 130
ethnicity, 1, 5–6, 13, 19, 30, 43, 46, 52, 61–62, 80, 84, 106, 157–61, 168, 180–81
ethnoi, 55
Euro-American, 129
Europe, 1, 4, 13, 19, 60, 110, 130, 144–45, 179
European, 19, 21, 23, 27, 48, 78–79, 103, 106, 111, 113, 137, 144, 152, 157, 159, 179
evangelical, 15, 31–32, 34–36, 56, 73, 81, 85, 87, 97, 100–01, 103–04, 107, 140, 142–43, 151–52, 154, 160, 181
  imperial. *See* imperialism.
Evangelical Alliance, 7, 91
Evangelical Movement of Wales, 31–32, 66, 168
Exclusion and Embrace, 164

F

"Fact and Faith" films, 32
Fellowship of Christian Unions (FOCUS), 161
Ffestiniog, 14, 20
Filipino, 129
Fisher, 81
France, 6, 22, 25, 110–11, 115, 145, 147
Frazer, James, 80
freedom, 3–4, 20–24, 27, 29–30,

35–36, 63, 68, 88, 103, 105, 123, 127–28, 152, 166
individual, 1, 3
French, 6, 22, 25, 62, 114, 145, 147, 152
French Revolution, 21–22, 145
fundamentalism, 35

G

Galicia, 110
Gambia, 114
Gellner, 14
genocide, 26, 28, 111, 114, 152, 157, 161, 163–64, 168, 173, 179, 181
Gentiles, 40–45, 55, 58
Gerald of Wales, 65–66
Gerald's Description of Wales, 65
German, 22–23, 25–26, 116, 141
    Moravians, 112
Germany, 25, 121, 127, 143, 152
Ghana, 159
global, 2
    village, 2
globalisation, 1–4, 39, 107, 151
globfrag, 1, 3
Glyndwr, Owen, 66
God
    Yahweh, 52–53, 121
Gomer, 48
Goth, 60
Gothic, 61
government, 18–19, 21, 25–26, 38, 65–67, 69, 75–77, 101, 111, 113, 126–27, 138, 151, 159–60
Graham, Billy, 32
Great Awakening, 68, 70, 72, 78, 143
Great Britain, 6, 13
Greek, 40, 44, 51, 59–61, 98–100
Griffiths, Ann, 67

Guinea-Bissau, 114
Gwamba, 79

H

Habyarimana, Juvenal, 163
Ham, 48
Hastings, Adrian, 61, 63
Hausa-Fulani military, 82
Havilah, 48
Heath Presbyterian Church, 36
Hebrew, 59
Hechter, 6
Henry II, 65
Henry, VII, 66
Henry VIII, 66–67
Hereford, 67
Hispanic, 116, 129
Holland, 115, 141
Hollywood, 2–3
Honduras, 112
human rights, 85, 87–88, 94, 105, 131, 159
humanity, 3, 21–26, 47, 49–50, 55, 58, 101, 103, 124, 129–30, 145, 154, 161, 167, 172, 174, 180
Hungarian, 4
Hurditch, Ruth, 81
Hutchinson, John, 5–6
Hutus, 26, 28, 51, 162, 164, 169, 177, 179

I

identity, 3, 7, 14, 18–19, 23, 26, 28–29, 40–47, 58, 62–63, 77, 81–84, 88, 94–95, 98, 100–04, 111, 115–19, 126–29, 131–32, 146, 153, 162, 165, 171–73, 175–76
    Anglo-American. *See* Anglo-American.
    ethnic. *See* ethnic.
    national. *See* national.

Index

immigrant, 6, 38–39, 44, 94–95, 102, 116, 119, 121, 127, 137
imperialism, 18, 24, 30, 76, 131
   imperial, 78, 106, 114
      authority, 81
      era, 115
      evangelicalism, 140
      legacy, 114
      politician, 103
      power, 50–51, 140
imposition, 1, 68, 102, 114, 159
India, 4, 23, 69, 91, 110, 114–15, 130, 146
Indian People's Party (BJP), 130
indigenous
   languages, 51
   peoples, 4, 39, 83, 110, 133–37, 139, 142–49, 151–54, 159, 166, 175
   tribal peoples, 3
individualism, 3, 104
Indo-European people, 48
Indo-Iranian people, 48
Industrial Revolution, 14, 22, 37, 74, 78, 135
industrialism, 14, 16, 19, 73, 102, 105, 114, 131, 140, 154, 158, 165
   industrialized
      economy, 15
international, 39
   community, 117, 180
   context, 135
   economy, 146
   law, 4, 105, 131
   peace, 105
   standards, 118
   unity, 16
InterVarsity Fellowship, 35
Iranian, 48
   plateau, 48
Irish, 6–7, 15, 37, 39, 58, 95, 98, 129–30, 135, 148, 152, 159, 175
Irish Republican Army (IRA), 30, 130
Israel, 41, 43, 45–46, 52–53, 55, 63, 109, 120–26
Israelites, 46, 52–53, 121–24
Italian, 25, 58, 129

J

James I, 21
Japheth, 48
Jenkins, Roy, 127
Jerusalem, 41–43, 46, 60
Jesus Christ
   ascension, 40
   Good Shepherd, 176
   Messiah, 41, 46, 174
   resurrection, 40, 60
Jewish, 40–44, 58–59, 99
   identity, 40, 45
Jews, 6, 26, 40–43, 46, 57–59, 99–100, 121
   American, 6
Johannesburg, 169
John, 54–55, 87, 174
John the Baptist, 174
Johnson, Samuel, 82
Jones, Emyr Llywelyn, 32
Jones, Geraint, 36
Jones, Griffith, 69–72, 75, 150
Jones, Martyn Lloyd, 36
Jones, Mary, 72–73
Jordan River, 52
Joseph, 122
Judaism, 41, 43, 125
judgement, 5, 49–53, 65, 109, 178
Junod, Henri, 79–81

K

Karen, 3, 114
Karnataka, 115
Kazakhstan, 112

Khan, Genghis, 113
King, Martin Luther, 91
Kinyarwanda, 51
Kosovars, 26
Kosovo, 1, 7, 26
Krajina, 26
Kurds, 6
KwaZulu Natal, 167
Kymlicka, Will, 6, 134

L

Lake Fyrnwy, 33
language, 1, 6, 9, 12–13, 15–16, 22, 26–27, 32, 35–39, 44, 48–52, 56–57, 59–61, 65, 67, 69, 73, 76–85, 87–90, 93, 95, 98, 100–02, 104, 107, 110, 113–14, 116–18, 125–26, 128, 133, 138, 141–42, 144, 146, 148–50, 152, 154, 162, 165
Latin, 51, 60–61
   Vulgate, 62
Latin America, 4, 114, 135, 137, 141, 145
Latin American Congress for Evangelisation, 141
Leicester, 115
Levites, 124
liberal, 15–16, 20, 29, 154
   tradition, 14
liberalism, 34
Liberia, 168
lingua franca, 80
Little Crow, 138–39
Liverpool, 15, 17, 35
   Association, 15
   Corporation, 33
Llanddowror, 69–70, 150
Llanfihangel y Pennant, 72
Lloyd, Rhiannon, 167–70, 172–73, 176–79
Llyn Celyn, 33

Llywelyn, Emyr, 32–34, 66
Luganda, 80–81
Lycaonian, 44
Lystra, 44
Lystran, 44

M

Macedonia, 1, 7
Macedonian
   Albanian, 1
Madai, 48
Maddox, 81
Manifest Destiny, 24, 30, 54, 137
Maoris, 137
Marx, Karl, 16, 23
Marxist, 16
materialism
   materialistic, 2
Matthews, Ann, 149
McDonald's, 2–3
Mdewkantons, 138
Medes, 48
Mee, Arthur, 10
Mendelsshon, Moses, 26
Merionethshire, 14
Merthyr Tudful, 74, 135
Mesopotamia, 48–49
mestizo, 135
Methodist, 15, 73
Methodist Revival, 143
Milosevic, Slobodan, 164
Minnesota, 139
minority, 4, 35, 81–82, 123, 133–34, 143, 147, 153
mission, 15, 41, 60, 65, 69, 78–81, 83–84, 104, 112, 132, 136, 140–44, 148
missionary, 44, 64–65, 69, 80–81, 84, 100, 103, 107, 125–26, 140–43, 149, 154
   journey, 44
Mizraim, 48

modern, 9, 14, 20, 22, 24–25, 29–30, 52, 63, 102, 105, 111, 113, 115, 118, 131, 135–36, 154
   Modernist, 19–20, 22–25, 27–30, 62, 77, 103–05, 114, 140, 146, 151, 158–59, 165, 180
Moldovan, 4
   republic, 4
Moltmann, Jürgen, 164
Mongol Empire, 113
Mongolia, 112
Mongols, 113
monoglot, 10–11, 15
Montenegro, 1
Montgomery, 66
Morris-Jones, John, 38
Moses, 123
Moskitu, 112
Mosquitia coast, 112
mother tongue, 60, 69, 71, 92, 118, 128, 147–48
   education, 147
Mozambique, 79–80, 114
MTV, 2–3
multiethnic, 27, 37, 39, 103, 114–15, 129, 131
Muslim, 82, 111, 113, 123, 166
   Arabs, 113
Myanmar, 4, 114

N

Narby, 136, 147
national
   development, 80
   identity, 14, 117
   law, 118
   minorities, 6, 117, 134, 154
   superiority, 152, 175
National Health Service, 27
National Young Life Campaign (NYLC), 32

Nationalism, 7, 14, 17–18, 20, 24–25, 27, 30, 53, 104–06, 152, 173
Nationalist, 7, 17–18, 27–29, 90, 94, 104, 111, 130, 135, 152, 155, 172
nationhood, 25, 28, 59, 61–62, 78, 84–85, 103
Native American, 4, 22, 54, 116, 129, 137–38, 142, 152
Nazareth, 46
Nazis, 26, 121, 152
   Nazism, 26, 30
Nebuchadnezzar, 50
New Age, 3–4
New Testament, 37, 40–41, 51, 54–55, 57, 60, 67, 71, 73, 83, 125
New York, 115–16
New Zealand, 137, 157
Newcastle, 169
Nicaragua, 112
Nigeria, 23, 82, 114
Nike, 2
Nimrod, 48
Nineveh, 48
Noah, 47–48
Nonconformist, 75–76
Non-governmental Organizations (NGOs), 154
Norman, 111
   Conquest, 62
   culture, 111
   dialect, 111
   identity, 111
Normandy, 111
North Africa, 60
   Berbers, 113
North America, 25, 137, 141–43
Ntintili, Prince Vuyani, 160

O

Obasanjo, 82

Old Testament, 54–55, 59, 62–63, 119, 125–26, 131
oppression, 20, 23, 30, 84, 99, 103, 105, 122–23, 134, 137, 139–40, 145, 153, 166, 171–73, 181
  violent, 122
Oruro, 151
Oyo, 82

P

Pakistanis, 115, 123, 129
Papua New Guinea, 114
Paul, 40–46, 52, 57, 60, 98–100, 110, 178
Penllyn, 110
Pentecost, 41, 59–60
Penybont ar Ogwr, 149
people movements, 111, 114
Persians, 53, 61
perspective, 7, 23, 53, 57, 59, 76, 85, 97, 102, 107, 125–26, 128, 134, 139, 146, 151–52, 159, 161, 167
  autobiographical, 9
Peru, 137, 153
Peter, 42
Pharaoh, 52, 122–23
Philipps, John, 69
Picton, 69
Pietism, 143
Pike, Edith, 81
Pilgrim's Progress, 10
Plaid Cymru, 18–19, 28, 90, 94
Pontypridd, 93–95, 97, 133, 149
Pope Gregory, 65
Portuguese, 27, 114, 157
postmodern, 3–4
  culture, 3
poverty, 145, 160
Presbyterian, 32, 36
primordialist, 19–21, 27, 30, 58, 130
  roots and fruits of, 23
Protestant, 21, 63, 78, 83–84, 100–01, 112, 137, 163
Providence Island, 112
Puritan, 63, 68, 112

Q

Quebecois, 6
Quechua, 148–51, 153
Quito, 141

R

race, 24, 45, 83
racism, 161, 171
radio, 9–10, 27
Rees, William, 73
Reformation, 20, 37, 63, 66–67, 81, 84
relativism, 3
religion, 3, 6, 31, 35, 48, 74, 84, 107, 117–18, 123–24, 138, 141, 162, 165, 172
Rhiwlas, 33
Rhys, Morgan, 67
Roman, 10, 40, 45, 60, 62, 64, 131
  centurion, 42
Roman Catholic, 20, 137, 163
Roman Empire, 41, 43, 51, 59–60, 64, 99, 111
Romania, 4
Romanian, 4
Rome, 10, 24, 41, 64–65, 110
Ronga, 79–80
Russia, 99
  southern, 48
Russian, 51, 129
  Caucasus, 110
  Federation, 4
Rutherford, Samuel, 21
Rwanda, 26, 28, 30, 114, 157, 161–64, 168–69, 173, 177, 179, 181

Belgian, 114
Rwandans, 114, 161, 163, 169, 179

S
Sahidic Coptic, 60
San Juanillo Bible Institute
   in Sucre, 148
Sandinista revolution, 112
Santa Cruz, 149
Sao Paulo, 148
Satan, 176
Schumacher, E. F., 146
Scots, 135, 159, 175
Scottish, 6–7, 58, 64, 129
Scripture Union, 31–32
   English, 32
Scythian, 99–100
Seba, 48
Second World War, 29, 115, 142
Senegal, 114
Serbo-Croat, 51
Serbs, 26, 51, 166
Shea, George Beverly, 32
Sikh, 130
   separatist movement, 130
Silas, 44, 60
SIM
   missionary, 149
Sioux, 138–39
Slavic, 111
   Peoples, 4
Slovak
   republic, 4
Small is Beautiful, 146
Smith, Anthony D., 5–6
Snowdonia National Park, 9
socialism, 14, 77
   impact of, 77
socialist, 14, 16, 77
   approach, 20
   forms, 29
   ideal, 16
manifestation, 154
theory, 14
view, 16
Society for the Propagation of
   Christian Knowledge (SPCK),
   68–70, 73
Solomon, 122–23
South Africa, 78, 80, 152, 160,
   167–69, 175–77, 180–81
   abuse of blacks in, 54
South American
   peoples, 27, 157
Spain, 7, 110–12, 148
Spanish, 83, 112, 114, 141,
   148–50, 157
   origin, 27
spiritual, 3, 99, 126
   awakening, 31
   darkness, 68, 176
   growth, 44
   life, 35
   reformation, 63
   superiority, 99
   unity, 40
   vitality, 15
Stalin, Joseph, 4
Sucre, 148–51
Sudan, 113
   Western, 113
Swiss Mission, 79
syllogism, 14
Symons, J. C., 76
Syrian Antioch, 41

T
Tamil Nadu, 115
Tarsus, 41
Tasmania, 27, 157
Tasmanians, 53–54
Tearfund, 148, 153
television, 2, 10, 91
Teutonic tribes, 62

migrants, 84
Thailand, 4
The Ecclesiastical History of English People, 62
The History of the Yorubas from the Earliest Times, 82
The Melting Pot, 115
theologian, 21, 165
theology, 66, 73, 98, 119
   mission/missionary, 142, 144
   political, 21
   theological
      approach, 164
      education, 91, 150
      foundation, 119, 123, 164
      liberalism, 34
      principle, 167
Tibetan
   identity, 3
Timothy, 44, 60
Toplady, 66
Toro, 80–81
Tranquebar, 69
Transvaal, 78–81, 83
Treason of the Blue Books, 75
tribalism, 158
Trinity, 170
Tryweryn
   river, 9
   valley, 12, 33
Tsonga, 78, 80
Tuanama, Artidoro, 153
Turkey, 41, 99
Tutsi, 26, 51, 162, 164, 169, 173, 175, 177, 179
Twa, 161
Tyndale, 63
Tynybont, 33

U

Uganda, 78, 80–81, 83, 114
Uighur, 112–13
identity, 113
language, 113
Ukraine, 4
Ulfilas, 60
United Kingdom (UK), 6–7, 12, 37, 89, 94, 115, 121, 127, 142–43, 175
United Nations (UN), 4, 85, 105–06, 159
   Commission on Human Rights, 117, 133
   Declaration of Human Rights Universal (UDHR), 88, 106
   Declaration on the Rights of Persons Belonging to National or Ethnic, Religious or Linguistic Minorities, 117, 131
   Emergency Response Division, 159
   rights of ethnic identities, 105, 117
United States of America (USA), 2, 22, 24–27, 54, 91, 115–16, 129–30, 137, 143, 157
   America(n), 6, 13, 24, 30, 116, 129–30, 133, 137
unity, 1, 39, 42–43, 47, 57, 62, 82, 98, 100, 140, 170–71, 179, 181
   artificial, 114
University College
   Aberystwyth, 32
   North Wales, 34, 66
University of Wales, 89, 172

V

Volf, Miroslav, 164–67

W

Wales, 15–19, 28, 32–34, 36–37, 39, 58, 64–71, 73–78, 84, 90–92, 95, 97, 102, 110, 118,

133, 135–36, 148, 150, 170, 172
  North, 18, 34, 66, 72, 89, 168
  North East, 19, 38
  rural, 10, 15, 74, 94
  South, 56, 64, 93, 95, 102, 135, 150
  South East, 37, 74
war, 54, 78, 106, 139
  class, 16
Washington D.C., 138
Watts, 66
welfare, 1427, 126
Welsh, 6–7, 9–13, 15–19, 28–29, 32–39, 56–58, 64–67, 69–71, 73–74, 76–78, 89–98, 101–02, 104, 118, 133, 135–36, 146, 148–50, 152, 159, 168, 172–73, 175, 179
  Bible, 64, 66–70, 72–74
  childhood, 9
  Christian heritage, 32
  Congregational, 15
  identity, 15, 19, 28–29, 56, 65–67, 73–74, 78, 102, 173
    decline of, 73, 92
  revivalism, 32
Welsh Language Society, 90–91, 172
Welsh Not (W. N.), 38, 172
Wesley, 66, 71
Wesleyan, 79
  Methodist, 15
Western, 135, 138, 146
  advance, 110
  civilization, 142–43, 154
  culture, 55, 140
  humanism, 131
  intrusion, 136
  modernization, 107, 114
  transnational companies, 2
Westminster Parliament, 34
Whitefield, George, 71

Williams, William, 67
Worcester, Samuel, 137–38
Wrexham, 32
Wright, Christopher, 52–53, 120
Wycliffe, 62
Wycliffe Bible Translators, 144–45
Wyoming, 24

X

Xinjiang-Uijgur Autonomous Region, 112

Y

Yoruba, 3, 82
Yr Amserau, 73
Yugoslavia, 4, 117, 157, 164–65

Z

Zacchaeus, 31
Zaire, 114, 169
Zangwill, Israel, 115
Zion, 54–55
Zulus, 170, 175–76, 178–79

SCRIPTURE INDEX

Genesis 1:9 .... 12, 18, 25, 31, 170
Genesis 1:28 47
Genesis 7:21 55
Genesis 9:7 47
Genesis 10 47–50
Genesis 10:5 .... 20, 31, 48
Genesis 11 49
Genesis 11:1–9 49
Genesis 11:4 50
Genesis 18:18 5
Genesis 26–34 122
Genesis 46:1–7 122
Genesis 47:1–5 122

Exodus 1:10 122
Exodus 9:14 .... 16, 29, 52
Exodus 20:10 123
Exodus 22:21 123
Exodus 23:12 123
Exodus 23:19 30

Leviticus 11 40
Leviticus 16–18 124
Leviticus 16:29–30 124
Leviticus 17:8, 10, 12–13 124
Leviticus 18:26 124
Leviticus 19:10 124
Leviticus 19:34 121
Leviticus 22:18 124

Numbers 15:14–29 124

Deuteronomy 1:16 124
Deuteronomy 2:9–12, 19–23 52
Deuteronomy 4:14 124
Deuteronomy 7:7 120
Deuteronomy 9:4–5 .... 53, 109, 120
Deuteronomy 10 123
Deuteronomy 10:8 178
Deuteronomy 10:14–19 119–20
Deuteronomy 14:3–21 40
Deuteronomy 14:21 40
Deuteronomy 16:9–14 124
Deuteronomy 24:14–15 124
Deuteronomy 24:17 124
Deuteronomy 24:19–21 124
Deuteronomy 26:1–13 124
Deuteronomy 27:19 124
Deuteronomy 32:8 52–53

2 Chronicles 2:17 123

Psalm 136:25 55

Proverbs 8:30–31 170

Isaiah 10:5 53
Isaiah 60:1–11 54

Jeremiah 18:1–10 53
Jeremiah 18:7–10 53
Jeremiah 27:1–7 53

Daniel 1:1–5 50	Acts 15:24 42
	Acts 17:26 .... 52, 105, 170
Jonah 3 53	
	Romans 3:1–2 45
Haggai 2:7 55	Romans 9:3–4 45
	Romans 9:4–5 46
Matthew 8:5–13 40	Romans 9–11 45
Matthew 11:6 174	Romans 11 46
Matthew 24:6–7 54	Romans 12:17–13:5 178
Matthew 24:14 40	
Matthew 28:18–20 40	Galatians 2:14 42
	Galatians 3:28 .... 40, 98–99
Mark 11:17 40	
Mark 13:10 40	Ephesians 5:22–33 57
Mark 14:9 40	
	Colossians 3:11 98–99
Luke 11:29–32 40	
	1 Peter 2:9 178
John 10:10–11 176	
John 16:10 40	1 John 3:17 87
Acts 10 42	Revelation 21:24–26 .... 54, 171
Acts 14:8–18 44	Revelation 21:26 55

www.ingramcontent.com/pod-product-compliance
Ingram Content Group UK Ltd.
Pitfield, Milton Keynes, MK11 3LW, UK
UKHW022237230426
12048UKWH00018BA/1305